A VICTORIAN EMINENCE

The Life and Works of Henry Thomas Buckle

By Giles St. Aubyn

LORD MACAULAY
THE ART OF ARGUMENT

With W. A. Barker and R. L. Ollard
GENERAL HISTORY OF ENGLAND 1688-1832
GENERAL HISTORY OF ENGLAND 1832-1950

With E. W. Gladstone and Brian Rees
THE UNIFICATION OF ITALY

Henry Thomas Buckle

A VICTORIAN EMINENCE

The Life and Works of Henry Thomas Buckle

Giles St. Aubyn

BARRIE

BARRIE BOOKS LTD.
3-4 Clement's Inn, London, W.C.2

Printed in Great Britain by
Taylor Garnett Evans & Co. Ltd
Watford, Hertfordshire

To my Mother and Father

CONTENTS

PREFACE

THIS biography is written in the belief that the life and works of Henry Thomas Buckle have fallen into undeserved obscurity. Neglected as Buckle is now, in his own day he was most influential, and so no student of Nineteenth-Century thought, or of English historiography, can afford to ignore him. The only previous life of Buckle has long been out of print, many of its judgements require revision in the light of new evidence, and its assessment of his work is out of date.

The present work consists of a mixture of biography, exposition and criticism. The first four Chapters retell the story of Buckle's life, the next Chapter consists of a summary of his thought, and the last considers the views of his critics. The book has been written in the conviction that Buckle and his contemporaries should, wherever possible, be allowed to speak for themselves. It is not intended that the expositionary Chapter should save the reader the trouble of studying the *History of Civilization*. On the contrary it is to be hoped that it may encourage him to do so. But, as Buckle's doctrines have so often been ignorantly misrepresented, and as they are anyway scattered over three volumes, it seems best to summarize them before discussing to what extent they have been misconstrued.

I am very grateful to the authorities of the British Library of Political and Economic Science, the Henry E. Huntington Library, the British Museum and the Public Records Office, for permission to print letters in their possession. In the course of my research I received generous assistance from Mr. N. Blakiston, Mr. A. Gray, Mr. G. Woledge, Mr. M. Packe, Dr. F. Toufar, Miss Y. Parnell and the Reverend J. W. Jones. I am also indebted to Mr. Raymond Carr, Mr. William Gladstone, Sir Harold Nicolson, Mr. Richard Ollard, Mr. Kenneth Rose and the Reverend Charles Tomkins, for reading the book in manuscript and for suggesting numerous improvements. They are, of course, in no way responsible for the faults of the work or for the views it expresses. Finally I should like to thank Mrs. Mary Nayler, who typed and retyped the manuscript and who helped in a hundred other ways.

Eton 1957 GILES ST. AUBYN

CHAPTER I

THE SOLITARY STUDENT

In 1857, the year in which *Barchester Towers*, *Little Dorrit* and *Tom Brown's School Days* appeared, Henry Thomas Buckle, after eighteen years of solitary study, published the first volume of his *History of Civilization in England*. At home the unknown student won instant fame among all classes of society; abroad his work was discussed from California to the Steppes. "Never, perhaps, among men who have made a name and left their stamp on the thought of their generation has anyone enjoyed so sudden a blaze and so brief a span of glory."[1] Both those who reverenced and those who reviled him agreed that his was one of the seminal minds of the age, and the extent to which he is at present neglected would have astonished his contemporaries.

Buckle belonged to that middle class of whose services to mankind he had so high an opinion. In the reign of Queen Elizabeth his family had moved from Westmorland to London and in 1593 one of his ancestors, Sir Cuthbert Buckle, became Lord Mayor. His father, Thomas Henry Buckle, was a partner in a shipping firm, Buckle, Bagster, and Buckle, which traded mainly with the West Indies. His mother, Jane Middleton, came from Yorkshire. She married in 1811 and had three children: two daughters and a son. Both the girls married. Mary Buckle married a Dr. Allatt, and Annie a Mr. Hutchinson. Henry was born on 24th November, 1821, at Lee in Kent, while his parents were visiting John Buckle, his father's brother and partner.

Buckle's father loved good conversation, read widely, and was a strong Churchman and Tory. Often in the evening he used to sit alone over his port reading books on theology, although sometimes he would recite Shakespeare to his family or discuss politics. As he grew older he became increasingly absent-minded and even passed his nearest relations in the street without noticing them. His intellectual legacy to his son was short-lived, for the boy soon rejected political and religious orthodoxy in favour of radicalism and free thought; but the £20,000 he left Henry, thereby enabling him to work and write without the distraction of earning a living, proved a more substantial inheritance.

In his youth, most of which was spent in London, Henry was very delicate, and therefore hardly ever met any boys of his own age, apart from his cousin, John, who was brought up with him. He showed no desire to learn to read until he was nearly eight. A present of the *Arabian Nights*, a book which both Gibbon and Macaulay had loved as children, inspired him to acquire the art to which he devoted so large a portion of his life, and which, once learned, he would not have exchanged for all the wealth of India. Until he was sixteen, Buckle read little except Shakespeare, and Bunyan's *Pilgrim's Progress*. The only sign he gave of his genius while still a boy was when playing "Parson and Clerk" with his cousin. According to Mrs. Buckle, who may be suspected of partiality, her son's eloquence was astounding.

Buckle's parents, on the advice of Dr. Birbeck, decided that it would be dangerous to overtax their son's brain and accordingly sent him to Gordon House School, on the understanding that he should be taught nothing he did not wish to learn. The Head Master, Doctor James Holloway, had married Miss Bentham, a relation of Jeremy Bentham, and it was to her care that Henry was mainly committed.[2] Although he learned very little indeed there, he became interested in geometry and won a mathematical prize. When he returned home with it at the end of the term, his father was so delighted that he asked him what he would like as an additional reward. "To be taken away from school," was the reply. As the request was granted, Buckle's formal education ceased at the age of fourteen and nearly all the knowledge he subsequently acquired was derived from reading. "I was never much tormented," he wrote later, "with what is called Education, but allowed to pursue my own way undisturbed. . . . Whatever I may now be supposed to know I taught myself."[3]

So anxious was Buckle's mother that Henry should not over-exert himself mentally that she taught him to knit as a relaxation requiring activity but little mental concentration. Indeed the indulgence she showed him, necessary as it may have been for his health, weakened his character, and only too often he behaved like the spoiled child he was. While staying at Tunbridge Wells, he lost a considerable sum of money playing Billiards, but his mother paid the debt for him so as to avoid unpleasantness with his father. Buckle's conduct in early life, gave "great pains and anxiety to his relations".[4] Once when visiting his old nurse, he turned everything in her toom topsy-turvy and threw her cat out of the window. Such uproariousness was unfortunately not exceptional. His cousin, John Buckle, writes: "He was weak in body from childhood and his education was very much neglected on that account. He grew up a spoiled child and as a youth was ignorant, self-opinionated and fond of Exeter Hall meetings."[5]

When Henry was seventeen his father decided to start him in the office of "Buckle, Bagster and Buckle". This plan commended itself neither to Henry nor his mother, but for once they were both over-ruled. Although he only worked with the firm for a short time, he always looked back on it with distaste. Accustomed to doing what he pleased, the discipline of office life was as repugnant as the work was dreary. He seems, however, to have relieved the monotony by falling in love with Annie Jane Holloway, his Head Master's daughter and a friend of his sister Mary. She was five years older than he was, but despite this considerable difference in age, he was none the less determined to marry her. "Buckle in making his proposal was seated with the young lady on a seat which entirely surrounded an old tree. He slipped off on to his knees in his anxious excitement. The lady fancied she heard a giggling and when they had both left the spot they found that two persons had been behind them, and ear witnesses to some extent at least of what had passed." Both Dr. Holloway and Mrs. Buckle would have welcomed the marriage; the lady herself was the sole impediment. "She did not encourage his advances as she had not formed an attachment for him and shrank from the life she would have to lead if she had married a man so devoted to his favourite pursuits."[6]

In 1840 Buckle's father, whose health had long been undermined by consumption, slipped on the kerb of his own front doorstep, broke his arm and became convinced that he would never recover. For a month after the accident he grew weaker every day. Only a few moments before he died, he sent for his son and told him to be a good boy to his mother. Henry was so overcome that he had to be carried from the room in a swoon and for some months afterwards had frequent fainting fits from which he only recovered after a long convalescence in his aunt's house at Brighton.

His father's death left Buckle free to travel and to write, and rich enough to give up his business career. In July 1840 Mrs. Buckle, Henry, and Mary, left England for the Continent. They spent the summer in Germany, and then by way of Switzerland, the Italian lakes and Florence, reached Rome, where they remained for several months. In April of the following year, they moved on to Paris for six weeks and then returned home. While travelling on the Rhine Buckle met the historian, Hallam. Hallam, who spoke little German, welcomed the services of an interpreter, and quickly recognized the genius of his young companion. In Rome the Buckles found living in the same house as themselves a Mr. Samuel Strickland and his family, with whom they became friendly. Although Strickland and his sister, Eliza, afterwards became close acquaintances, the first impression Henry made on them was bad. "I should be very sorry to recall," writes Samuel Strickland, "much that was then very objectionable in his conduct. The child however, is not *always* father to the man. . . . Mr. Buckle was never strong and travelling fevered him and made him a fretful and irritable companion."[7]

Throughout this journey, and during all his subsequent travels, Buckle studied the language and literature of the countries which he visited. By 1850 he could read eighteen foreign languages, and speak and write at least six of them;* but he only considered a knowledge of languages valuable "as the stepping-stone to other learning, and spoke with contempt of a person who was mentioned to him as speaking eight languages familiarly. 'Has he done anything?' 'No! Then he is only fit to be a courier!' "[8] Although he had a wonderful facility for learning languages he always pronounced them with an English accent. Once, when travelling in Holland he began talking to a Dutchman, partly to improve his conversation in that language, and partly because he always liked talking to strangers. At first, the man apologized for not speaking Italian, and it was a considerable time before he realized that he was being addressed in fluent, but ill-pronounced Dutch.

During his early travels Buckle spent a certain amount of time looking at paintings. In Munich he passed hours gazing at the pictures and trying to think himself into the whole idea of the master he studied. But, as he became increasingly immersed in his work, his interest in art, and his sensitivity to beauty declined. What appealed only through the senses lost its power to move him. Music he never enjoyed for he could not tell one tune from another. Once he astonished his friends by standing to attention while "Rule Britannia" was played.

When Buckle came back to England in the summer of 1841 his outlook had greatly altered. He had gone abroad a Tory and a Churchman: he returned a Radical and Freethinker. The change was partly effected by what he saw of foreign despotism, and what he heard of

* French, German, Italian, Spanish, Portuguese, Dutch, Danish, Walloon, Flemish, Swedish, Icelandic, Frisian, Maorian, Russian, Anglo-Saxon, Hebrew, Greek, Latin.

German theological criticism, but it was equally the result of his own reading and thought. He had immense confidence in his power to educate himself and disliked the idea of going to a University where his lack of conventional schooling would have proved a severe handicap, and where he would be excelled by his contemporaries. "I made up my mind when I was a boy," he once said, "that whatever I took up, I should be first in. I would rather be first as a Shoe-black, than second in anything else." Moreover the Universities were still steeped in "port and prejudice". Oxford, it is true, had been roused from her slumbers by the Tractarians but that scarcely made her more attractive to a Free-thinking Radical. He describes Oxford in his history as "that ancient University, which had always been esteemed as the refuge of superstition, and which has preserved to our own day its unenviable fame".[9]

The fact that Buckle's early life was so solitary, and his education so unconventional, helps to explain the originality and independence of his views. "Probably if he had gone for a few years more to school, and eventually to College, he would have been quite a different man, and we should never have had the *History of Civilization*."[10] On the other hand, "he did not possess that knowledge of society which comes from practical intercourse with men. . . . He had lived too much alone, or at least his graver life had been too solitary. He knew most of what was written, he often did not know enough of what was said and done. . . . He had not been forced, as most men are, in the actual contact of the working world, to see, and learn to appreciate at their real value, influences foreign to his own life. . . . In many ways, the influence of self-education and of a retired home-life was apparent in the tone of Mr. Buckle's opinions and character. . . . Having won everything by his own exertions, and never tried his strength against others, he sometimes appeared to underrate, sometimes to overrate, the common average of ability and of attainments. Accordingly, in his work we occasionally find points elaborately dwelt upon and enforced by repeated quotation, which few would have been inclined to dispute; and occasionally, on the other hand, a belief in the ready acceptance of some principle which the majority of men are still far from acknowledging."[11]

The idea of writing a History of Civilization occurred to Buckle very early in life. "Between the ages of eighteen and nineteen," he writes, "I conceived the plan of my book—dimly indeed—but still the plan was there, and I set about its execution."[12] His original idea seems to have been to write a History of the Middle Ages. On 15th October, 1842, he began to keep a diary and the very first entry in it refers to his resolve to write such a book. "Being this day settled in my new lodgings, No. 1, Norfolk Street, I determined to keep a journal of my actions—principally, for the sake of being able to review what I have read, and consequently to estimate my own progress. My reading has, unfortunately, been hitherto, though extensive, both desultory and irregular. I am, however, determined from this day to devote all the energies I may have, solely to the study of the History and Literature of the Middle Ages. . . . Ambition whispers to me the flattering hope that a prolonged series of industrious efforts, aided by talents certainly above mediocrity, may at last meet with success."[13]

Gradually, as he began to amass his material, his early scheme of a History of the Middle Ages was transformed into a design for a History of Civilization. One of his intermediate plans seems to have been to concentrate on the reign of Elizabeth, but as on 7th March, 1843, he writes in his journal, "Began my life of Charles I", it is clear that he frequently changed his mind about the scope of his work.[14] Exactly when he finally decided to write a History of Civilization is impossible to determine. There is, however, one entry in his Journal, respecting his reading, which suggests that by 1850 his mind was made up. "June 24, 1850.—Read Simon's Animal Chemistry. The more I read of this great work the more delighted I am, particularly at the new views it opens to me, and of which Simon seems to have no idea, I mean the connexion between his researches and speculations, and the philosophic history of man."[15]

Buckle's aim in writing his history is well expressed in a letter he wrote to a friend who had asked for news of its progress. "You wish me to write a few words upon the object and tendency of that *History of English Civilization*, on which I have been now for some years engaged. It is very difficult to give in two or three lines a clear idea of so extensive a subject. But I may say generally that I have been long convinced that the progress of every people is regulated by principles—or, as they are called, Laws—as regular and as certain as those which govern the physical world. To discover those laws is the object of my work. With a view to this, I propose to take a general survey of the moral, intellectual, and legislative peculiarities of the great countries of Europe. . . . This is the general scheme of my work; and its merits, if it has any, will depend on the fidelity with which I carry that scheme into execution, and on the success of my attempt to rescue history from the hands of annalists, chroniclers, and antiquaries."[16]

So great was Buckle's ambition that he would let nothing interfere with his writing, except his own, or his mother's illness. He preferred to postpone his work twenty years rather than endanger his reputation by premature publication. Although he might have made several thousand a year by casual writing—he had offers of five pounds a page for anything he chose to print—nothing was ever allowed to distract him from writing his *History of Civilization in England.*

"This intense earnestness of pursuit," says Miss Shirreff,* "was part of his power. It might offend the idle, or occasionally weary at a dinner-table, where lighter subjects of conversation would have been more acceptable; but it seized upon those who lived with him more intimately, and it may safely be said that no mind at all alive to intellectual impressions, ever was brought into much communion with his, without being in some small measure interpenetrated with his spirit; without feeling the grandeur and power of truth, and the littleness of mere worldly success compared with the lofty objects to which the lover of knowledge may aspire. . . . What the real worth of Mr. Buckle's speculations, and whether he overrated them or not, is not for me to examine; but I do know that having, as he believed, attained some valuable principles, some glimpses of truth not hitherto recognized, such a possession was to him the call to an apostleship in as true and earnest a sense as ever was realized by missionary or philanthropist. He believed, as they do, that men should not 'put their light under a bushel', but rather so toil as to place it where it shall light up the dark corners of the earth. Widely, indeed, did he differ from them as to the means of doing good among men, but he was not the less kindled by the noble desire that by his labours he might leave the world better than he found it[17]".

When he was seventeen Buckle began forming a library and, from then onwards, used to wander all over London in search of rare volumes. A considerable part of his income was given to books, but he was always careful not to spend money unnecessarily, sometimes even making comparative lists of the prices in different booksellers' catalogues. His journal is full of references to his purchases. "Bought Caird's *Life of Charlemagne*, whole bound, very neat, 1 vol., 2s. 6d.;

* Miss Emily Shirreff, the author and educationalist, first met Buckle in 1854. They quickly became close friends. See below p. 23.

Crabb's *History of Common Law*, 1 vol. 8vo, 4s.; Barrington on More's Ancient Statutes, 1 vol. 8vo, calf, 2s. 6d.; Mills' *Travels of Theodore Ducas*, 2 vols. 8vo, in boards, only 2s.; also Johnson's *Memoirs of John Selden*, one vol. 8vo. new bds., uncut, portrait, only 2s. These two last books were bought at Stocklers', who when he *has* anything to sell, is extremely cheap." "To Holywell Street, to look among the bookstalls there, but only bought a copy of *The History of Helvetia*, two vols. 8vo, for which I paid 1s. 6d.!!!"[18]

In 1843, Henry and his mother moved to 59 Oxford Terrace, now 115 Sussex Gardens. At the back of 59 was a large room cut off from the rest of the house by four doors. This was turned into a library. Buckle worked in it at a specially constructed table which had shelves fitted all round so that the books he needed for writing were always to hand. As he bought more and more books, every room in the house was soon lined with them and even the butler's pantry had its share of learned tomes. Each volume was numbered and catalogued and consequently a servant, if necessary, could be sent to fetch any particular work required. Buckle, who demanded absolute quiet while he worked, could not endure reading or writing in public libraries.

Mr. Charles Hale, who met the historian in Cairo in 1862, records that he told him "about his library in London, which is surpassed (among private libraries) only by that belonging to Mr. Van Weyer, the Belgian Minister.... Buckle has twenty-two thousand volumes, all selected by himself; and he takes great pleasure in them. He spends eight or nine hundred pounds a year upon his library.* He owns copies of all the books referred to in his History; some of them are very old and rare."[19]

Long before Buckle became known as an historian, he was internationally famous as a Chess player. By the time he was only twenty he had defeated many acknowledged masters of the game, and was equally skilful at Whist and Draughts. When his book was published and he became the literary lion of the day, Herbert Spencer was taken to see him. Spencer at once recognized him as a man he had often seen in Simpson's Chess Divan in the Strand. Before Buckle got really immersed in his book and gave up regular Chess, he used to go to the divan nearly every evening and play several games. He was "a player of extraordinary power, daring originality, and calm self

* Hale is wrong in saying that Buckle spent "eight or nine hundred pounds a year on his library". Such a sum exceeded half his income. He did, however, spend between three and four hundred a year on books.

reliance".[20] "Nature had gifted him," wrote his friend Captain Kennedy, "with a superlative aptitude for the game of chess, and he brought the powers of a rare intellect—clear, penetrating and sagacious beyond that of most men—to bear upon it. His imagination was that of the poet, 'all compact', but subservient to the dictates of a logical judgment. His combinations accordingly, under such guidance, seldom if ever, exhibited a flaw, and were characterized by exactitude of calculation and brilliant device. . . . He gave large odds, such as Rook and Knight, with wonderful skill and success, appearing to have a sort of intuitive knowledge of a strange opponent's chess idiosyncrasy, which enabled him precisely to gauge the kind of risks he might venture to run. The rendering of heavy odds, as every experienced chess-player knows, necessitates hazardous and unsound play on the part of the giver. These contests of his at odds, were always full of interest and entertainment to lookers-on, and a gallery two or three deep often surrounded his board in the Strand Divan. . . . I have occasionally seen roars of laughter elicited from the spectators by the crestfallen aspect of some poor discomfited Rook-player, who, with much care and solicitude, having obtained, as he fondly believed, an impregnable position, had suddenly found his defences scattered like chaff, and himself accommodated with a mate, after the sacrifice, by his keen-witted opponent, of two or three pieces in succession. Whether winning or losing, Mr. Buckle was a courteous and pleasant adversary, and sat quietly before the board, smoking his cigar, and pursuing his game with inflexible steadiness."[21]

If Buckle was good-natured at Chess it was partly because he avoided severe trials of his patience. When asked why he had refused to play with a very slow opponent, he replied: "Well, sir, the slowness of genius is difficult to bear, but the slowness of mediocrity is intolerable." Buckle could never spare the time to study printed games, and did not even possess a chess-board. Although too busy to compete, he became a member of the committee of the Chess Tournament which was held in conjunction with the Great Exhibition of 1851. Afterwards, however, he played a series of fifteen games with Anderssen, the winner of the Tournament, and won eight. In 1851 Buckle was entitled to the championship of the world, a rare feat for an amateur who played only for amusement and gave no time to studying the game. But such victories took more out of him, as he said, than he was prepared to give to any such "frivolous triumph" again.[22]

Soon after moving into Oxford Terrace Buckle went to Holland, where he fell ill. When he recovered, he came back to England, to be presented at Court. In June 1843 he returned to the Continent, where he spent much of his time with Lord Kimberley, whom he had found staying in the same hotel at Hamburg. Kimberley at first thought his new friend very conceited, but soon realized how much justification Buckle had for feeling confidence in his own powers. Wherever Buckle went, he played Chess. At Dresden, a well-known player, jealous of the Englishman's extraordinary skill, went around saying that he was not nearly good enough to bother about. Buckle immediately posted up a large placard challenging him to a game for a considerable sum, but the man never again appeared in public until he knew that his opponent had left the city.

On his way to Italy, Buckle had an adventure at the Austrian frontier which he much enjoyed relating. The customs officer, on finding that his luggage contained a large number of books, examined it with meticulous care. When at length the official discovered a copy of Copernicus' *De Revolutionibus Orbium Caelestium* he at once confiscated it. Buckle vehemently protested, but was told by the Austrians that they did not care *where* the revolution was; they had their orders, and their orders were, to confiscate all revolutionary books. After extricating himself from the frontier, he travelled by stages to Rome. Once, while he was watching a game of Chess outside a café there, one of the players challenged him to a game. This man, seeing that he was very young, proposed a scudi as the stake. Buckle agreed. "Or perhaps a couple of scudi?" he added. Buckle assented. "Well, perhaps it would make a better game if we were to play for five scudi?" Upon this Buckle began to get annoyed, and exclaimed: "I'll play you for a hundred scudi if you like." The Italian beginning to grow cautious asked the stranger his name. "Buckle," came the reply. "Ah, Booclay!" was the answer, "then I won't play with *you*."

From Rome he went to Naples, and thence to Capri, where the boatmen who took him to see the island's Blue Grotto refused to take him out of it again unless he paid more than originally agreed. He gave them what they demanded, but when he got back to Naples, prosecuted them and got them punished. This refusal to be bullied or blackmailed was characteristic of him. A similar story is told of his finding himself alone with a young man in a compartment of a train travelling to Brighton. As the train approached a station, the man suddenly disarranged his clothes and threatened to accuse Buckle of assaulting him unless he gave him five pounds. When the train pulled up, Buckle seized the man and took him straight to a policeman, to whom he told the whole story. It turned out, after the case had been tried, that the prisoner had constantly used this trick but had found that other victims preferred to pay rather than risk a scandal.[23]

From Italy he travelled back to Germany where, at Munich, he fell ill of rheumatic fever. His mother hastened out to nurse him and never again were they parted for any length of time. On his recovery, they travelled home together through Holland. Although this tour had to some extent been undertaken for pleasure and reasons of health, it was one of Buckle's theories that travel was an essential part of education. He conscientiously studied the language of every country through which he passed, talked to as many people as he could, and visited art galleries and museums. But if he learned much from travel he learned more still from books. He was never happier than when reading in his library. "I am just like a child," he once wrote, "come home for the holidays, in the midst of my toys. What lovely things books are! I suppose sometime or other I too shall publish a book. . . ."[24] "He was an omnivorous reader," wrote Captain Kennedy, "no book of any kind seeming to come amiss to him; and he had the power, accorded to few, of plucking out, as it were, the heart of a book by doing little more than turning over the pages, with here and there an occasional halt. I remember his borrowing off me *Burder's Oriental Literature*, a two-volume octavo, of anything but light reading. He brought it back next day, whereon I remarked that I supposed it did not interest him? He said he had read it, and began to expatiate on its contents in a way which satisfied me that he, at any rate, knew more about them than I did."[25]

Buckle used to sit up late at night, reading, with a wet towel round his head: on one occasion, at about two o'clock in the morning, he suddenly saw by the light of the candle a white figure gazing at him. It proved to be his landlady sleep-walking. He read nearly all the books he possessed, which meant finishing about three a day. He covered every book he read with notes, and moreover took a pocket-book with him on his walks, full of dates and long quotations he wanted to be sure of remembering. His memory, however, was so capacious, that this industry was a precaution rather than a necessity. In addition to the notes he took on his reading in the books themselves and on bits of paper, he kept Common Place Books, which in accordance with his wishes were published in 1872 by Helen Taylor, John Stuart Mill's stepdaughter. Like Gibbon's and Southey's "his Common Place Books were well-ordered arsenals which yielded without stint or confusion the weapons and munitions required by him."[26]

Buckle was a very methodical worker. Every day he recorded in his diary the number of pages he had read and the exact time he had spent on them.

"*Monday*, *November* 24, 1851, *Brighton.*—Rose at 8. Walked half an hour and then breakfasted. From 10.5 to 12 read German. From 12 to 1.30 read Mill's Analysis of Mind, i., 66–140. Walked one hour and a half, and from 3.40 to 4.30 made notes from Leigh Hunt's Autobiography. From 4.30 to 6.20 read Lord Lyttleton's Memoirs and Correspondence, i., 246, to vol. ii., p. 580 (the paging of the two volumes is continuous). Dined at 6.30. In bed at 10.20, and to 11.30 read Beattie's Campbell, ii., 61–236."

"*Saturday*, *May* 19, 1855, 59, *Oxford Terrace.*—Rose at 8.30. Walked half an hour, and then breakfasted. From 10.40 to 1.50 finished the chapter in which I pass from physical laws to inquire into metaphysical resources. Walked one hour and a half, and from 5.30 to 7.10 finished Transactions of Asiatic Society, iii., pp. 138–585. Dined at 7.15. In bed at 10.40, and to 11.40 read Journal Asiatique, i., series., 82–335."

This meticulous routine was forced upon him by ill health. "He could have gone on reading or writing hours beyond his fixed time without any immediate danger, but he knew as a result of previous illness that he dared not overtask his brain; thus he worked with his watch on the table, and resolutely stopped when the appointed hour came."[27] To keep his brain clear he ate only bread and fruit for lunch, and to avoid wasting time over the meal he would often eat it while he took his afternoon walk. Exercise was essential to him. When he was younger he sometimes rode, but he never enjoyed it. Once, while riding at Hastings, he became so absorbed in his own thoughts that he let his horse take him into the library on the Parade. Every morning, whatever the weather, he took at least a quarter-of-an-hour's walk before breakfast, and every afternoon he went out for an hour or two, in search of books. He enjoyed walking alone, for it enabled him to talk to himself.

Darwin, after meeting Buckle, wrote the following account of his method of work. "I was very glad to learn from him his system of collecting facts. He told me that he bought all the books which he read, and made a full index, to each, of the facts which he thought might prove serviceable to him, and that he could always remember in what book he had read anything, for his memory was wonderful. I asked him how at first he could judge what facts would be serviceable, and he answered that he did not know, but that a sort of instinct guided him. From this habit of making indices, he was enabled to give the astonishing number of references on all sorts of subjects, which may be found in his *History of Civilization*."[28] Charles Hale, who met Buckle in 1862, also discussed his method of work with him. "He has long since abandoned the practice of writing at night," Hale records, "and now does not put pen to paper after three o'clock in the afternoon. . . . When he is engaged in composition, he walks about the room . . . until he has composed an entire paragraph, when he sits down and writes it, never retouching, nor composing sentence by sentence, which he thinks has a tendency to give an abrupt and jerky effect to what is written. Traces of this, he thinks, may be found in Macaulay's style."[29] If a passage he had written did not satisfy him he preferred re-casting to alteration.

Buckle took great pains in studying literary style, and analysed and contrasted that of the best English and French writers. "It ought to be a lesson," wrote Helen Taylor,* "to young writers, that a style so brilliant as Mr. Buckle's was built on a foundation of so much drudgery and scrupulous attention to detail."[30] He was a severe critic of the writings of others and it was a valuable lesson, says Miss Shirreff, "to hear him dissect an ill-constructed sentence, and point out how the meaning could have been brought out with full clearness by such or such changes".[31] The trouble he took over his style was not unappreciated. "He is the very best writer of the English Language that ever lived,"[32] Darwin declared.

If it was Macaulay's ambition to find his History in the drawing-rooms of young ladies, it was Buckle's intention to be read by the working class. "I want my book," he told Miss Shirreff, "to get among the mechanic's institutes and the *people*; and to tell you the honest truth, I would rather be praised in popular and, as you rightly call them, vulgar papers than in scholarly publications."[33] He believed that unless his book was well written it would prove of little value as it would find few readers, and thus his plan to popularize his ideas

* Helen Taylor was John Stuart Mill's stepdaughter. After Buckle's death she edited his literary remains. See below p. 102.

would be frustrated. "I am deeply impressed," he told his publisher, "with the importance of a clear and popular style, and I have made great and constant efforts to attain it."[34] Buckle attributed much of the criticism he attracted to the clarity of his style. "If I had written more obscurely," he once told a friend, "I should have excited less anger."[35]

For a short time Buckle seems to have considered taking the bar examination as a legal career would have given him time for writing, while the study of the law would not have been irrelevant to his historical work. But his cousin, whose advice he greatly valued, argued that his health was too uncertain. "He consulted me," wrote John Buckle, "about the law as a profession. I dissuaded him on the ground of health alone. Except one I never knew so quick a man and his quickness and industry would have commanded ultimate success—but his physique would have given way."[36]

Miss Strickland, whom Buckle first met in Rome, has left the following description of his life in London during the years in which he was working at the first volume of his History. "Mr. Buckle always spent one evening in the week with us, more frequently two. His mornings were always passed in his library, indeed the flower of his youth was passed alone, and the labour of his mind was so great during the day that it was absolutely necessary he should have some little relaxation in the evening, and then with all the audacity of genius, he would talk in the wildest and most amusing manner possible; all the time petting his mother, who was quite well then and so happy by his side. We used to talk after dinner until tea was over, and then he used to read to us. It is impossible to describe the pleasure of those evenings. Mr. Buckle read well and liked an audience, so we were frequently joined by some neighbours at that time. Shakespeare, Macaulay, Sydney Smith, Francis Horner and Charles Lamb, were the authors he generally chose, at least they were those I best remember. At that time his book was not sufficiently advanced, but later, he generally read portions of what he had been writing in the morning. Mr. Buckle and his mother paid us a visit at Hastings, and we all went to stay with them at Brighton. But soon after these pleasant visits, a shadow seemed to come over dear Mrs. Buckle, frequently for two or three days at a time, she was confined to her room with most distressing headaches, and I cannot help thinking *now* that she lived in too abstemious a manner, taking very little for Breakfast and a piece of dry bread, and a glass of water *only* for luncheon and no early tea before a seven o'clock dinner. But at times she seemed perfectly well, and then they used to have most delightful dinner parties, and many were the clever and distinguished people I have met there."[37]

Miss Strickland was not alone in thinking that he read beautifully. "His voice and intonation," writes Miss Shirreff, "were peculiar; his delivery was impassioned, as if another soul spoke through his usually calm exterior; and it has seemed to me of many a familiar passage, that I never had known its full power and beauty till I heard it from his lips."[38] Although he was tone deaf, his voice was extremely musical, and certainly every woman who heard him recite was deeply moved by the experience. Mrs. Augusta Huth, whose son was later to be Buckle's biographer, describes how one evening the talk turned to Shakespeare's plays, and how Buckle said that *Richard II* was the most poetical. Then, leaning against the chimneypiece, he began to illustrate this assertion by quoting the speech: "No matter where, of comfort no man speak!" Mrs. Huth doubted whether anyone had heard it rendered so perfectly.

Nearly all accounts agree that Buckle was an exceptionally good conversationalist. "One could not be five minutes in a room with him without being aware that a talker unusually informed with book knowledge was present. From the news of the morning to the most recondite and curious recesses of learning, Mr. Buckle ranged freely. . . ."[39] He was anything but a recluse by nature and loved London dinner-parties. During the season he gave dinners to between eight and eighteen guests, two or three times a week. Long before he became famous for his writing, people were struck by his conversational powers. His remarkable memory enhanced his talk, since a great deal of English literature had become part of his mind.

Delightful as most people found his conversation, there were those who were bored by him. He was inclined to be self-assertive, and was so anxious to get to the root of a subject that he sometimes wearied those who did not share his zest for truth. His tendency to monopolize conversations, and his persistence in pursuing themes to their logical conclusion, in time decreased. As he mixed more in society, he grew more willing to listen and less inclined to controversy or to monologue. "During many years' wanderings throughout the world," wrote Alexander Gray, who travelled for a time with Buckle in the East, "I have never met anyone, whose general knowledge or conversational power could be compared for a moment with that of Buckle. Whether in botanizing up Sinai, or geologizing at Petra, in astronomy, medicine, chemistry, theology, or languages, everything and every subject appeared to me to be handled as if by a professional."[40] It is true that by 1862 everyone who met him on his travels had already heard of his fame, but wherever he went he nevertheless made a very profound impression. Miss Marguerite Power, who met Buckle at Cairo, a few weeks before his death, wrote: "I have known most of the celebrated talkers of—I will not say how many years back—of the time, in a word, when Sydney Smith rejoiced in his green, bright, old age; and Luttrell, and Rogers, and Tommy Moore were still capable of giving forth an occasional flash; and when the venerable Lord Brougham, and yet more venerable Lord Lyndhurst, delighted in friendly and brilliant sparring at dinner-tables, whose hosts are now in their half-forgotten graves. I have known some brilliant talkers in Paris—Lamartine and Dumas, and Cabarrus, and brightest, or at least most constantly bright of all, the late Madame Emile de Girardin. I knew Douglas Jerrold; and I am still happy enough to claim acquaintance with certain men and women whose names, though well known, it were perhaps invidious now to mention. But, for inexhaustibility, versatility, memory, and self-confidence, I never met any to compete with Buckle. Talking was meat, and drink, and sleep to him; he lived upon talk. He could keep pace with any given number of interlocutors on any given number of subjects, from the abstrusest point on the abstrusest science to the lightest *jeu d'esprit*, and talk them all down, and be quite ready to start fresh."[41]

Mr. Longmore, who like Miss Power met Buckle in Cairo, also found him the best talker he had ever met. "I never longed but when in his company," says Longmore, "for my countryman Bozzy's somewhat questionable talent of reporting private conversation. He was, however, not merely a good talker, he was an excellent listener as well. He even liked a little modest contradiction, as serving to bring out his own dialectic skill to greater effect. If, indeed, he saw symptoms of conceit or of impudent dogmatism on the part of an opponent, he was down upon him like a sledge-hammer; and I have often pitied a poor wretch who had to submit to be pounded by him to pieces, though I must say the victim generally richly deserved it. He had, besides, another admirable trait of a good conversationist—he never prosed, and woe betide him who became prosy in his company. In a single lucid sentence or two he took up the threads of the arguments over which the proser was drivelling, and completely shut him up, by clearly explaining to the company what there seemed no prospect of his being able, in any reasonable time, to make clear himself."[42]

Although even those who found Buckle persistent and overbearing agreed that his conversational powers were remarkable, not everybody was of the same mind about some of his other characteristics. Several people found him egoistical and selfish. Kate Stanley (later Lady Amberley) liked him when she met him dining with George Grote, but her mother found him rather a bore. "I enjoyed my evening at Mrs. Grote's very much," Kate wrote to her brother. "We went at 10 and everyone went away at 11 so it was not late. There were about 30 people: Buckle, Lacaita, Motley, Huxley, Garcia—Aunt Kitty and Eliza. I talked to Mr. Grote a little and I liked him. . . . Buckle talked a long time to Mama and said he disliked the prize fight but disliked more the government interfering with it. They talked of Mill on Liberty and he approved very much of my reading it; Mama did not like him as he was very egoistical and told her how many hours he slept without turning in his bed and what exercise he took; he interested me very much and I liked talking to him."[43]

John Buckle, a few years after his cousin's death, told John Stuart Mill that Henry was "intensely selfish, and his own personal comfort and safety were always the first consideration. . . . I cannot say that I ever knew him sacrifice his plans or personal comfort even to his Mother."[44] If Buckle appeared to his cousin to be so utterly self-centred, others who knew him as well, if not better, thought otherwise. Miss Shirreff, who saw John Buckle's letter, indignantly denied the charges it contained. "If Mr. J. Buckle," she wrote, "never knew him to postpone his plans or wishes for his Mother I can only say that he knew him less than I did."[45] "I have known him," wrote Miss Strickland, "to sit for hours by her bedside, in a darkened room, and that in the middle of the day too, when no pleasure in the world would have tempted him to leave his library except in the evening."[46]

Often he would set aside his work to help his friends. He offered to read some school textbooks, for example, to help Miss Shirreff in her work on education. "I will gladly read them," he wrote, "and give you the best opinion I can form of their merit. This, or anything else in my power, I shall be truly happy to do; but never again use me so ill as to write me a note doubting whether or no I grudge giving up time in order to help you. There is no particular reason why I should hurry in my own work, and there is reason why I should assist you, if I can; the reason being simply the selfish one of doing myself a pleasure."[47] Not content merely to help Miss Shirreff, he offered his assistance to her friends. "I can never be too busy," he writes, "to help a friend of yours."[48] An old lady who knew him from his boyhood, said that his kindness and sympathy was almost more than human. "I shall never forget," she said, "what he was to me when I found myself suddenly alone in the world, and what he was to me ever afterwards. Even though he had only a few days in town to prepare for his Eastern journey, he walked across the park to see me, and to bid me farewell. He asked about my health; he gave me advice. He did it as if it were both a pleasure and a duty to see that I did the right thing for myself before he left England. I am neither handsome nor clever, nor have I rank or title, but he never forgot that his mother had been fond of me! And I have often been made a good deal of by other people, simply because they saw that the celebrated Buckle treated me with such respect."[49]

The divergent impressions that Buckle left on those who knew him were particularly marked in the matter of money. He was on the whole extremely tolerant, but he hated extravagance and deplored financial disorder. There were those who thought that he was excessively interested in money, and that he was miserly. It is true that he kept his accounts very accurately, and often used to say that there was no one passion which has done so much good to Mankind as the love of money, but he had good reason to be frugal. If he was to devote himself to writing, to buy the books he required for his work, and to look after his invalid mother as he desired, he could only do so by avoiding extravagance. Moreover he had decided not to marry until his income was £3,000 a year, and as it originally did not exceed half that amount, strict saving was necessary.

Careful as he was about his expenditure, he was never greedy for money and did not extend his parsimony to any but himself. At a time when he was teaching his servants to rebind his damaged books in brown paper, he was offering to pay for a holiday for a convalescent friend. All his charities were secret and those most ready to accuse him were the least likely to know about his generosity. It was his custom when accosted by a beggar to ask him his name and address; nine times out of ten he was given a false one; but although the slums he had to visit were very disagreeable, yet the pleasure of giving food to a starving family repaid him many times over for his trouble. "He was fond," says Miss Shirreff, "of the comforts and luxuries of life and indeed his health made many things necessary to him which are luxuries to others, but he could give generously and his charities were as large as they were secret."[50] Once, Mrs. Huth, after meeting him at the house of a mutual friend, offered to take him home in her carriage. He asked to be taken to an out-of-the-way street, saying that he had business there. It was only long after that she accidentally discovered that the business was one of those errands of charity to which he devoted so much of his time.

Another charge made against Buckle was that he was effeminate and old maidish. It is true that he was meticulous. On Mondays he ate only toast because no fresh bread was obtainable. In his opinion no woman could make tea properly until he had taught her. The cups and even the spoons had to be warmed. "It's the only time my servants are afraid of me," he said, "when I am at my meals." Mrs. Grote, the wife of the historian, went so far as to tell Sir William Hardman that Buckle "was a great gourmand even to the extent of fearful gluttony, and that he drank large quantities of Champagne and Port wine to 'repair the waste of mental fibre'."[51] He was not only fastidious about food. When Mrs. Huth asked him to stay in a furnished house she had taken for the season at St. Leonards, he remarks in his letter of acceptance: "You will, I know, be careful to have the bed thoroughly aired. This I should not mention, except that lodging-houses at this time of the year have often been long unoccupied, and I am subject to pains in the limbs, which are half rheumatic and half neuralgic."[52] The trouble he took to look after himself was very necessary, as his health was always precarious, and he took exactly the same care of others. When in the last year of his life he took Mrs. Huth's two boys with him to the East, he never stopped fussing about their health.

Buckle was not without a sense of humour, and many people noticed a boyish playfulness in him, particularly when with his mother. A friend of Mrs. Huth, who met Buckle for the first time at her dinner-table, was struck "not by his brilliancy, which he had expected, but by his delightful humour. . . . Poor Mr. Capel as the representative of the Clergy among us, had to serve as butt to Mr. Buckle's clever sarcasms against them. Mr. Capel defended them valiantly. . . . At the end of the discussion Mr. Buckle said, quite seriously, that he considered the evil inflicted by the Clergy on Mankind outweighed any good they had done."[53] Even ten weeks before his death at Damascus his cheerfulness had not deserted him. Edward Huth, the elder of the two boys Buckle took on the journey, apologized for careless spelling in his letter home by saying: "You must excuse mistakes because

Mr. B. will sing 'ri too, rall oo rall oo ralloo'." Only during the very last days of his life did Buckle's high spirits and flow of fun fail.

All his life he was very fond of smoking. "There are two things," he said, "for which I never grudge money—books and cigars." For a time he tried a pipe but found it rather too strong. So soothing was the influence of tobacco upon him that unless he had three cigars a day, one after breakfast, one before dinner and one in bed, he said that he could neither read, write nor talk. As he could not smoke when walking, the effort being too great for him, he never went to stay in any house where smoking was objected to, and more than one house which had never tolerated a cigar before, bore with it for his sake. "Those who delight in the exquisite flavour of Tobacco," he observes in his Common Place Book, "and above all those who have experienced its soothing influence over an irritated brain, may form some idea of the enthusiasm with which it was welcomed by all classes."[54] Buckle was as particular about his cigars, as he was about his bed, or his tea. Henry Huth once sent him some to try. They were returned with the following note. "I return the sample of cigars which you kindly sent to me. I have smoked three or four in the hope of getting accustomed to their peculiar flavour, but there is a sort of earthy taste about them which I cannot relish."[55]

Although Buckle had no pretension to good looks, "he had fine eyes, and a massive, well-shaped head; but premature baldness made the latter rather singular than attractive; and beyond a look of power, in the upper part of the face especially, there was nothing to admire".[56] In the last year of his life he was described as "tall and slender, although he is a large man; he stoops a little in standing; his head, well shaped, is partly bald; and although his features are not striking in themselves, they are rendered so by his animated expression".[57] For much of his life Buckle looked very much older than he was. Mr. Longmore, who met him in Egypt, describes him as: "a singularly old-looking man for his years. Extremely bald, and very much bent, he would have easily passed for nigh threescore, while he was in reality twenty years younger. Among the Nile travellers of that year he always went by the appellation of 'old Buckle', when in reality he was a juvenile when compared with many of us."[58]

That Buckle looked so much older than he was, must partly have been the result of bad health. There seems to have been little organically wrong with him, and his illness was almost certainly nervous in origin, resulting partly from overwork. Even his recreations, such as Chess and conversation, stimulated rather than rested his brain. It was almost impossible for him not to work.* When he was a child his doctors had advised that his brain should not be overtaxed, and it is therefore hardly surprising that his industry as a grown man should often have exhausted him. "I have been suffering from weakness and depression of spirits," he wrote to his sister, in 1860, "with all sorts of odd sensations, and strange bodies flitting before my eyes. Mr. Morgan says, what in fact, is obvious, that the brain has been seriously overworked, and that nothing will restore it but complete rest and the most bracing air I can get."[59] Anxiety over his mother's health was a source of constant worry to him. During the last months of her life, her mind would sometimes wander. Unable to endure it, he would rush from the house.

Buckle was subject to attacks of fainting. "Coming home through Hyde Park," he writes in his journal on 24th June, 1856, "I suddenly felt ill, and fell down insensible."[60] During one illness, as the result of "complete and sudden nervous exhaustion", his hand shook so much that he could hardly write, and "his overworked nerves showed their state of weakness by his constant little groans, as if he were going to speak and stopped himself suddenly".[61] So restless a sleeper was he at the time of this collapse, that one night he fell out of bed, and his voice was heard so loud, that the servants thought he was calling, and came down to see what he wanted.

Because of his ill health, Buckle was tormented by fears that he would not finish his work, and by the thought of how vast a distance there was between his talents and achievements. When, in 1856, Dr. Allatt, his brother-in-law, urged him to put aside his first volume for a time, Buckle wrote: "To lose another season would be a great vexation to me; and then, too, these early checks make me think mournfully of the future. If I am to be struck down in the vestibule, how shall I enter the temple?"[62] "I will not be so affected as to conceal from you," he wrote to a friend, "that I am a little alarmed, and at times very depressed, to think that with such large hopes I have such little powers. My head is at times weak and slightly confused; but it

* During his month's tour of Brittany in 1850, he read amongst other books: Montesquieu *De L'e'sprit des Lois*; Corneille's Plays; Shakespeare; Capefigué, *La Reforme et la Ligue*; Voltaire *Louis XIV*; Schiller *Geschichte des Abfalls der vereinigten Niederlande von der spanischen Regierung*; Todd *Life of Cranmer*; Blackstone *Commentaries on the English Law*; Reeve *History of English Law*; Caumont *Architecture Religieuse au Moyen Age*; Knight *Architectural Tour in Normandy*; Dawson Turner *Tour in Normandy*; and Murray's Handbook.

goes off (the feeling, not the head—I will have my joke) again directly. They tell me that I have nothing to fear, and I am not apprehensive except of my future. To break down in the midst of what, according to my measure of greatness, is a great career—and to pass away, and make no sign—this, I own, is a prospect which I now for the first time see is possible; and the thought of which seems to chill my life as it creeps over me. Perhaps I have aspired too high; but I have at times such a sense of power, such a feeling of reach and grasp, and if I may so say, such a command over the realm of thought, that it was no idle vanity to believe that I could do more than I shall now ever be able to effect."[63]

His mother's health, which so greatly affected his own, first broke down in June of 1852. "From 10.20 to 2," he notes in his journal, "wrote my book, but could do little being detained by a long conversation . . . and thinking about dearest Jenny, who, I fear, is very poorly."[64] How seriously ill she was, appears from the following account which he sent to Eliza Strickland. "Dr. Roupell has just been. He says my mother is better but he refused to hold out any hopes of her recovery beyond those which he expressed last Sunday. . . . Disease properly so called she has none—that is to say none of the organs are affected in their structure—but she is labouring under a complete prostration the result of which Dr. R. says it is impossible to predict. . . . Annie* goes to Oxford Terrace on Tuesday. . . . Perhaps you would call and see her. Do not show this note to her—for I never tell her the whole of Dr. Roupell's opinion. She has not sufficient command over her countenance and any appearance of grief would alarm my mother who still remains cheerful and sanguine. . . . Dr. Roupell says if she ever were to be alarmed he would not answer for the consequence."[65]

Besides Dr. Roupell, Mrs. Buckle consulted a number of medical men, including Macaulay's physician, the celebrated Dr. Bright, who lived at 11 Saville Row, next door to the Grotes. But no amount of expensive advice seems to have effected any permanent improvement. "She is slowly recovering," Buckle wrote in 1854, "from a very serious illness and has not called this season even upon her nearest relations."[66] But a year later she was no better, and "her weakness was so great that the few stairs she had to mount she literally crawled up, holding, not by the rails, but by the stairs themselves".[67]

Buckle's anxiety for his mother's health made him sleep badly

* Annie Hutchinson, Buckle's sister.

and distracted him from his book. In answer to a letter from Miss Shirreff, he says, "You asked me to write about my mother; she is indeed altered, and I am becoming very uneasy. . . . You, who can form some idea, and only some, of what my mother is to me, may imagine how unhappy I am. It is hardly worth while, with this hanging over me, to say anything about myself; but I am not at all well—sleeping badly, and having painful, nervous feelings at night. . . .

"This is a sad note, but it is the only sort of one I can write. Still, I shall be glad, and indeed anxious to hear about you, what you are doing, and if you are going abroad? And Mrs. Grey, too: it will, I am afraid, be long before I see either of you. If I can give you any advice about your book, do not let the tone of this note prevent your asking me. I think the more miserable one is, the more willing one becomes to draw nearer to others."[68]

Buckle and his mother spent a lot of time living in furnished houses, which they took for a few months, while they let 59 Oxford Terrace. Sometimes they stayed with Mrs. Buckle's sister, Mrs. Ward, at Brighton, and quite often they visited Mary Allatt, who lived at Boulogne, or Annie Hutchinson, who had a house in Kent. In 1850, before Mrs. Buckle became an invalid, she toured Britanny with her son, Henry having first read a number of guide books and histories of the places they proposed to see. They started from Paris, and then went on to Orléans, Blois and Tours. They saw the Bayeux tapestry, and visited Mont St. Michel, "with which we were delighted". In 1853 Buckle went to Ireland alone, having been ordered a change of air for his health. There, he poked about the book-shops in Dublin, played some Chess, and explored the country-side. But apart from these occasional holidays, his life was a placid one, lived mostly in London.

Soon after he returned from Ireland, Buckle met Miss Shirreff and her sister, Mrs. Grey. These talented ladies had already written some books together, and were pioneers in the cause of women's education. In 1850 they had published a two-volume work entitled *Thoughts on Self-Culture Addressed to Women*, which Buckle admired. Long after his death the sisters carried on their good work. They supported the foundation of Girton, started the Maria Grey Training College for Women Teachers, and helped to found and run the Froebel Society. Maria Shirreff married her first cousin, William Grey, a nephew of the Prime Minister who carried the first Reform Bill. She was an early advocate of Women's Suffrage, and also the authoress of *Last Words to Girls on life in School and after School.* Her sister, Emily, was too busy improving the minds of young ladies to find time for romance, but if Buckle had lived longer, he might have married her.

"It was in the spring of 1854," writes Miss Shirreff, "that we first made acquaintance with Mr. Buckle. The intimacy became so close, and occupied so large a place in our lives while it lasted, that it seems strange, on looking back, to realize how short a time actually witnessed its beginning and its close. . . . The period during which we were in the habit of frequently meeting or corresponding was little more than five years. Three years later, he who had been the life of our circle lay helpless and friendless amongst strangers, and the utterances of his genius were hushed for ever in that silence nothing mortal can break. . . .

"A valued friend of ours had known Mr. Buckle and his mother for some time, and paid us the compliment of thinking we should appreciate him, unknown as he then was to the world. Accordingly he arranged a dinner-party for the purpose of making us acquainted. It was a house in which good conversation was valued, and where consequently guests contributed their best. Talk flowed on, mostly on literary or speculative subjects, and Mr. Buckle was brilliant and original beyond even what we had been led to expect. . . .

"That first meeting led to many others, at our own house or among friends; quiet evenings or long afternoon talks, in which he sometimes was led to forget the rigid method of his hours. It was less easy to know his mother, for she was even then an invalid; but he was very eager to bring us together, and succeeded ere very long in doing so. The acquaintance thus begun, rapidly extended to all our familiar circle, grew into intimacy with other members of our family, and ripened into one of those friendships which are not reckoned by years, but are felt early in their growth to be beyond the power of time to alter.

"In the course of that spring we spent several weeks in the neighbourhood of London, and Mr. Buckle, like other friends, was invited from time to time to spend a day with us. We did not know then what a rare exception he was making in his habitual life when he came down before luncheon and stayed with us till the late evening. Pleasant days they were; and, like a boy out of school, he seemed to enjoy strolling in the garden, rambling in Richmond Park, roaming also in conversation over every imaginable subject, and crowding into the few hours of his visit food for thought, and recollections of more amusing talk, such as weeks of intercourse with others can seldom furnish. . . .

"Another and still more unusual break in Mr. Buckle's habits was a day spent with us at the Crystal Palace, then lately opened, which he always said he never should have seen but for our taking him, and which he never re-visited. It was a day more rich in many ways than mortal days are often allowed to be. We were a large party, all intimates, and all ready for enjoyment, and for the kind of enjoyment which the Crystal Palace offered for the first time. It was a lovely summer's day, and the mere drive some miles out of London—for there was no noisy, whistling railway then—was a delight. . . .

"We were not altogether disabused at that time of the illusions of a new era of peaceful progress which the first Exhibition of 1851 had seemed to inaugurate. . . . None shared the illusions of that period more fondly than Mr. Buckle. He thought he had reached philosophically, and could prove as necessary corollaries of a certain condition of knowledge and civilization, the conclusion which numbers held, without knowing why; and it was this train of thought which made the opening of 'The People's Palace' interesting to him. . . . We had wandered through the different courts, reproducing in a manner as new then as it was striking, the memorials of the past. From Nineveh to Egypt—Greece—Imperial Rome—Moslem Granada, and Italy through her days of glory to her decline—all had been passed in review; and he then turned, as he loved to do, to the future, with its bright promise of reward to man's genius, and of continued triumph over the blind powers of Nature; and it seemed but a natural transition from his own speaking, as if still uttering his own thoughts, when he took up Hamlet's words: 'What a piece of work is man! How noble in reason! How infinite in faculty!' . . ."[69]

Buckle shared with Miss Shirreff and her sister an interest in education. He once told Kate Stanley that he liked "women to be highly educated but not masculine", and that he thought that "all men of genius have a great deal of women in their nature and are always gentle and tender".[70] Many of his letters to Miss Shirreff and Mrs. Grey are about women's education. "I take great interest," he writes to the latter, "in what she is doing,* or about to do, on female Education. The grand thing would be to make women more ashamed of ignorance; but that is perhaps too difficult a task to undertake. The

* Miss Shirreff was working on her book *Intellectual Education, and its Influence on the Character and Happiness of Women*. 1858.

next best thing to seeing the ignominy of ignorance is to feel the beauty of knowledge—and there I think something might be done. And in this point of view I might caution Miss Shirreff against advising too much to be learnt."[71]

Buckle told Mrs. Huth very much the same thing when he discovered that her daughter was taught Latin. "My dear Mrs. Huth," he exclaimed, "what induced you to make her study one of the most difficult of languages? She will teach it herself, if she wishes to know it, by the time she is twenty; and for the present the best thing you can do is to make her forget what she has learned, as fast as possible. Let her read books on travels: they will teach her pleasantly, and without fatigue, much that is valuable. If she does not care to read these, let her read story-books. It is of the greatest importance to foster a habit of reading; the rest will come of itself."[72]

Buckle showed a realism about education which was, and is, singularly lacking in most of the literature on the subject. He particularly warned Miss Shirreff against considering too much what ought to be, rather than what can be. "My fear is," he tells her, "lest you should place the standard of excellence too high, and thus intimidate those you wish to allure. . . . I cordially agree with all you say about a wide range of study . . . but remember that you are addressing minds, most of which either do not perceive this, or, at all events, perceive it very faintly. The feeling of intellectual sympathy is by no means a very early step even in minds of some power, and in ordinary cases the step is never taken at all. I doubt, therefore, whether in this line of acquirement you can make proselytes. For those who are capable of being convinced will already be converted. Your mission is with the heathen; why, then, preach to the regenerate and baptize the elect? If you deal with average minds you must hold out average inducements—such, for example, as the value of knowledge, as a discipline in the acquisition of it; or, as a disgrace not to have it."[73]

Wherever Buckle went, it was his custom to talk to local schoolmasters and find out about their methods of teaching and discipline. Perhaps because he had been spared it himself, he was an advocate of corporal punishment. "You must deal with boys either in a rational or in an irrational manner," he told a parent. "If they will listen to the arguments of their superiors, you do not require punishment; but if they will not listen to reason, you must treat them as irrational beings, and flog them."[74] On one occasion he got into conversation with a teacher who praised the boldness of the authors of *Essays and*

Reviews and then remarked, "But there is another, even bolder man, of whom, I dare say, you have heard, and whose book you have probably read, I mean Buckle." "What has he done?" asked Buckle. "Buckle," came the reply, "don't you know Buckle?" "I saw," Buckle said in telling the story afterwards, "that I was falling in his esteem through my ignorance, so I said, 'Oh yes, Buckle to be sure'; and took my leave."

At one time Buckle had hoped to publish the first volume of his History as early as 1852, but as he progressed his horizon enlarged, and it was five more years before it was finished. So hard did he work that his friends feared he would break down under the strain. But, as he pointed out to Miss Shirreff, to rest would be only to waste time as his mind would always be active. By July of 1855 the first volume was finished, and Buckle records in his journal: "Began at length the great task of copying my work for the press."[75] In January of the following year, he turned to copying the notes. This task proved more formidable than he expected, particularly as he checked them so thoroughly. "How unhandsome it is of mankind," he complained, "to expect authors to give proof of what they assert, and how silly it is of authors to give it." While he was working on the notes, he began to negotiate with the firm of J. W. Parker for the publication of his history. John Parker had been Printer to the University of Cambridge, and had made his name there by introducing steam-power to the press, a step which for some reason proved so controversial that the Bible Society long declined to circulate books thus printed. Then he established himself on his own, published *Fraser's Magazine*, and, amongst others, the works of Froude, Charles Kingsley and John Stuart Mill. In 1863, the year after Buckle's death, Parker sold his business to Longman.

Unfortunately Buckle could not agree with Parker on terms for future editions of the book, should they be demanded. "In regard to any future edition," he writes to Parker, "it will naturally be my wish to remain in your hands; but I cannot formally bind myself down to any such engagement, because to do so would in fact be surrendering the control of my own property: it would be equivalent to selling the copyright without reaping the advantages of the sale, since it would be a compact which would bind me without binding you."[76] Parker, however, was not prepared to make the desired concession, and so Buckle decided to print at his own expense. "As you were unwilling," he writes to Parker, "and perhaps reasonably so—to run the risk of printing my work on conditions which I was equally unwilling to accept, I have determined to print it at my own expense. . . .

"My object in writing to you at present is to ask if you would be disposed to publish on commission the 1,500 copies which I am printing. In this way you would avoid the risk of loss, and, should the work prove tolerably successful, you will have a criterion by which to estimate any proposal you might like to make for the subsequent volumes, or for subsequent editions of the first volume. Should the book fail, you will, of course, not be bound to continue your connexion with me after the first edition; and if, on the other hand, it should succeed, it will be for your interest and for mine that the connexion should be a permanent one. We should in this way be united by the bond of self-interest. . . ."[77] Parker agreed to this proposal, and a first impression of 1,500 copies was prepared.

The decision to bring out the first volume alone was reached after much discussion.* Buckle at first had intended to complete the whole introduction rather than publish it in parts, but his mother prevailed on him to change his mind. She suspected that she could not afford to wait, and although she tried desperately to conceal from her son the fact that she was dying, she daily betrayed to Miss Shirreff "her knowledge that her days were numbered, and her anxiety to see her son take his right place in the world. She had had no vulgar ambition for him; she had been content that he should hide his bright gifts in their quiet home so long as the serious purpose of his life required it, but now that it was partly attained, that a portion of his work was ready, she grew eager to see those gifts acknowledged before she herself went forth to be no more seen on earth. Chapter by chapter, almost page by page, had that first volume been planned with her, criticized by her; every speculation, as it arose, talked over with her; and now her mind was oppressed with the fear that she might never know how those pages, so unutterably precious to her, would be welcomed by those whose welcome would crown her beloved with fame. Yet, to spare him, she never would betray in his presence the real secret of her growing impatience; only when we were alone she would say to me, 'Surely God will let me live to see Henry's book;' and she did live to see it, and to read the dedication to herself, the only words there that she was unprepared to meet. Mr. Buckle told

* This first volume was only part of an introduction to the work which Buckle planned to write. Although he lived to bring out another volume, he never completed even the introduction to his History.

me he bitterly repented the rash act of laying the volume before her to enjoy her surprise and pleasure; for he was alarmed at her agitation. Even the next day, when showing it to me, she could not speak, but pointed with tears to the few words that summed up to her the full expression of his love and gratitude. She thus saw her ardent wish gratified, and her impatience was but too well justified. The second volume was dedicated to her memory alone!"[78]

Miss Shirreff seems to have been one of the very few people, apart from his mother, whose criticism Buckle valued or invited. "I have adopted," he writes to her, "at least five out of six of every emendation you proposed."[79] The Reverend George Capel was another friend to whom he always listened seriously.* "I have just received your truly friendly and indeed affectionate note," he writes to him. "If anything could increase my esteem for you what you have written would do so—for I completely appreciate your motives. But I *cannot* promise to blot out a passage which contains my honest opinions, until I hear what your objections are. . . . Meanwhile I promise two things. First that no one else shall hear the passage. Secondly that I will listen with earnestness to whatever you can urge against it."[80]

Early in 1857 the long-delayed book at last appeared and was instantly successful. Although Buckle was attacked by many reviewers, the public was struck by his originality, boldness and industry. "Not a line from his pen," says Miss Shirreff, "had ever been seen till this volume of 800 pages, purporting to be the first of a long work, took the public by surprise. He sprang at once into celebrity; and singularly enough, considering the nature of the book, he attained not merely to literary fame, but to fashionable notoriety. To his own great amusement, he became the lion of the season; his society was courted, his library besieged with visitors, and invitations poured in upon him, even from houses where philosophical speculation had surely never been a passport before. To himself, as to the public, his previous obscurity added to the glare of his sudden triumph. . . . He had been proudly confident in his own power, and he felt a natural pleasure in seeing it for the first time publicly acknowledged; but his mind was too earnestly bent on what he yet hoped to achieve, to dwell with complacent satisfaction on the social distinction won by past exertion; and in the first flush of his triumph he refused the most flattering

* The Reverend George Capel was a clergyman who kept a small boarding-school at Carshalton. He was a friend of the Huths, who sent their sons to his school.

invitations to different parts of the country, in order to spend the few weeks of absence from his mother with friends in a small country parsonage, where his time was divided between study, playing and talking with children, and long evening conversations, into which he threw the same richness and animation as if the most brilliant circle had been gathered round him."[81]

After the publication of his History Buckle became the lion of the season. "Let me hear what you think of Buckle," wrote Meredith to Janet Ross, "who has become a topic!"[82] "I have not read any part of Buckle on Civilization," Clough admitted to William Allingham, "which is however the great literary success of the day. Nothing of the size and substance has had anything like the favourable reception which this big volume has met with—and the author has become Chief Lion for the time being."[83] Buckle was soon introduced to many of the great men of his day: Thackeray, Huxley, Darwin and Herbert Spencer. "I am dining out a good deal," he admits, "and hear much of my own success; but it moves me not. Often could I exclaim with Hamlet, 'they fool me to the top of my bent'."[84] Huxley, who met Buckle at Herbert Spencer's house one Sunday afternoon, was much struck by the historian's feeble gait and remarked: "Ah, I see the kind of man, he is top-heavy." "I suspect," Spencer comments, "that the analogy suggested was not without truth. He had taken in a much larger quantity of matter than he could organize; and he staggered under the mass of it."[85] Buckle, himself, realized that his book was too discursive, "and what is worse, the discursiveness is too ostentatiously displayed".[86]

The ubiquitous Charles Greville met Buckle dining with the Grotes. "He is not prepossessing in appearance," Greville records in his memoirs, "but he talks very well and makes a great display of knowledge and extensive reading, though without pedantry or dogmatism."[87] John Tyndall also met him and thus described the encounter. "On Friday last I was invited to meet Livingstone, the African traveller. I found him a man full of sound practical sense. I sat beside a Mr. Buckle, who has recently published a book that has caused a very great sensation in London: a *History of Civilization in England*. He is the literary lion of the day. His conversation is wonderfully energetic, and his voice at table generally masks all other voices. Soon after sitting down, we had a little sparring as to the influence of moral agents in the culture and advancement of the world. After the ladies left the table, our differences broke out into open war. It was thoroughly good-humoured but energetic in the extreme. He talked loud, and I responded with corresponding vigour."[88]

Charles Darwin was one of Buckle's contemporaries who greatly admired the *History of Civilization*, which he described as "wonderfully clever and original, and written with astonishing knowledge."[89] So much did he value the book that he studied it again later. John Stuart Mill also recognized Buckle's exceptional powers, and thought that "he was performing a most valuable function in popularizing many important ideas, and stimulating the desire to apply general principles to the explanation and prediction of social facts".[90] James Russell Lowell was yet another who predicted that Buckle's History would exercise a profound influence on the thought of his time. "I have employed," he writes, "all the spare time of my gouty week in reading it through. Six hundred and seventy-two pages octavo! And only the beginning of the Introduction after all! . . . As Ellery Channing said of the Bible, 'It is a book worthy to read'. . . . I think Buckle's book is going to exercise a vast influence on thought in this country, where we have a hundred hasty generalizers for one steady thinker. But if it does not lead to a stupid fatalism and a demand-and-supply doctrine for everything, it will do good. . . . What I like about Buckle's book especially is that there is no Buncombe in it—that his conclusions, whether right or wrong (and many of them seem to me to be wrong and even dangerous), are set forth fearlessly and without passion. Perhaps the reason why I like the book is that I disagree with it so much as I do. At any rate, it is a book to be read, for it will certainly influence opinion. . . ."[91]

The impact of the book was by no means confined to England. It quickly found its way all over Europe, and in the year when it was published, Buckle had a visit from a Russian gentleman who told him of its great success at Moscow. The *History of Civilization* was so widely discussed in Russia that its author's name and ideas are mentioned in Chekov's play, *The Cherry Orchard*, in a way which assumes the audience's familiarity with the work.[92] Buckle particularly appealed to young Russian intellectuals, although even peasants read him.[93] "Several times I encountered peasants," wrote Mackenzie Wallace of his travels in the province of Yaroslavl, "who had a small collection of books, and twice I found in such collections, much to my astonishment, a Russian translation of Buckle's *History of Civilization*! How, it may be asked, did a work of this sort find its way to such a place? . . . At the commencement of the present reign there was a curious intellectual movement . . . among the Russian educated classes. The movement assumed various forms, of which two of the most prominent were a desire for encyclopaedic knowledge, and an attempt to reduce all knowledge to a scientific form. For men in this state of mind, Buckle's great work had naturally a powerful fascination. It seemed at first sight to reduce the multifarious, conflicting facts of human history to a few simple principles, and to evolve order out of chaos. Its success, therefore, was great. In the course of a few years no less than four independent translations—so at least I have been informed by a good authority—were published and sold. Every one read, or at least professed to have read, the wonderful book, and many believed that its author was the great genius of the present generation. During the first year of my residence in Russia, I rarely had a serious conversation without hearing Buckle's name mentioned; and my friends almost always assumed that he had succeeded in creating a genuine science of history on the inductive method. . . . In books, periodicals, newspapers, and professional lectures, the name of Buckle was constantly cited—often violently dragged in without the slightest reason—and the cheap translations of his work were sold in enormous quantities. It is not, then, so very wonderful after all that the book should have found its way to two villages in the province of Yaroslavl."[94]

In America the History was received with similar interest and enthusiasm. When it became known that its author intended to treat the New World in his next volume, the Governor of Rhode Island, himself a writer, hastened to invite Buckle to visit his State. "I wish sincerely," wrote the Governor, Samuel Arnold, in February 1862, "that you could come to America to observe for yourself, before writing that portion of your work. Although you would see a nation in arms fighting for its existence against one of the most formidable rebellions recorded in history, and might hear much to wound your pride as an Englishman, arising from the vindictive feeling provoked by the unfriendly policy of Palmerston, yet I am persuaded that the philosopher who has so skilfully analysed the tortuous course of British history in the days of the Stuarts would know how to make a proper allowance for these unfortunate circumstances, and would know better how to discuss American civilization after a few months of personal observation than he could by a lifetime of reading. . . . I promise you a hearty welcome if you will come, for in our camps as well as our cabinets you will find congenial spirits who will hail the historian of Civilization."[95]

Theodore Parker, an influential writer and preacher, whose father, John Parker, had fired the first shot at Lexington, was another enthusiastic American admirer of Buckle. Possibly Parker's love of freedom which led him to advocate the emancipation of slaves and to help John Brown, encouraged him to regard the Englishman as a fellow spirit. "Have you seen," he writes to a friend in England, "a quite remarkable book by H. T. Buckle? It is a *History of Civilization in England.* It is one of the most remarkable and instructive books I have seen from the English press in this century. I do not always agree with him, but he is a great man—learned too in many departments of thought. I have read only the first part of his book. . . . The work is not less significant in its department than the *Vestiges of the Natural History of Creation* in another sphere."[96] Three weeks later Parker had finished reading the History. "I think it is a great book," he says, "and I know none so important since the *Novum Organum* of Bacon. I mean none in English. Of course I except the *Principia* of Newton. This is a *Novum Organum* in the department of history."[97]

CHAPTER II

FAME AND MISFORTUNE

So highly was Buckle regarded after the publication of his history that he was made a member of the Athenaeum, a great distinction for so radical a thinker. For a time it seemed unlikely that he would be elected, as the clergy believed that it was their duty to blackball him. The opposition of those maintaining "endowed doctrines"[1] was thought to be so formidable that Buckle was advised to allow himself to be elected by the Committee. He refused, however, to accept this easy way out, and, as it happened, only nine of the two hundred and seventy-three members who voted opposed him. One member who was asked to vote against Buckle because of his religious views, replied: "If that is your reason I shall certainly go and vote—for him." It was hinted at the time that Buckle's opponents only withdrew at the last moment because they were given to understand that if he was not elected, every clergyman put up would be blackballed.

Soon after his election to the Athenaeum Buckle was invited to lecture at the Royal Institution. The theme he chose was "The Influence of Women on the Progress of Knowledge." It was a subject to which he had given much thought, and about which he held strong views; partly because he recognized what he himself owed to his mother, and partly because Miss Shirreff had convinced him that mankind was seriously harmed by its neglect of women's education. As Buckle had never before been seen, let alone heard, in public, a vast crowd came to his Friday evening lecture, delivered on 19th March, 1858. "The place was crammed," wrote Sir Frederick Pollock, "and he spoke without notes and in the most fluent manner—a very remarkable discourse, the more wonderful because it was his first appearance as a speaker in public, and his life had been that of a secluded student of books, without the discipline of school or University."[2] Applications for tickets had to be refused, and even Buckle could not get as many as he wanted. So great was the crowd outside the Royal Institution that the doors were opened before the usual time and the hall was soon crammed from floor to ceiling. He spoke without hesitation or pause for an hour and forty minutes, and although he had notes in his pocket in case the audience unnerved him, he did not consult them. At the conclusion of the lecture congratulations were showered upon him, Faraday personally thanking him for a delightful evening.

This triumph was the result of much painstaking preparation. Buckle began preparing his talk two months before its delivery. Not only did he write extensive notes on the subject, but he attended the Royal Institution's Friday evening lectures in order to study the methods of experienced speakers. "I cannot make up my mind," he wrote to Parker, "to write the lecture, because, if I were to do so, I am sure that new views or expressions would open themselves to me in speaking, and I should deliver something quite different from what I had written. But I intend to take notes, and as I have a pretty good memory, I am certain that with their aid I could write out the lecture in two days after it was delivered; and, as you appear anxious to have it,* I should not object to do so."[3] In the end Buckle decided to write a rough, preliminary draft. After delivering the lecture, he sent a revised version to Parker, which he completed by sitting up very late one night and working most of the following day.

Busy as Buckle was, writing his next volume, and bringing out a second edition of his first, he nevertheless found time to help and encourage Miss Shirreff in writing her book: *Intellectual Education and its influence on the Character and Happiness of Women.* Miss Shirreff, disheartened by poor health and the difficulty of her subject, nearly gave up. "What! Faint at the eleventh hour!" Buckle writes to her; "Impossible! Surely you do not mean that you despair about your book because it cannot be all that you wish. And as to your other objection, that your system of education is different from others and that therefore you will not get a hearing; I do not believe that these are days in which a view of education (or of any other subject) can be suppressed because it is new. Pray go on: then let me see it: and trust the rest to me, to Mr. Parker, and to the public. Me first! and the public last! Observe the vanity of the man. Seriously, I want to know that you are advancing, as the right publishing season will soon be at hand."[4]

Thus encouraged, Miss Shirreff went on with her book, and as soon as it was finished, she sent it to Buckle. He at once began reading it. "I am delighted," he wrote to her, "you have come up to my

* Parker wanted an advance copy of the lecture in order to print it in *Fraser's Magazine* as soon as possible after it was delivered.

expectations, and that is saying much. I have now (2 p.m.) read to page 70, and therefore will delay no longer telling you what I think. When I saw you last night I purposely abstained from giving you an opinion, though I saw that you wanted one. I abstained because your opening did not satisfy me and does not quite satisfy me now; and seeing you so unwell I could not find it in my heart to tell you so: and I should ill repay the confidence you place in me if I were to flatter you; therefore I said nothing. But the latter half of Chapter I and what I have read in Chapter II is truly admirable. . . . I intend first to finish the whole; and then carefully read again, and if necessary, study the first chapter and we will then look it over. It is possible that I may change my mind: but I do not think I shall. You may rely upon my giving your work such earnest and patient attention as real friendship can secure. Remember that I am only discontented with a small part; and that only because I compare you with yourself."[5]

Very soon after the publication of the first volume of the History, Mrs. Buckle's health rapidly declined. "Month after month she is now gradually altering for the worse," Buckle told Mrs. Grey, "at times slightly better, but on the whole perceptibly losing ground. Her mind is changed, even since I was here last; she is unable to read, she confuses one idea with another, and nothing remains of her, as she once was, except her smile and the exquisite tenderness of her affections. I while away my days here doing nothing, and caring for nothing—because I feel that I have no future.

"Dear Mrs. Grey, I did not intend to write a note to make you feel uncomfortable; but my mind is now full of one idea, and I cannot help dwelling on it. When you too are suffering, it seems selfish in me; but you would not care for my writing if I did not speak what was within."[6]

His mother's illness so worried Buckle that he was unable to write for days on end. "For the last three weeks," he says in October 1858, "I have been unable to write a single line of my history, and I now confine myself to reading and thinking, which I can do as well as ever, though I am too unsettled to compose. My mother is just the same as when I wrote last, caring for nothing but seeing me, though she is too unwell to converse. . . .

'While she is in this state, nothing could induce me to leave her, even for a day, without absolute necessity. She has no pleasure left except that of knowing that I am near her, and as long as that remains, she shall never lose it."[7]

Although Buckle worried so much about his mother that he made himself ill, he did not fully realize how near death she was. For the last six months of her life she was often delirious, but such was the strength of her will that when her son came into the room she became perfectly rational. Her illness deprived him of all enjoyment of his success. "What can I care about fame," he wrote, "when I see the only person who would have gloried in it perishing before my eyes, her noble faculties wasting away, the very power of expressing her affection almost gone? And this is called success! Rather call it cruel and bitter humiliation, and failure at the last moment of all my cherished hopes."[8]

On 31st March Mrs. Buckle grew rapidly worse, and the following evening Buckle recorded in his journal: "My angel mother died peacefully, without pain."[9] Her death left him lonely and desolate. "I remain quite well;" he told a friend, "but my grief increases as association after association rises in my mind and tells me what I have lost. One thing alone I cling to—the deep and unalterable conviction that the end is not yet come, and that we never really die. But it is a separation for half a life; and the most sanguine view that I can take is, that I have a probability before me of thirty years of fame, of power, and of desolation. . . ."[10] When he called on Mrs. Grey less than a fortnight after his bereavement, he was so distressed by the associations which her house recalled, that he did not dare to visit it again for many months.

One comfort was left him: his belief in immortality, and his faith that the separation was not final. Immediately after his mother's death he wrote the passage on immortality with which his review on Mill's "Liberty" concludes. "When the very signs of life are mute; when the last faint tie is severed, and there lies before us nought save the shell and husk of what we loved too well, then truly, if we believed the separation were final, how could we stand up and live? We have staked our all upon a single cast, and lost the stake. There, where we have garnered up our hearts, and where our treasure is, thieves break in and spoil. Methinks, that in that moment of desolation, the best of us would succumb, but for the deep conviction that all is not really over; that we have as yet only seen a part; and that something remains behind. Something behind; something which the eye of reason cannot discern, but on which the eye of affection is fixed. What is that, which, passing over us like a shadow, strains the aching vision as we gaze at it? Whence comes that sense of mysterious companionship in the midst of solitude; that ineffable feeling which cheers the afflicted? Why is it that at these times, our minds are thrown back on themselves, and being so thrown, have a forecast of another and higher state? If this be a delusion, it is one which the affections have themselves created, and we must believe that the purest and noblest elements of our nature conspire to deceive us. So surely as we lost what we love, so surely does hope mingle with grief. . . . Most earnestly would I again urge upon those who cherish the doctrine of immortality, not to defend it, as they too often do, by arguments which have a basis smaller than the doctrine itself. I long to see this glorious tenet rescued from the jurisdiction of a narrow and sectarian theology, which, foolishly ascribing to a single religion the possession of all truth, proclaims other religions to be false, and debases the most magnificent topics by contracting them within the horizon of its own little vision. Every creed which has existed long and played a great part, contains a large amount of truth, or else it would not have retained its hold upon the human mind."[11]

Buckle had begun to read Mill's essay on "Liberty" a few months before his mother's death, and his friend, the Reverend George Capel, seeing that the book helped to divert his attention from her suffering, suggested that he should review it. Accordingly he wrote to Parker offering to do so in *Fraser's*. Early in February he began work on the review. "I am now engaged in earnest on the Essay on Mill," he wrote to Parker in March, "it will be ready for the press by the middle of April at the latest. I am afraid you must make up your mind for a long article, both the subject and the man being of the highest importance. Had I foreseen the labour it cost me, I confess that I should not have undertaken it."[12]

Buckle greatly admired Mill, whose mind he considered to be the most powerful of the age. When Parker, on Mill's instructions, sent Buckle some of Mill's books, he replied that they had "exercised immense influence over most thinking men of our time," and that he was himself more indebted than he could well express to Mill's thought.[13] The essay was finished, as promised, by the middle of April although, to complete it, Buckle had to work about six hours a day throughout the fortnight following his mother's death. It appeared in *Fraser's Magazine* on 1st May, and instantly created a stir, which, for an author who had never reviewed a book before, was almost without precedent.

Mill in his essay on "Liberty", referred to a recent case of religious persecution in these words: "Penalties for opinion, or at least for its expression, still exist by law; and their enforcement is not, even in these times, so unexampled as to make it incredible that they may some day be revived in full force. In the year 1857, at the summer assizes of the County of Cornwall, an unfortunate man, said to be of unexceptionable conduct in all relations of life, was sentenced to twenty-one months' imprisonment for uttering and writing on a gate some offensive words against Christianity."[14] "It was with the greatest astonishment," wrote Buckle in his review, "that I read in Mr. Mill's work that such a thing had occurred in this country, and at one of our assizes, less than two years ago. Notwithstanding my knowledge of Mr. Mill's accuracy, I thought that, in this instance, he must have been mistaken. I supposed that he had not heard all the circumstances, and that the person punished had been guilty of some other offence. I could not believe that in the year 1857, there was a judge on the English bench who would sentence a poor man of irreproachable character, of industrious habits, and supporting his family by the sweat of his brow, to twenty-one months' imprisonment, merely because he had uttered and written on a gate a few words respecting Christianity. Even now, when I have carefully investigated the facts to which Mr. Mill only alludes, and have the documents before me, I can hardly bring myself to realize the events which have actually occurred, and which I will relate, in order that public opinion may take cognisance of a transaction which happened in a remote part of the kingdom, but which the general welfare requires to be bruited abroad, so that men may determine whether or not such things shall be allowed."[15]

Buckle went to immense trouble to discover the full story of the prosecution and sentence of Thomas Pooley, the Cornish well-sinker, and to report it fully and accurately.[16] The facts of the case as stated by Buckle were that "in the summer of 1857, a poor man, named Thomas Pooley, was gaining his livelihood as a common labourer in Liskeard, in Cornwall, where he had been well known for several years, and had always borne a high character for honesty, industry, and sobriety. His habits were so eccentric, that his mind was justly reputed to be disordered; and an accident which happened to him about two years before this period had evidently inflicted some serious injury, as since then his demeanour had become more strange and excitable. Still, he was not only perfectly harmless, but was a very useful member of society, respected by his neighbours, and loved by his family, for whom he toiled with a zeal rare in his class, or indeed in any class. Among other hallucinations, he believed that the earth was a living animal, and, in his ordinary employment of well-sinking he avoided digging too deeply, lest he should penetrate the skin of the earth, and wound some vital part. He also imagined that if he hurt the earth, the tides would cease to flow; and that nothing being really mortal, whenever a child died it reappeared at the next birth in the same family. Holding all nature to be animated, he moreover fancied that this was in some way connected with the potato-rot, and, in the wildness of his vagaries, he did not hesitate to say that if the ashes of burnt Bibles were strewed over the fields, the rot would cease. This was associated, in his mind, with a foolish dislike of the Bible itself, and an hostility against Christianity; in reference, however, to which he could hurt no one, as not only was he very ignorant, but his neighbours, regarding him as crack-brained, were uninfluenced by him; though in the other relations of life he was valued and respected by his employers, and indeed by all who were most acquainted with his disposition.

"This singular man, who was known by the additional peculiarity of wearing a long beard, wrote upon a gate a few very silly words expressive of his opinion respecting the potato-rot and the Bible, and also of his hatred of Christianity. For this, as well as for using language equally absurd, but which no one was obliged to listen to, and which certainly could influence no one, a clergyman in the neighbourhood lodged an information against him, and caused him to be summoned before a magistrate, who was likewise a clergyman. The magistrate, instead of pitying or remonstrating with him, committed him for trial and sent him to jail. At the next assizes, he was brought before the judge. He had no counsel to defend him, but the son of the judge acted as counsel to prosecute him. The father and the son performed their parts with zeal, and were perfectly successful. Under their auspices, Pooley was found guilty. He was brought up for judgment. When addressed by the judge, his restless manner, his wild and incoherent speech, his disordered countenance and glaring eye, betokened too surely the disease of his mind. But neither this, nor the fact that he was ignorant, poor, and friendless, produced any effect upon that stony-hearted man who now held him in his gripe. He was sentenced to be imprisoned for a year and nine months. The interests of religion were vindicated. Christianity was protected, and her triumph assured, by dragging a poor, harmless and demented creature from the bosom of his family, throwing him into jail, and leaving his wife and children without provision, either to starve or to beg.

"Before he had been many days in prison, the insanity which was obvious at the time of his trial ceased to lurk, and broke out into acts of violence. He grew worse; and within a fortnight after the sentence had been pronounced he went mad, and it was found necessary to remove him from the jail to the County Lunatic Asylum. . . .

"No writer on important subjects has reason to expect that he can work real good, or that his words shall live, if he allows himself to be so trammelled by expediency as to postpone to it considerations of right, of justice, and of truth. A great crime has been committed, and the names of the criminals ought to be known. They should be in everyone's mouth. They should be blazoned abroad, in order that the world may see that in a free country such things cannot be done with impunity. To discourage a repetition of the offence the offenders must be punished. And, surely, no punishment can be more severe than to preserve their names. When we hear that a poor, a defenceless, and a half-witted man, who had hurt no one, a kind father, an affectionate husband, whose private character was unblemished, and whose integrity was beyond dispute, is suddenly thrown into prison, his family left to subsist on the precarious charity of strangers, he himself by this cruel treatment deprived of the little reason he possessed, then turned into a madhouse, and finally refused such scanty redress as might have been afforded him, a spirit of vehement indignation is excited, partly, indeed, against a system under which such things can be done; but still more against those who, in the pride of their power and wickedness of their hearts, put laws into execution which had long fallen into disuse, and which they were not bound to enforce, but of which they availed themselves to crush the victim they held in their grasp.

"The prosecutor, who lodged the information against Pooley, and had him brought before the magistrate, was the Reverend Paul Bush. The magistrate, who received the information, and committed him for trial, was the Reverend James Glencross. The judge who passed the sentence which destroyed his reason and beggared his family, was Mr. Justice Coleridge."[17]

That Pooley was mad there can be no doubt. All his life he had been eccentric, but after a rock fell on his head while he was climbing down a well, his behaviour became even more unpredictable. When he was in Bodmin jail he tore his prison clothes to shreds and was left naked in his cell. On a previous occasion, when he had been brought before the Liskeard bench, "he placed a rope round his neck and walked into court with it, and told the magistrate to pull it and have done with it". George Holyoake,* who investigated the case for the Secularist Society, and who had himself once been sent to prison for six months for making flippant references to God, reported that "all Liskeard knew there was something wrong with Tom Pooley". The words which had provoked the prosecution in the first instance scarcely indicated that their author was in his right mind. The most offensive remark Pooley made was to the constable who arrested him. "If it had not been for the blackguard, Jesus Christ," he told him, "when he stole the donkey, police would not be wanted. He was the forerunner of all theft and whoredom." Holyoake found that working-men in Liskeard regarded the sentence as disgracefully severe, and as yet another proof that "justice is not to be had of gentlemen".[18]

Sir John Taylor Coleridge, who sentenced Pooley, was a nephew of the poet. Learned in the law—he edited Blackstone's Commentaries—his insight into human nature does not seem in this instance to have been very penetrating. In vindicating himself, he disclaimed any knowledge that Pooley was mad. "There was not the slightest suggestion," he wrote to the Home Secretary, "made to me of his being other than perfectly sane, nor was there anything in his demeanour at the trial, or in the conduct of his defence by himself, which indicated it. . . . Had I been informed of anything which had led me to enquire into his sanity during the trial, it is probable I might have discovered enough to have led to an acquittal on the ground of insanity, which on such a charge I should have been very glad to have arrived at."[19] As Buckle was quick to point out, it says little for the judge's perspicacity that he should have overlooked what was obvious to less practised eyes.[20] Even *The Law Magazine and Law Review*, which was horrified by Buckle's attack on an eminent judge, went so far as to admit that "the absurd and incoherent

* George Holyoake (1817–1906) was one of the most fearless radicals of the nineteenth century. He was a friend both of Buckle and Mill. He was an Owenite, Chartist, and Socialist, and at different times advocated a secret ballot, extension of the franchise and support of Garibaldi. He invented the word "Secularism", and it was his suggestion that a light should shine above Big Ben during sessions of Parliament. He had his own publishing firm at 147 Fleet Street. His wife died of "drink madness", having worn herself out trying to look after their family without enough money.

character of the language employed by Pooley—his remarkable appearance and gestures—would all have contributed to confirm the impression of his being mad, if the idea had once been suggested."[21] It is difficult to resist the conclusion that Coleridge was guilty of serious negligence in sentencing an undefended, ignorant, and crazy man, without apparently observing at the trial manifest signs of the well-sinker's lunacy.

Buckle's attack on Coleridge was widely resented, and he was forced to justify himself to a number of his friends, including Charles Kingsley. Parker had been apprehensive from the beginning and had suggested toning down parts of the essay, but Buckle was not prepared to muffle his arguments. "Three weeks ago," he wrote to Parker after the *Review* had come out, "I said, what I now repeat, that I wished you to state to whomever it might concern that you suggested my softening the expressions respecting Sir John Coleridge and that I refused to do so. As I said then, I would far rather have withdrawn the whole article than cancel a single word I had written on a transaction respecting which I felt so strongly. In justice therefore to your own interests you ought to make this known, and I hope you will. You can keep this letter, and show it to whomever you like. I wrote the remarks on Sir John Coleridge deliberately. I carefully considered them afterwards. I consulted upon them a friend in whose judgment I repose great confidence; and now that I read them again in print, I have nothing to withdraw or regret. I have some little knowledge of the history of England, and I do deliberately say, that, considering all the circumstances of Pooley's case, the sentence passed by Sir J. Coleridge is the greatest crime and the foulest cruelty which has been perpetrated in any country under sanction of the law since the seventeenth century. Holding this opinion, I have stated it with the indignation which I felt, and still feel. The fact that the culprit is powerful and influential produced no effect, except to make me apply to him stronger language than I would have done had he been weak and insignificant. There are, unhappily, innumerable instances of religious intolerance in our judicial history; but in such cases the age was intolerant, and public opinion sanctioned the cruelty. The peculiarity of this case is, that a judge drives a poor man to insanity, and beggars his family, for the sake of enforcing a persecuting principle with which men have lost their former sympathy. He goes out of his way; he runs counter to the liberal tendencies of his time; and in doing so perpetrates an act of cruelty. I ask, 'Is that act a crime? and, if so, is it wrong to denounce the author of it as criminal?' Our laws do not call it a crime; but God forbid that we should form our notion of crime according to the maxims of criminal law. As to motives, these lie out of our reach, and no human eye can discern them. But if intolerance and oppression are crimes, I do not see how the act of Sir J. Coleridge can escape that appellation."[22]

Even Miss Shirreff was shocked by the violence of Buckle's attack on Mr. Justice Coleridge, and wrote its author a disapproving letter. "What you say," came the reply, "about my notice of Justice Coleridge does a little surprise me. I knew at the time that most persons would think I had shown too much virulence; but I believed then, and I believe now, that in this case, as in other cases where I have taken an unpopular view . . . those who object to my treatment have not taken as much pains to inform themselves as I have done. You know that I have no personal animosity against Coleridge, and yet I say that, to the best of my judgment, his sentence on Pooley is the most criminal act committed by an English judge since the seventeenth century. . . . I never have and never will attack a man for speculative opinions; but when he translates these opinions into acts, and in so doing commits cruelty, it is for the general weal that he should be attacked. A poor, ignorant, half-witted man, sentenced to be imprisoned for a year and nine months, for writing and speaking a few words against the Author of the Christian religion! And when I express the loathing and abomination with which I regard so monstrous an act, you, my dear friend, 'regret the extreme violence' of my expressions. To me it appears that your doctrine would root out indignation from my vocabulary; for if such an act is not to rouse indignation, what is?"[23]

Three days later, in answer to another letter from Miss Shirreff, he says: "We are both agreed that the sentence was wrong; but you consider that the judge, not having bad motives (but who can penetrate the heart and discern motives?), and not being a bad man, diminishes the *criminality* of the sentence, and therefore should have prevented me from using such strong language. Now, in the first place, hardly any amount of evidence would induce me to believe that, in THIS AGE, a judge who could pass such a sentence on such a wretched creature as Pooley could have either a good heart or a good head . . . as a public writer (not as a private or practical man) I estimate actions solely according to their consequences. The consequence of this sentence I deem far more pernicious than I have been able to state in my Essay, because I could not, for want of space, open up all the topics connected with it. Dealing, as I always do, with the interest of masses, and striving to reach the highest view of the subject, I hold that when an act is pernicious—when it is done in the teeth of the liberal tendencies of the time—when the punishment far exceeds the offence—when it is not only cruel to the victim, but productive of evil consequences as a public example—when these qualities are combined in a single transaction, I call that transaction a great crime, and therefore the author of it a great criminal. . . . You say that I should not have used language which one 'gentleman' would not have employed to another in conversation. Here we are altogether at issue. My object was not merely to vindicate the principle of toleration (for that, to all persons of competent understanding, was done before I was born), but to punish a great and dangerous criminal. Whether I am able to punish is another question. If I am not able, my remarks are ridiculous from their impotence, and I have been foolish from incapacity . . . It formed no part of my plan to use nice and dainty words. Instead of confining myself to writing like a *gentleman*, I aimed at writing like a *man*. I intended to smite Justice Coleridge, and the anger of his friends is one of many proofs that I have succeeded. Had I, or had I not, a right to smite him? Is it the business of literature to chastise as well as to persuade? I think it is; and I follow the example of many who have done the greatest good and left the greatest names. . . . You also think that I weaken my own influence and reputation by making such an attack; and in that respect I am inclined to agree with you in part. Many will be offended; but it is not the verdict of London drawing-rooms that can either make or mar a man who has a great career to run, and a consciousness of being able to run it. I would not willingly seem arrogant, but I think you will understand me whan I say, that I feel that within me which can sweep away such little obstacles, and force people to hear what I have to offer them."[24]

Buckle's indignation at Pooley's persecution and Coleridge's complicity in it, was matched by the outraged feelings his observations provoked. "The sentiment throughout the legal profession," says *The Law Magazine*, "is one of indignation, not unmingled with shame. Of indignation that a judge, among the eminent men who were his contemporaries on the bench pre-eminent for his great learning, sterling ability, and judicial virtues, should be thus attacked in an unjustifiable libel; of shame that a man, venerable and venerated, possessed in a remarkable degree of a pure love of justice . . . should have been subjected to slander so virulent, mistaken, and foolish, as that into which Mr. Buckle has unfortunately been betrayed."[25]

John Duke Coleridge, the Judge's son, who later became Attorney-General, wrote a letter to *Fraser's* defending his father's conduct. Hearing this, Buckle wrote to Parker saying: "I fully approve of your inserting the two articles attacking me.* Indeed, under the circumstances you were bound to do so; and under any circumstances it is advisable that the fullest latitude should be given to the expression of all opinions, however offensive and unreasonable they may be to those who dislike them."[26]

Coleridge's letter to *Fraser's* began by abusing Buckle, whose references to his father he describes as: "a tissue of . . . coarse personal malevolence. . . . It is certainly hard that a person like Mr. Buckle should be able to put a man of blameless life on his defence by reckless accusation. . . . Dirt thrown by the meanest hand may sometimes, if it is not removed, soil the highest reputation. . . . 'Crime' and 'criminal', 'stony' and 'cold heart', 'shallow understanding', 'gross and prodigious iniquity', 'tyranny in high places', 'insolence of office'; such and like expressions applied to a living person by way of angry vituperation . . . are not the language of gentlemen. . . ."[27]

Coleridge accuses his adversary of formidable ignorance. "That Mr. Buckle should have thought such conduct possible in an English advocate of any standing, that he should have made such a charge without evidence and without inquiry, is a proof that his learning (if he be a learned man) is not education, and has not raised him above the feelings and prejudices of a thoroughly vulgar mind. . . . The man Pooley was there to be tried on a charge which neither Sir John Coleridge nor I had any more to do with, nor knew any more about before the assizes took place at Bodmin, than Mr. Buckle himself. That a judge selects whom he will try, and where he will try them; that he can try or not try at his pleasure persons who are arraigned before him; that he can refuse, if he pleases, to put in force the law he is sent to administer, and choose which laws he will enforce and which he will not; that he or the counsel for the prosecution, or both of them, have anything whatever to do with getting up cases against prisoners, are matters which Mr. Buckle really seems

* John Duke Coleridge's letter and an article entitled: "Concerning Man and his Dwelling-Place". A. K. H. B. (Boyd). *Fraser's Magazine*, No. 59, June 1859.

as if he believed, but as to which he displays ignorance to a degree hardly credible. . . ."[28]

Before Buckle saw John Coleridge's attack he made up his mind not to answer it. "Whatever Mr. Coleridge may write, I shall make no reply."[29] His resolution, however, melted, when he read what his antagonist had to say. "You know that I dislike controversy," he tells Parker, "as a waste of time, and that I have always abstained from replying to attacks made upon me. But the tone of the daily press, and my own private letters, convince me that it is absolutely necessary to take notice of what Mr. Coleridge has said. He has imputed to me many things which I never meant, and which I desire to state that I never did mean. I also wish to withdraw the language which I have used in intimating that Sir J. Coleridge knew of Pooley's madness: while, on the other hand, I shall sum up, and state more clearly the evidence that he *was* mad."[30] In the end it was decided that Buckle's rejoinder should not be printed in *Fraser's* but should be published as a separate pamphlet with the title: "Letter to a Gentleman respecting Pooley's case."

"Sir," the letter began, "You are quite right in supposing that I have read a letter which is signed 'John Duke Coleridge', and published in *Fraser's Magazine* for the present month. But you are wrong in thinking that the tone of the letter surprises me. When I held up to public opprobrium that, for our time, almost incredible transaction in which the name of Coleridge was painfully conspicuous, the indignation which I felt prevented me from measuring my language, and I did not care to search for soft and dainty words in relating how, under shelter of the law, an outrage had been perpetrated upon a poor, an honest, a defenceless, and a half-witted man. I wrote as I thought it behoved me to write, and I rejoice that I did so. Since, however, I did not spare the principal actors of that deed, I could not expect that Mr. Coleridge should wish to spare me. And I must, in common justice, acquit him of any such intent. He has done his utmost. He is so anxious to be severe that he has not only expressed anger, he has even tried to express contempt. He has imputed to me nearly every kind of baseness and of folly. He has ascribed to me sentiments which I never entertained, and language which I never used. He has charged me with ignorance, cowardice, malignity, and slander. He has attempted to ruin my reputation as an author, and to blast my character as a man, by representing me as a perverter of facts, a fabricator of falsehoods, a propagator of libels, and a calumniator of innocence. To all this I shall make no reply. Whatever I have done in the matter of Sir John Coleridge, or in other matters, is open and before the world. I live merely for literature; my works are my only actions; they are not wholly unknown, and I leave it to them to protect my name. If they cannot do that, they are little worth.

"The first thing which strikes me in Mr. Coleridge's apology for his father is, that some of the most serious charges which I have brought are passed over in complete silence. They are not only unanswered, they are not even noticed. On the other hand, several charges which I did not bring are satisfactorily refuted. Indeed the greater part of Mr. Coleridge's letter is occupied with repelling imaginary accusations. He ascribes to me assertions which I neither made nor intended to make; and then he decisively proves that those assertions are false. . . .

"Meanwhile, the real accusation remains. To that he makes no reply. Perhaps he was right. Perhaps he found it easier to answer what I had not said than what I had said. . . .

"I charged Sir John Coleridge with passing a sentence which, independently of the other objections against it, was alien to the spirit of the age. To this I find no reply. I charged him with bringing the administration of justice into disrepute, by encouraging the prevailing and most dangerous notion that the poor are more harshly treated than the rich. Again, I find no reply. I charged him with doing this on the person of an unhappy, but most industrious man, whose family were, consequently, left either to starve or to beg. Still, no reply. I charged him, and the result has proved that I charged him truly, with exasperating the friends of liberty, and rekindling old animosities. No reply. I charged him with taking as his victim an undefended prisoner, whom our law humanely supposes to have the judge for his counsel, but who on this occasion had the judge for his oppressor. No reply. I charged him with inflicting a punishment which, severe at any period, is particularly so in our time, when all humane and thinking men aim at lessening penalties, rather than increasing them. This, too, Mr. Coleridge being unable to deny, passes over in silence. . . .

"The judge, says Mr. Coleridge, could not choose 'what laws he would or would not put in force'. Unhappy judge! he had no choice. His hands were tied. His leaning was on the side of humanity; he longed to be merciful; but he was in the melancholy position of being obliged to enforce an odious law. He was so straitened and circumscribed that he was, in fact, a victim rather than an oppressor. Really, sir, it is humiliating to read such arguments; it is still more humiliating to have to answer them. What! no choice! Has an English judge no option? Has he no latitude? Is no discretion vested in him? Must he always exact the letter of the bond, and take the last ounce of flesh? Mr. Coleridge is indeed in difficulties if this is his best defence. The fact is that an assize is rarely held without an instance of the judge imposing a light, and often a mere nominal, punishment, when the law allows him to impose a severe one. That part of our common law which coerces the expression of opinion, was established in a barbarous and ignorant age, when the very amusements of men were brutal, and when they delighted in inflicting pain and in seeing it inflicted. It was an age in which human life was disregarded, and human suffering made a jest. To suppose that an English judge is bound to follow with servile acquiescence all the decisions of such a period, is to suppose what is not only absurd in itself, but is contradicted by the judicial history of this country. . . .

"Yet in a few years, and Sir John Coleridge and Thomas Pooley will be numbered with the dead. But though the men will die, the principles which they represent are immortal. The powerful and intolerant judge seeking to stop the mouth of the poor and friendless well-sinker is but the type of a far older and wider struggle. In every part of the civilized world the same contest is raging, and the question is still undecided, whether or not men shall say what they like; in other words, whether language is to be refuted by language, or whether it is to be refuted by force. Disguise it as you will, this is the real issue. In this great warfare between liberty and repression, Sir John Coleridge has chosen his side and I have chosen mine. But he, being armed with the power of the executive government, has been able to carry matters with a high hand, and to strengthen his party, not indeed by arguments, but by violence. Instead of refuting, he imprisons. My weapons are of another kind, and shall I not use them? Am I for ever to sit by in silence? Are all the blows to be dealt from one side, and none from the other? I think not. I think it is but right and fitting that Sir John Coleridge, and those who agree with him, should be taught that literature is able to punish as well as to persuade, and that she never exercises her high vocation with greater dignity than when, upholding the weak against the strong, she lets the world see that she is no respecter of persons, but will, if need be, strike at the highest place, and humble the proudest name. . . ."[31]

Buckle's letter was not widely read, partly owing to the form of its publication. "The little publicity given to it, is, I think, unfair towards me," he wrote to Capel, "and still more unfair towards the cause which I advocate. Of course I can do nothing; and the great dislike which I have to circulate my own writings, prevents me from sending copies to people."[32] The attack on Judge Coleridge and the defence of Pooley, was one of Buckle's bravest and most generous acts. His language at times was somewhat extravagant but he felt that to be temperate was to condone the crime. Surprised as he was by the amount of criticism he attracted, he none the less knew quite well, when he wrote his account of the trial, that many people would object to his views and to his manner of expressing them. Holyoake, writing long after Buckle's death, said: "His brilliant defence of the poor, crazed, but intrepid well-sinker of Cornwall, is the only example in this generation or this century of a gentleman coming forward in that personal way, to vindicate the right of Free Thought in the friendless and obscure. Mr. Mill would give money, which was a great thing, or use his influence, which was more, to protect them, but Mr. Buckle descended personally into the arena to defend and deliver them."[33]

While working on his "Letter to a Gentleman respecting Pooley's case" Buckle stayed with his aunt at Brighton. There is little doubt that the controversy in which he became involved was a fortunate distraction and did something to mitigate his grief and loneliness. Nevertheless his mother's death seriously affected him. "He often had great fits of depression," said his aunt, describing this visit, "and excessive weakness also. I very much fear for his brain: and I am sure he does so himself. One morning he was out of bed dressing half an hour before he knew where he was—he thought he was in Oxford Terrace. . . . He had no settled plan. When he left me he talked of doing different things every day."[34]

So shaken was he in mind and body that he was unable to meet Theodore Parker who visited England in the summer of 1859. "I cannot tell you," he wrote to Parker, "how much I regret that we should not have met. The great respect which I feel for you, as the most advanced leader of opinion in one of the two first nations of the world, would of itself suffice to make me eager for the pleasure of your personal acquaintance.

"And when I add to this the memory of your obliging and friendly letters to me, you will easily believe me when I say how much I have been disappointed at being unable to call upon you, and make arrangements to see you.

"But the severest of all calamities has befallen me, and has so prostrated my nervous system that I am now enjoined the strictest quiet.

"Your conversation would arouse in me so many associations, and excite me to so many inquiries respecting your noble country, that I feel myself, alas! unequal to meeting you; and, as you might possibly hear from some of my friends in London, I have been compelled to give up all society."[35]

After staying with his aunt at Brighton, Buckle took lodgings at Blackheath. Capel visited him there and wrote to Mrs. Huth to tell her how the philosopher fared. "He is very much satisfied with his quarters," wrote Capel, "as you will have seen from his note. He advertised stating his wants, and of course got numerous replies. He was disposed to go to Bexley Heath, lower down in Kent, but was determined by the shady avenues of the fine Spanish chestnuts in Greenwich Park. Other things have conspired to justify his choice, for his landlady, who has been a widow four or five years, turned out a somewhat remarkable person. She reads Italian, quotes Tasso and Dante, &c., is well up in French, and knows its literature, and when necessary can produce Virgil and Cicero. There's for you! She did not know anything particularly of her inmate till I went down, and found her rather astonished, and holding her breath at him. She told me she had known me well in the Church in London, and she was evidently glad to have her excited curiosity as to her guest set at rest. So I let the light fully in upon her, and called up her anxiety to make atonement for having ventured to disagree with him in something he had said to her as to the mental influence of women—the old topic you see. On going the next day (for they could not take me in there) I told her I had three copies of the *History of Civilization*, and would lend her one; but she had lost no time, and had been to the book-seller and ordered a copy.

"Such then is his hostess mentally, and in manners she is very much of the gentlewoman. So you will not wonder that in the evening, after dinner, he sometimes drops the *solitaire*, and invites her to converse, as he takes his ease on the lawn in the shade behind the house. Nor is this, when so disposed, his only resource, for she has two or three children living with her, whose parents are in India; and he has made great friends with these—especially with one, a little girl about five, a quick, intelligent thing; and, as you may suppose, she has not been slow to show how sure she is of his predilections; for she climbs up on him, gets on his back, and pats him on the face, and glories in her liberties, which pleases him the more. So, at present, time goes on."[36]

From Blackheath, Buckle moved on to Margate. "After I left Brighton," he writes to Miss Strickland, "I took very comfortable lodgings between Blackheath and Eltham, but after staying there about six weeks, felt tired and restless as I now do of everything, and determined to try this place, as one of the very few English watering places on the north coast. And certainly the air is even more bracing than I had expected and has done me much good; while as to the vulgarity of the people, that disturbs me not. Why should it?"[37]

From Margate he returned to London on his way to spend Christmas with his sister, Mrs. Allatt, at Boulogne. He hated seeing 59 Oxford Terrace again. "I cannot tell you," he said to a friend, "how I dread the idea of going to London, to that dull and dreary house which was once so full of light and of love!"[38] After his mother's death he only once summoned up courage to go into her drawing-room to fetch a book he required. "You don't know how I miss my mother," he told Capel, who had discovered him in a flood of tears. For a long time he was unable to talk of her, particularly to those who had known her well. But in Egypt, in the last year of his life, he referred to her so frequently and enthusiastically that he gave the impression she was still alive. His Christmas at Boulogne only increased his sorrow; while he was there, Robert Allatt, his favourite nephew, died of a sudden illness. Robert had been his constant companion out walking, and the conversations they had gave Buckle so high an opinion of the boy's ability that he planned to leave him his library in his will. "When you talk to me, Uncle," his nephew once said, "it seems like a dream."

Partly because he had become famous, and partly because after his mother's death loneliness drove him to seek company, Buckle dined out more often than hitherto. Thackeray, who first met him at a party given by Priauex, found him "very diverting"[39] and subsequently often dined with him. "It is agreed," he writes to Buckle, "I am yours for Wednesday. You are mine for Thursday. But I cannot give you such a feast as Lucullus (i.e. Priauex) prepares for us. Can you? I hope you do rather."[40]

Buckle also dined frequently with George Grote, the historian, whose wife collected celebrities, Mendelssohn, Mill, and Hallam, being among her guests. Mrs. Grote had a weakness for the nobility, and it was unfortunate for her that her radical husband had so strong an aversion to it. He would probably have been left a considerable estate had it not been for his undisguised distaste for his aristocratic relations. Mrs. Grote, however, was never happier than when, as on one occasion at Christ Church, she found herself in a room "half filled with . . . scions of English families."[41] Sydney Smith thought her behaviour so remarkable that he maintained she was the origin of the word "grotesque".[42]

Sir William Hardman, who happened to meet the Grotes in an hotel at Neuchatel, described George Grote as "a prosy, precise sort of old gentleman whom I should have supposed to be an effete country squire and member for his county, instead of the author of the *History of Greece*." Mrs. Grote he found to be a "most disagreeable woman both in manner and appearance. She seems unable to say an unqualified kind thing of anybody. Her under lip projects half an inch in advance of the upper, and she is fond of her glass of wine. They were talking of Buckle, and Mrs. Grote said to Phillimore, with a pseudo-manly voice like the notes of a post-mortem bassoon, 'I hope you loved him as we did'. . . . She quoted Buckle as saying to her, 'Ah! I wish I had seen more and read less!' Buckle himself thought he had injured his brain and constitution by excessive chess-playing; he would play several games at one time: he seems also to have injured his health by attention to his mother during a long illness; he scarcely ever was absent from the house. You may perhaps have wondered that Mrs. Grote found fault with the Buckle whom she 'loved' so well. She blamed him so much for not making a will, that I greatly suspect she had rather anticipated a legacy!"[43]

It was at a dinner-party given by the Grotes that Kate Stanley, who was soon to marry Lord Amberley, first met Buckle. "I went there," she records in her journal, "with Mama Maude & Henry on Friday, 27th April, 1860, at 10 o'clock; it was quite a small party, about 30 people. I enjoyed it very much as I saw and talked to Buckle; he seemed very pleasant, very easy to get on with as he does most of the talking himself. He talked to me about Mill on Liberty and approved of my having read it, he liked it very much and said it had influenced many persons. He had not read Darwin* as he says he is too hard at work to read anything at all not even the papers. . . . I liked him as I found him very agreeable but he is certainly conceited. He is bald and makes ugly faces when he talks but otherwise is not ugly."[44]

One of the places Buckle most enjoyed visiting was his friend Capel's house at Carshalton. The two Huth boys, who were pupils of Capel's, at first were awed by Buckle, but they learnt to appreciate him when they found that he threatened Capel that he would lead a rebellion if their hours were not shortened. Edward Huth, the elder of the boys, wrote to his mother telling her about Buckle's stay at Carshalton. "I have not written to you," he begins, "for such a long time that I suppose you think you are going to punish me by not writing to me, but ha ha ha I did have a letter and . . . it was better than all your letters put together. Who do you think it was from? Why from *Mr. Buckle* to be sure. . . . Mr. Buckle when he was here was a jolly chap." Eddy then goes on to explain how he wrote to Buckle saying how sorry he was that he had gone, "and lo and behold Lud, an answer comed and it was a better letter than Mr. Buckle sends you, so my eye wont you get jealous, ha ha ha. Praps as a great treat I'l let you read it so I enclose it. . . . Mr. Buckle says we ought to get up the chimney and bob our heads out at the top and then all the people would think it was the Devil. I told you this that you might understand the letter better."[45]

"My dear Boys," ran the letter which so delighted Eddy, "I received your letter this morning with great pleasure, as it showed that you had not forgotten me; and it is always agreeable not to be forgotten. The next time I stay at Carshalton all three of you will, I hope, be at Mr. Capel's and we shall be as merry as ever. And I expect that before then you will have learned to go up the chimney in the way I told you of. I have not tried it myself, but I hear that it is very pleasant, and it must be funny to see a fellow covered with black gradually rising out of the chimney at the top of the house.

* Kate Stanley was almost certainly mistaken in saying that Buckle had not read Darwin. He recommended the *Origin of Species* to Mr. Woodhead shortly after its publication. Huth II, 28. Moreover Darwin himself thought that Buckle had read the book. "I hear," he wrote, "that the great Buckle highly approves of my book." *Life and Letters of Charles Darwin*, Vol. II, 315. The point is of some importance because Buckle was frequently attacked for "not having the Darwinian Clue". (See, for example, Maitland: *Life and Letters of Leslie Stephen*, 452.) Darwin's book, however, came out two years after Buckle's first volume was published.

Mind you don't do too many lessons, it's very bad to work too hard, and particularly unwholesome for boys, especially when they are growing.

"The weather here is very wet and disagreeable, and so windy that I had my hat blown off yesterday, and very nearly lost it in the sea. But I was too quick, and, after a sharp race, I succeeded in capturing it. Such things never happened to me at Carshalton. And now I must say good-bye, because I have my lessons to do, and as I am not growing I have no excuse for being idle, as you have."[46]

Buckle's kindness to children was one of the most engaging things about him. "I cannot refuse anything to children," he once said, having worn himself out playing cricket with his nephews. He even seems to have considered adopting some children. He told Mrs. Huth that he wished someone would make him the guardian of two or three boys. He could not, he said, adopt children of the working class because they were badly brought up. What he would like would be gentlemen's sons of about thirteen or fourteen. Once when Mrs. Huth visited Carshalton unexpectedly she found that Capel had gone to London, but the maid told her that she knew where Mr. Buckle and the young gentlemen were. "We waited," she says, "and after a short time saw them coming across the field, laughing, talking, and running, as if they were all boys together. They had been at a strawberry gathering, and one of the boys . . . told us that they 'had been allowed to eat as many as they liked'. 'You ought to say, you ate as many as you could,' interrupted Mr. Buckle; and then turning to me, 'Edward filled himself with them till I saw a strawberry come out of each eye.' "[47]

Buckle first met the Huths in 1857, and very soon, according to Herbert Spencer, "all members of the family were worshippers".[48] The Huths were originally Hanoverians. Henry Huth's parents after moving from Germany to Portugal, were driven out by the French in 1809, took refuge in England, and became naturalized British subjects by Act of Parliament. Henry was born in the year of Waterloo, and as a young man spent some time as a merchant banker in the family firm. After giving up business, owing to illness, he travelled all over the world, and became a great collector of rare books which he lent generously.* He married Augusta Westenholz of Waldenstein

* Henry Huth's library was inherited by his son Alfred Huth, the biographer of Buckle. After Alfred's death, the British Museum was allowed to choose fifty books from his library. The remaining books were then sold for over £100,000. Alfred Huth was one of the founders, and a President, of the Bibliographical Society.

Castle in Austria and had six children. Buckle was introduced to the family by Capel. "Our friend Mr. Capel," wrote Mrs. Huth, "would not borrow a book from us to read without first asking 'my friend Buckle' whether it was worth reading, as *he* knew *all* books. If I praised a favourite author, I was told that my admiration was misplaced, as 'my friend Buckle' saw imperfections in him. 'But would not Mr. Huth like to call on my friend Buckle?' Mr. Huth decidedly objected, saying that if that gentleman's library contained 22,000 volumes, and he had read them all, as Mr. Capel assured us, it would be an impertinence for a man, who had not anything very extraordinary to recommend him, to intrude upon him. I was very glad of this answer, for I hated that 'friend Buckle', whose name was constantly in Mr. Capel's mouth, and bored me intensely; who was always put forward to contradict me; who was said to know everything, and who had seemingly done nothing. We were therefore considerably surprised when Mr. Capel came one day and said, 'I have told my friend Buckle that you wish very much to make his acquaintance, and he will be glad to see you if you like to call upon him.' My husband looked very black, but he had nothing for it but to go to 59, Oxford Terrace, where he was told Mr. Buckle was not at home, and he left his card. Later, when our dear friend made his last stay with us, I told him how we had been forced into our acquaintance with him; and he explained that he had only agreed to see us, as he thought it would be of advantage to Mr. Capel, who was going to have a son of ours at his school. At that time he had never expected our acquaintance to develop into friendship.

"One morning Mr. Capel came in, looking very much excited, and asked whether I was going to remain at home that afternoon, for, if so, he would call with Mr. Buckle. When he came, the conversation turned chiefly on education, especially on the bad methods in which languages are generally taught. . . .

"At Mr. Buckle's first visit he spoke of the immoderate admiration most people have of the past; and that was why, the more remote the times, the bigger, better, and longer-lived the people were supposed to have been—a subject then new to me, as his first volume had not yet been published.

"Mr. Buckle had on a thick, fluffy overcoat, which I never saw again till we accompanied him to Southampton, where he was to embark for Egypt with our sons. He sat leaning back on a sofa, which pushed his coat collar up over his ears, and gave him the appearance of a short, fat man.

"The next time I saw Mr. Buckle I asked his advice about historical reading. He remarked on that occasion, that most people read too much and think too little; and said that it was necessary to take copious notes while reading, and look them through very often. Of Prescott he observed, that that part of his works which treats of the Netherlands was inferior to the Spanish part, because he had never taken the trouble to learn Dutch, and therefore had been unable to study those documents and works which were as yet untranslated. He advised me to read Lingard, not only because he was a good writer, but also because I lived in an atmosphere of Protestant opinion, and therefore ought to be careful to get acquainted with the opposite views. . . .

"I saw from that very first visit that Mr. Buckle's intellect was something extraordinary. But he seemed to me a cold, unfeeling man, with no sympathy for individuals, and caring only for what was beneficial for mankind as a mass. When, soon after his first volume was published, I read his biographical sketch of Edmund Burke, I began to take a different view. . . . By degrees I got more and more puzzled about him. I kept a note-book, from which I was prepared categorically to question him whenever I knew he was coming; and the kindness, patience, care, and sympathy with which he answered greatly astonished me. It was a rule with him, never to pay more than one visit a day among his friends—on acquaintances he only left cards—and his visits, when they happened to be to me, generally lasted about twenty minutes. But if, on any subject on which we happened to be talking, I was not yet quite clear, he went on combating my arguments point by point, and never moved from his chair until he had made it perfectly plain to me. But no sooner had I grasped it than he took up his hat, said good-bye, and hurriedly left.

"The conversations which I had in this way with him, made me see that there were two Buckles—one cold and unfeeling as Fate; who invariably took the highest and widest view; to whom the good of the individual was as nothing compared to the good of the mass. This man was heard in the *History of Civilization*, and at dinner-tables where many people were present. The other Buckle was tender, and capable of feeling every vibration of a little child's heart; self-sacrificing to a degree which he would have blamed in another; and habitually concentrating his great intellect on the consequences of individual actions to the actor."

Mrs. Huth goes on to describe a visit Buckle paid her at St. Leonards where she had taken a house for Easter. "When going out for a walk or drive we never asked whether he would come with us. Sometimes he invited himself for a drive, but his walks he always took alone. Once, indeed, he met my husband on the beach, and they walked on together, talking on Political Economy. Mr. Buckle got interested in the questions he was asked, and went on walking and talking for an hour; but when he came home he was quite ill for the rest of the day. My husband did not then know how slight a frame bore that powerful intellect; he himself had forgotten it in the interest of talking. He retired to his bedroom to sleep if possible for a couple of hours. When the two hours were nearly over my husband went softly upstairs to see if he was moving; but before he reached his door he heard our landlady's children singing loudly and jumping violently, as it seemed just over Mr. Buckle's room. He stopped the noise, and then went to inquire if he had slept. Mr. Buckle said, 'No, the noise had prevented it.' Why did he not ring the bell? 'Oh, no, poor little things! It was their time for singing and jumping, not their sleeping time.'

"The fulness of his mind was something wonderful. Every evening the talk turned on a different subject. One evening, in a sentimental mood, he would talk of poetry. . . . But the next he would be full of fun and anecdote. . . . His reading of French Memoirs had furnished him with a number of amusing stories, and among others he told us many that Lord Lyndhurst had got from Talleyrand. They were mostly clever answers of the witty Frenchman. Another time we asked him a few questions about the children, and it led to special medical advice for every one of our little flock: the diet requisite for each different age and constitution, the amount of exercise, of sleep, &c., &c., was all considered. Later I got much of the advice confirmed by Dr. Mayo, and none at variance with it.

"That Easter, on account of the recent death of the Duchess of Kent, everybody was in mourning with the exception of Mr. Buckle. 'People do question me about it sometimes,' he said, 'but I always answer that I never do wear mourning for anybody but those who have been my personal friends.' 'What with going against the stream in this way,' said one of us, 'and the opinions expressed in your book, you will never be Lord Buckle.' 'No,' he answered, 'nor do I wish it.' Yet he greatly admired the character of the Duchess of Kent, and the way in which she had educated the Princess Victoria. . . .

"Talking of the so-called 'Working Classes', Mr. Buckle thought that they would always exist, but would be better paid than they now are. 'At present fortunes are still unequally divided. It is not right that any man should have two thousand pounds a year and his housemaid only twenty. Such things, however, can never be altered but by the gradual rise of the standard of wages. It would avail nothing were a few well-meaning persons to give their servants higher wages.' These remarks led to my telling him how much the extravagance of my coachman and his family vexed me, and that I was not at all sure but that it was my duty to interfere as far as I could. 'Would your coachman like your advice?' he asked. 'No, he would not.' 'Then don't give it. I always give advice freely when I am asked, but not otherwise, excepting to those whom I love. . . .'

"We accompanied him to the station when he was leaving us, and saw him take a second-class ticket, which, he told us, he often did. 'I always talk,' he said, 'and often find very intelligent people in those carriages; the first-class travellers are so dull; directly you broach a subject they are frightened.' Later in the year, when he came to us from a tour in Wales, he told us that he had picked up a great deal of information in this way from commercial travellers, who generally have a thorough knowledge of the country through which they are in the habit of travelling."[49]

The publication of the second volume of the History was much delayed by Buckle's ill health. "I have been very unwell," he wrote in January 1860, "but am now regaining strength, and am busy with my next volume, which I much desire to publish this season. . . ."[50] The improvement turned out to be only temporary. By the summer he was a little better and had nearly completed his work on the second volume, but his progress proved slower than he expected. "I see too surely how changed I am in every way, and how impossible it will be for me ever to complete schemes to which I once thought myself fully equal. My next volume is far from being ready for the press; and when it is ready it will be very inferior to what . . . I expected."[51]

Despite weakness and depression he began to send the completed manuscript to the printers early in January 1861. This time, instead of printing the book at his own expense, he negotiated with Parker an outright sale of the first edition. It was agreed that three thousand copies should be printed and that Buckle was to be paid £600. Buckle's dealings with his publisher combined meticulousness with bluntness. "I received your letter yesterday," he wrote to Parker during the course of negotiations, "in which you offer to undertake my next volume and to pay me five hundred pounds for an edition of three thousand copies—supposing that it contains about 450 pages and is published at 12/6. I am not quite willing to accept this proposal; and as I think that all matters of business should be conducted with great plainness and simplicity, I will frankly tell you the reasons of my objection. The first edition of my first volume, I published at my own risk; and on referring to my account with you respecting that edition, I find that after deducting your commission and the cost of advertising, I received £917.9.0. I also find that by my account with Messrs. Robson and Levey,* I paid them (after deducting 5 per cent. discount) £410.17.0. It therefore appears that by the sale of 1,500 copies of a guinea book I netted £506.12.0. Hence if I were to print at my own expense 1,500 copies of a 12/6 book I should nett a little over £300. But as the cost of printing and advertising 3,000 copies is much less than double that of printing 1,500, I should if I took the matter into my own hands, receive on a moderate estimate £700. . . . To you the cost of printing and binding would be less: but on the other hand I have to consider that by printing on my own account, I should lose a year's interest on the sum you would pay me for the edition. I should likewise lose the interest on the sum I pay the printers. Putting all these things together, I hope that you will not deem me unreasonable in saying that I should expect Six Hundred pounds for the edition of 3,000; that sum to be paid as soon as the volume is published. . . ."[52] Parker accepted these terms and the book came out in May 1861.

Buckle found that the effort of getting the book out was too much for him. "The moment I had got my second volume through the press," he writes, "the excitement which had kept me up being withdrawn, I suddenly collapsed. . . . Already I am better, but still miserably nervous, and tormented by the thought of how little I can do, and how vast an interval there is between my schemes and my powers."[53] He was ordered by his doctor to go to Ramsgate, where the air was reputed to be bracing, and Capel, who joined him there, found him nervy and quick-tempered; little things which would formerly have amused him, now caused him annoyance. When, after a miserably cooked dinner, his landlady brought in doilies and

* A printing firm.

finger-bowls, he observed: "Now they are coming with their vulgarities." Once, when Capel asked him some questions about Mill's philosophy, Buckle nearly fainted with the exertion of answering. From Ramsgate he went to Brighton, and from thence to London, but he was still unable to work as was shown by his visiting friends in the middle of the day. "I told him how anxious we had all been about him," writes Mrs. Huth, "and that the first we had heard of his illness was from Mrs. Bowyear, who told me that he had called on her, and was obliged to sit down for twenty minutes before he was rested enough to speak. He laughed, and said: 'What? I did not talk for twenty minutes? You must have thought that a very bad symptom!' "[54]

In June, he told Mrs. Grote: "I feel like a worn-out old man."[55] A month later he wrote to Samuel Strickland, "I wish I could tell you that I am better, but my head is as weak and incompetent as when I left town."[56] A tour of Wales, however, seems to have assisted his recovery. From there he slowly travelled to Berwickshire where he had been invited to stay by his friend Mrs. Mitchell.* "Again I begin to feel human," he tells her. "At all events, human or not, I am quite unable to resist the temptation you hold out to me. I shall hope to be with you somewhere about the middle of August; but you will perhaps let me leave the time open as the rate at which I travel Northwards will depend on the weather and my health, and, I fear I must add, on the caprice natural to a solitary and unthwarted man."[57]

"I am really better," he writes to Mrs. Grey after his stay with the Mitchells, "but think it prudent to abstain from all work. . . . Everywhere I go I soon feel restless, and, after the first novelty has passed, want to go elsewhere. This, I believe, is caused by the absence of that stimulus to which my brain has been so many years accustomed; I seem to cry out for work, and yet I am afraid of beginning it too soon. . . . This letter is very dull; but how can a man help being dull when he neither reads nor thinks?"[58]

Difficult as it was for him to rest, there was no other cure. By September he was able to tell his aunt, "My health has improved greatly, indeed I may say, I am almost well, having lost all my nervous symptoms. I greatly enjoyed my trip in Wales and Scotland. My new volume is selling famously in England and America. The German

* Fanny Mitchell was married to Alexander Mitchell, M.P., of Carolside, Earleton, Berwickshire. Some years after his death she married Lord Reay.

translation is being prepared. The Russian translation has been prohibited, it not being thought right that so mischievous a book should pollute the pure minds of the Russians. You see that it is your misfortune to have a bad and dangerous man for your nephew. The second edition of my *first* volume is all sold, and a third edition is being printed."[59]

From Berwickshire he went, in September, to stay with the Huths, who had taken a house at Sutton. "On the 15th we met Mr. Buckle at the station," Mrs. Huth writes, "and saw him get out of a third-class carriage with his little dog 'Skye', who had been specially invited. Skye had never travelled by rail before; and when Mr. Buckle had to change at Croydon, and saw him taken out of the dog-box trembling all over, he preferred rather to get into a third-class carriage with him than have him put back, and consequently caught a cold, which he did not get rid of for a week.

"He told us that he felt much stronger, and intended to try to work for a couple of hours every day. In the evening he brought a heap of newspapers and other periodicals, and letters, into the drawing-room which he had found awaiting him at Oxford Terrace, and had not had time to read before coming on to Sutton. They all had reference to his second volume; the periodicals containing reviews which the publisher or friends had sent him, and the letters from people in almost every class of society, all saying something about his book.

"One of the most curious among them was from a public-house keeper at Glasgow, who said that every word of Mr. Buckle's character of the Scotch was true, and that he himself would have written it just as Buckle had done, but that he had not learned to write books. . . . Another letter was from a young American lady, who was pained to think that the author of the *History of Civilization in England* was so little valued in his own country. Would it comfort him to know that a heart was beating for him on the other side of the Atlantic—a heart full of admiration and warm and lively sympathy?

". . . 'Do you mean to answer all those letters?' I inquired. 'No, not all,' he said; 'there are too many. But I always answer the mis-spelled ones.' We read as many of the reviews out loud as we could get through in one evening. Among them was one which said that the second volume was as full of platitudes as the first; while as for that *truism* which he dwelt so much on in his first volume, that the progress of civilization depends not on moral but intellectual progress, it was known and recognized by everyone long before his book was thought of. Mr. Buckle laughed, and said, 'I have been attacked on this point more than all the others put together; and now it is called a truism.'

"The drawing-room was given up to him during the morning as a study; and for the first few days of his visit he attempted to read German for a couple of hours, in preparation for his third volume, for he was always re-studying the languages of those countries on which he wrote. He soon found, however, that his brain was still too weak. It was not a question of prudence in taxing it, but simply of possibility. In place of it, he frequently indulged in the 'luxury' of thinking. The greater part of his two volumes, he told us, he had thought out while out walking; and here, he would go out and sit in some field thinking over such subjects as whether Germany or America should be first treated in his next volume. Even Skye was not allowed to accompany him on 'thinking mornings', but delivered over to the custody of one of the boys. Sometimes the dog escaped and went for long excursions on its own account; but Mr. Buckle would never allow him to be beaten when he returned, as the boys advised: he gave him a gentle tap with one finger, talked to him reprovingly, and pointed in the direction in which he had run away. And Skye really looked as if he understood it. . . . For his dog he had a great affection; indeed, he said that he could not conceive it possible for anybody to have much to do with any animal without getting fond of it.

"Whenever he travelled about he always got into conversation with the police and school-teachers of every place he stopped at. He used to inquire what particular crimes were prevalent in each district; and found that they were much the same all over the country: 'People have so little imagination,' he complained with a grave face—as if this want of imagination in criminal acts were a matter of serious concern to him. In large towns, such as Birmingham, he used to walk through all the worst parts, to observe manners for himself; and remarked that he might, as in the well-known anecdote, put down under the head of manners—none. In answer to a question, he said it might have been dangerous for a weak man like himself, but he was tall and carried a good stick, and always walked in the middle of the road to give less opportunity to people to pick a quarrel. It was necessary to see everything he wrote on, especially concerning England, with his own eyes. . . .

"It is impossible to describe how thorough a master he was of the art of pleasing; how he was as ready to amuse the children, as he was grown people; his joyous nature; his inexhaustible, but never tiring, talk; his wealth of anecdotes, and especially the *way* in which they were told, which made them as amusing when he repeated himself (as he sometimes did), as when heard for the first time; or to describe his appreciation of every little attention; and the warm interest he took in what were matters of moment for others. How naturally he entered into all the hopes and fears of his hostess concerning her family, asking questions, giving advice, and all with the deepest interest! We remember how touched and soothed we felt when one of our children fell ill, and we, hearing its cries, rushed up to the nursery, leaving him alone in the drawing-room. We stopped there some time, and quite forgot our visitor; but when we came out he was standing, waiting patiently, outside the nursery-door, to learn from us what was amiss."[60]

Although Buckle had recovered considerably from his illness he still could not work, and the prospect of spending an idle winter in London so depressed him that he decided to go to Egypt.

Believing that travel was the best form of education, he offered to take Eddy and Alfred Huth, aged thirteen and eleven respectively. In his Common Place Book he says: "Even in our own times the importance of travelling is obvious, and we rarely find an untravelled man who is not full of prejudice and bigotry."[61] Mrs. Huth was delighted with the idea, and sensibly refused to listen to her friends and relations who said that her children were too young to make so long a journey. She realized that no ordinary person had Buckle's knowledge, or gift of interesting boys, and she decided that this rare opportunity should not be missed.

Buckle took great pains preparing for the journey, and was particularly solicitous of the health of his young charges. "I have just had a long talk," he writes to their mother, "with the dear, kind old man, Dr. Mayo—*extremely satisfactory* in every respect, particularly as to the good, both physical and intellectual, which he anticipates for the boys. But he suggests one or two things of importance.

"In the first place, they are to be sponged all over, every morning and, in order to ensure an immediate reaction, each boy is to have a flannel gown reaching nearly to the ankles and fastened round the neck by a single button so as to be quickly put on and off—the gown must have arm holes, but no sleeves. It will remain on while their arms and legs are being dried.

'Then, in the next place, you will if you please, supply them with some of the very best mustard, in case a mustard poultice is wanted. Also a 3-ounce pot of Emplastium Lyttoe and some fine leather to put it on—so that we may be provided if a blister should be wanted.

"My conversation with Dr. Mayo has confirmed my confidence in being able to meet any event which can arise in the ordinary course of nature. And as impunity and absence of risk are always impossible, this is all we can expect. Give my love to the boys, and read this note to the little men. I am sure they will be very obedient, and, by their docility, will help my endeavours to secure their health and happiness."[62]

"Early tomorrow," he told Mrs. Grote on 18th October, 1861, "I leave for Southampton, and sail thence for Alexandria. I shall ascend the Nile to the first cataract, and thus gratify one of the most cherished wishes of my childhood. I am literally pining with excitement at the prospect of seeing the remains of that powerful but imperfectly developed nation, whose existence has always been to me as a dream.

"I am much better, and, indeed, quite well in every respect, save the most important. I cannot work, and therefore my life has not been very happy. . . .

"I wish for the next few months to sever myself, if possible, from all old associations, and, as it were, begin life afresh. Consequently, I shall write no letters, and shall not have any forwarded to me. After Egypt, perhaps I may go to Greece, perhaps to Algiers, perhaps to Jerusalem: but wherever I may be, I shall retain a lively sense of the pleasant hours I have passed with you. Sometimes I fear that I have permanently hurt myself, and form plans of leaving London altogether—but time will show."[63]

Happy and excited as Buckle was, to many he seemed a pathetic figure. Forced to travel because he could not work, so lonely after his mother's death that he took two boys as companions on what proved to be his last journey, he excited the pity of those who met him. Too late he realized that he ought to have married, but as he once said: "What I love I lose; and now that I am forty I am alone."

CHAPTER III

THE NILE VOYAGE

ON Sunday, 20th October, 1861, Buckle embarked at Southampton in the steamship *Ceylon*, bound for Alexandria. Mrs. Huth came to see her sons off, and after watching the ship until she could no longer distinguish individuals in it, returned to the hotel. "I looked into the rooms of the travellers," she wrote to her boys that evening, "they were so empty. The sitting-room was dull, and the whole house seemed changed.... 'Bless your little hearts,' as Mr. Buckle says, and bless his own little heart too, and may you behave to him in such a way that he will never regret having taken you."[1] In this hope she was not disappointed for Buckle told her in his first letter: "Both your sons are very good boys, and do everything I bid them without the least hesitation."[2] "Your sons," he wrote a little later, "are everything I could wish; they attach themselves much to me, and I to them. A Scotchman on board said, 'Why, dear me, sir, how fond those boys do seem of you!' And so I am sure they are. I hope and believe that this journey will be an epoch in their lives, morally and intellectually. They are very diligent in reading; but I never prescribe any hours or daily task, merely telling them that the only reward I require for watching over them is, that they should acquire knowledge."[3]

On the very first day of the voyage Buckle persuaded the two gentlemen sharing his cabin to change berths with the Huth children and so for the rest of the journey they all lived together. The sea was very rough as far as Gibraltar and both the boys were ill. "Alfred and I got sick on Sunday evening," Eddy wrote to his mother, "and I have only just got over it. Today's breakfast was the first meal I enjoyed since I have been on board. Mr. Buckle would not let us do anything for ourselves whilst we were ill, and he was always running downstairs to fetch things for us."[4] The Mediterranean, however, was calmer, and they began to eat so heartily as to alarm Buckle for the solvency of the Steamship Company.

Buckle and the boys spent a lot of time on the way out reading about the countries they were going to visit, and it says much for the education of the children that Alfred, aged eleven, apparently enjoyed reading Herodotus, and Martineau's *Egypt, Past and Present.* Buckle, as was his custom, spent many hours in conversation with his fellow passengers, and otherwise amused himself by playing Draughts with a gentleman on board, who being an expert player, was much astonished by his repeated defeats. The only entertainment officially provided was a sensational melodrama acted by the crew, entitled *Red-hand, the Gypsy*. The orchestra shut out all view of the stage so the performers were invisible.

The *Ceylon* reached Gibraltar on the 25th. After inspecting the fortifications, Buckle and the boys agreed that the rock was impregnable. "We saw lots of convicts working there," Eddie wrote home. "Two were in chains and walking up and down a platform, which they are condemned to do all their lives, for raising a mutiny among the other convicts."[5] The ship called at Malta on the 29th and reached Alexandria at half past six on the morning of 2nd November. Eventful as the boys' arrival proved to be, it was not as catastrophic as the Huth family nurse feared, for she told her mistress that she had seen in the papers that they were busy killing all the Christians at Cairo. Fortunately the trouble was at Karak, but this only partially reassured the good lady, who was finally consoled by being told that Mr. Buckle would not go into the way of killing—a probability which her experience endorsed. She remained convinced, however, that the children would be stolen by Arabs and held to ransom.

As soon as the *Ceylon* dropped anchor at Alexandria it was surrounded by dozens of small craft whose owners offered to take passengers and luggage ashore. "On the banks," according to Alfred, "were lots of Arabs bawling to the boatmen. As soon as the boat touched the bank all the Arabs began fighting for the luggage and a Sheik kept whacking them all with a long stick. At last each of them got a bit of luggage and marched off to the Custom House. As soon as we were near it, the officer came and opened our boxes in the open air. He opened the wine box and another one, but Mr. Buckle gave him five shillings not to open any more and not charge for the wine. As soon as it was done all the Arabs shouldered the luggage and we started for the hotel."[6] On the way they were accosted by a dragoman, Hassan Vyse,* who showed them bundles of testimonials

* Hassan, who had accompanied Major-General Richard Howard Vyse on his celebrated exploration of the Pyramids (1835), subsequently adopted his name, as is the Arab custom.

given him by former travellers. After careful inquiries had been made, Hassan was engaged to accompany the party up the Nile.

For several days Buckle stayed in Alexandria, spending the time sightseeing and making final arrangements. The children's letters home already showed how rapidly their education was proceeding. "Yesterday we went to Heliopolis," Eddy writes, "the palace which Joseph is said to have been Governor of, where Moses was taught the wisdom of the Egyptians, and where Plato took lodgings. . . . Nothing remains of Heliopolis now but an obelisk and two stones with hieroglyphics on. It took us two hours and a half to ride there on donkeys, and when we got there we sat down under a weeping willow close by the obelisk, and ate the oranges which grew in the gardens of the natives. Mr. Buckle smoked three pipes and I put tobacco in and lighted them for him."[7] Alfred's letter, written on the same piece of paper, was less erudite. "The donkey boys," he says, "keep bothering us. Everywhere they call out, 'this the best donkey', and 'this donkey been to London Tower', 'this donkey English donkey', 'this donkey speak English'. One of the donkeys' name is 'Snookes', another is 'Yankee Doodle'."

While at Alexandria, Buckle, having tried in vain to find a good European servant, decided to look after the boys himself, and in particular to make sure that they washed and changed their clothes. Their health was his constant anxiety, and he personally supervised every detail of their diet. Again and again he assures Mrs. Huth that her sons are well, and tells her of the precautions he has taken to keep them fit. "In hot countries, fruit and vegetables are more wholesome than meat, and I let the boys eat all kinds of both—I carefully watch the effects on their stomachs, and I never let them eat any uncooked fruit without first satisfying myself that it is perfectly ripe. Hitherto this plan has completely succeeded; Alfred has not had the least symptom of the disorder to which he is subject, and Eddy's liver has for the last 8 or 9 days acted properly without medicine, which in these climates should always if possible be avoided. I stint them as to their meat and forbid all veal and pork."[8] Indeed there was a danger that he might do more harm than good by his precautions, and one lady, who met the young Huths at Alexandria, was filled with pity for the poor children whose hats were swathed in endless folds of muslin, and whose eyes were hidden behind huge blue goggles.[9]

Buckle spent part of the time at Alexandria hunting for a suitable *dahabeeyah* in which to travel up the Nile. In the end he found one belonging to a European. It was an iron craft, shaped something like a house-boat, carrying one enormous sail and drawing only two feet of water. It had the reputation of being fast and was certainly expensive. This vessel was ordered to sail to Boulak, where Buckle and his charges, who travelled in advance to Cairo by train, later joined it. At Cairo the party stayed at the Hotel d'Orient where they divided their time between visiting the city and reading about Egypt. In the evenings Buckle played Backgammon with one or other of the children, insisting upon a halfpenny stake in the belief that it discouraged reckless play.

The journey and the sunshine soon began to have their desired effect. "I feel better," he told Mrs. Huth, "in health and spirits than at any time during the last three years. Especially I am conscious of an immense increase of brain power,* grasping great problems with a firmness which, at one time, I feared had gone from me for ever. I feel that there is yet much that I shall live to do."[10] As a result of this improvement he decided to extend his proposed journey to Palestine, and wrote to the boys' mother from Cairo telling her of his plans. "We hope to leave here for Thebes tomorrow, provided the boat can be provisioned by then. It is a first-rate boat; and as we shall be in it three months, I am doing what I know you would do if you were here, sparing no expense in laying in every comfort that can ensure health. I feel the responsibility of your dear children, perhaps more than I expected, but I am not anxious; for I am conscious of going to the full extent of my duty, and neglecting nothing; and when a man does this, he must leave the unknown and invisible future to take care of itself. They are *most excellent boys*, and their behaviour does great credit to Capel who has had the charge of them so long. All that I see of them satisfies me that his treatment of them has been judicious: otherwise they would not be what they are. . . . If the boys improve still further in health, and if I find that they are reaping real intellectual benefit, I propose taking them in February to Jerusalem, and thence making excursions in Palestine—explaining to them at the same time the essential points in Jewish history, and connecting it with the history of Egypt. . . . I shall want a letter of credit on Constantinople, as I propose sailing for that city direct

* Less than a fortnight before he died he told Longmore that "his health now being re-established, he was anxious to get home to finish his work on Civilization, which he anticipated he could not complete, according to the plan he had laid down in his own mind, in less than sixteen volumes". J. A. Longmore. *Reminiscences of Mr. Buckle*. Athenaeum, 1873, 116.

from Palestine, and then ascending the Danube to Vienna (now a very easy journey), and meeting you all there in May or June. . . . I could draw all the money here, but there is the chance of robbery in the desert. There is NO FEAR OF VIOLENCE, for I shall have the best escort that money can procure. My maxim is economy, not parsimony; and though I never throw away money, I never spare it on emergencies. If in the spring there are any disturbances in Arabia or Syria, be you well assured that I shall not set forth there. . . .

"I am better than I have been for years, and feel full of life and thought. How this country makes me speculate! I am up at six o'clock every morning, and yet there seems no day—so much is there to see and think of. I try to pour some of my over-flowings into the little chaps; time will show if I succeed, but I think I shall do something towards making them more competent and finished men than they would otherwise be."[11]

After many delays, the party joined their *dahabeeyah*, *El Ableh*, the "Wild One", at Boulak. Here they resided on board for four days until 25th November; a contrary wind and difficulties in provisioning preventing their starting for Thebes earlier. The routine followed at Boulak was much the same as at Cairo. Before breakfast Buckle took his customary walk and then read throughout the morning, or catalogued the antiquities he had begun to collect. After lunch he smoked, read, played Backgammon or Draughts, and generally took another walk, during which he questioned the boys on their morning's reading or told them stories. Dinner was at six o'clock. Afterwards "he sat with the boys in semi-darkness for a quarter of an hour or so, playing and joking with them, till they generally ended in a violent romp, and now and then a smash of crockery or windows".[12] Such breakages had to be paid for. Buckle boasted that except for one tumbler which had slipped through his fingers on a very cold day, he had never broken anything since he was a child. The ill effects of Buckle's rule were somewhat mitigated by the allowance he gave the boys to pay for possible damage. As the Huths had plenty of uses for this money, accidents were infrequent. The boys, like Buckle, bought many antiquities, and although he helped them to make their collection, they were encouraged to regard the assistance as reciprocal.

Living conditions on board *El Ableh* were luxurious. The saloon was large enough to dine eight persons, the bedrooms were comfortable, and the boat proved to be as fast as was claimed. Hassan was an excellent dragoman, and Buckle contrived to engage the cook employed by the Rothschilds when they had been to Egypt. Alfred was particularly appreciative of the food. "We have got a very good cook," he tells his mother. "He can make plum-pudding, and he can make Irish stew as well as Mr. Buckle's cook. We often have roast Turkey, so on Christmas we can have Turkey and plum-pudding. . . . We always have Marmalade and curry for breakfast."

Buckle's education of the Huth children was not confined to telling them about the history and geography of the country they passed through. "Mr. Buckle," continues Alfred, having concluded all he has to say on the subject of food, "has been explaining to us the relation of minerals and plants and animals to each other, and the way in which while animals are poisoning the air, plants are purifying it."[13] By the same post Buckle himself writes to Mrs. Huth explaining his system of teaching her sons. "The boys, I am truly pleased to say, are most anxious to instruct themselves, and without any pressure on my part they read quite as much as I wish. Lest the long confinement should be injurious, I stop the boat twice every day, and we walk with an escort on shore. Then, and in the evening, I talk to them about what they have seen and read, and having encouraged them to state their opinions, I give them mine, and explain how it is that we differ. They have accumulated a great number of historical and geographical facts. But that is not my chief object; what I aim at is, to train them to consider everything from the largest and highest point of view that their years and abilities will allow. To this I make everything subordinate, save and except their health. . . .

"Besides the general history and geography of the East, I am teaching the boys by conversation (for I have no books on the subject) the elements of physiology, and explaining to them the general laws which connect animals with plants. Two or three days ago I first began to proceed further, and opened up the relations which the animal and vegetable kingdoms bear to the mineral world. Alfred was never weary of listening, and asking questions. Eddy, his eyes quite sparkled, and beamed with light, as he traversed (though of course very indistinctly) the field of thought. . . .

"The boys' Bible has no Apocrypha; and I want to explain to them the character of that most remarkable Maccabean revolution which broke out two centuries before Christ. If, therefore, you can buy the Apocrypha separate, and in a portable form, do so; but it is not worth while to send out another whole Bible, as my memory will enable me to explain the main points without it."[14]

By the same post Mrs. Huth received a letter from Eddy telling her about his lessons. "You cannot think how jolly it is," he writes. "Mr. B. lets us do what we like; and the only lessons we do as yet is reading. . . . We have got about the best boat on the Nile, and the best cook, and a very good dragoman. . . . I have read Sharpe's *History of Egypt*, and Martineau and Russell's *Egypt*, and Herodotus, and now I am reading the *History of the Jews*. I shall not tell you anything about Mr. B.'s plans for Syria and Palestine and Mount Sinai, as he will most likely tell you more about it than I could; but won't it be jolly, and Bucky is a brick. . . . Tell Nurse that Mr. B. says there is no fear of the Arabs stealing us, because it would not be worth their while; but he is afraid they will steal him, because he is such a nice little fellow."[15]

On 14th December *El Ableh* reached Thebes. Buckle and the boys immediately landed and explored the remains of the ancient City. Then they hired donkeys and set out for the temples of Karnak, taking the road once lined with sphinxes. The prodigious ruins of Karnak, which they visited by moonlight, moved Buckle deeply. "To give you even the faintest idea," he writes to a friend, "of what I have seen in this wonderful country, is impossible. No art of writing can depict it. If I were to say that the temple of Karnak at Thebes can even now be ascertained to have measured a mile and half in circumference, I should perhaps only tell you what you have read in books; but I should despair if I were obliged to tell you what I felt when I was in the midst of it, and contemplated it as a living whole, while every part was covered with sculptures of exquisite finish, except where hieroglyphics crowded on each other so thickly that it would require many volumes to copy them. There stood their literature in the midst of the most magnificent temple ever raised by the genius of man. I went twice to see it by moonlight, when the vast masses of light and shade rendered it absolutely appalling. But I fear to write like a guide-book, and had rather abstain from details till we meet. . . . If you were here, and felt as I do what it is to have the brain every day over-excited—be constantly drunk with pleasure—you would easily understand how impossible much letter-writing becomes, and how impatient one grows of fixing upon paper 'thoughts which burn'. But, as you know of old, if my friends were to measure my friendship by the length of my letters, they would do me great injustice."[16]

Two days later *El Ableh* set sail for Aswan, the voyage taking six days. The boat stopped, as was then customary, at Esneh, to allow the crew to land and bake bread. Here Buckle met Mr. Longmore who afterwards published an account of their discussions. "Though he smoked continuously during our interview," wrote Longmore, "he was by no means solely occupied with that recreation, for he talked nearly as continuously. A good deal of the time . . . he spent in maintaining that a constitutional country like England was never so well governed as when the sovereign was either a debauchee or an imbecile. . . . With the Pharaohs and Ptolemies of Egypt, and other absolute monarchs, it was different, for they, if energetic men, could do what they liked with the resources they governed, and thus leave to posterity such wonderful monuments of their magnificence as we had recently been admiring on the banks of the Nile."

Longmore then goes on to record Buckle's description of a seance he attended shortly before leaving London. "This seance took place in the house, he said, of a Cabinet Minister,* who, he was quite satisfied, would not have lent himself to any collusive trickery to facilitate the proceedings of the mediums. The chief of these was Mr. Home; and various marvellous phenomena were produced, more particularly the floating of a large circular drawing-room table in mid-air. These manifestations Mr. Buckle was unable to explain on any known physical laws. 'But,' he added, 'while I cannot admit there is anything supernatural about them, I think it quite possible there may be a development of some new force, well worthy of scientific investigation.' He afterwards mentioned that Mr. Home called on him shortly after the seance, and told him that he was anxious that he, a man well-known in the literary world, and recognized as no granter of propositions he had not duly examined for himself, would take up the subject of spiritualism, and after sufficiently testing the reality of its phenomena—in doing which Mr. Home offered every assistance in his power—announce to the world to what conclusion he had come. Mr. Home volunteered that, whenever Mr. Buckle wished it, he would readily come to his house, and perform his experiments there, so that there might be no suspicion of apparatus

* The Cabinet Minister was Milner Gibson, whose wife collected celebrities, amongst whom were Mazzini and Louis Blanc. She gave several parties to show off Daniel Home, "King of the Mediums"—the "Mr. Sludge" of Browning's poem. Buckle, who attended one of these seances, was "much struck with what he saw". The subject is one which seriously occupied his thoughts after his mother's death. Other travellers who met him on his last journey have recorded conversations with him on the same theme.

or collusion being employed to deceive him. In conclusion, Mr. Buckle told us he was so pleased with Mr. Home, that he was quite willing to agree to his proposal; but that the second volume of his book being then nearly ready for the press, his time had been so occupied with it that he was quite unable to take the subject of spiritualism up before his health broke down, and he was compelled to leave England. But he was resolved to investigate it on his return home. . . . The next occasion on which I came into contact with Mr. Buckle was a few days afterwards, in the island of Elephantine, where we found him surrounded by a crowd of women and children purchasing at enormous prices questionable scarabaei and other antiques. So far from appearing narrow, as he has been accused of being, he seemed to me rather too lavish. Indeed, he paid 3,000 piastres for a common country boat, in an unclean and dilapidated condition, to take him from Mocatta to the second cataract. His own *dahabeeyah* being iron, could not be taken up the first cataract without great risk of damage, which, had it occurred, could not be repaired so far up the river. All the resources of Aswan were put in requisition by the governor, to whom Mr. Buckle had a letter, but not an inch of glass could be found, and the faulty windows had to be pasted up with old newspapers which he had brought with him."[17]

Buckle arrived at Aswan on 22nd December and after transferring stores from his *dahabeeyah* to the very much less luxurious craft he had hired, started on the last stage of his Nile journey on Christmas Eve, returning on 8th January. Despite the considerable discomfort of the boat, the voyage to the second cataract was so full of interest that he did not for an instant regret making it. "The journey into Nubia," he tells Mrs. Huth, "notwithstanding its many discomforts, was in the highest degree curious and instructive; and, as I took extra precautions as regards diet and health, it did us no harm. . . . The heat in Nubia was intense. On Christmas day, at half past eight in the evening, it was in my cabin 81° Fahrenheit, though the sun had been excluded all day. Not one Egyptian traveller in ten enters Nubia; but, as you see, I felt confident in bringing us all well out of it; and now that we have been there, I would not have missed it for £500. I feel very joyous, and altogether full of pugnacity, so that I wish someone would attack me—I mean, attack me speculatively. I have no desire for a practical combat."[18]

The day after Buckle's return to Aswan, he met John Stuart-Glennie, who was later to accompany him to the Holy land and to write a book about the journey. Glennie was born in Scotland, and had inherited more than a pleasant share of the assertiveness of his compatriots. Since Dr. Johnson's prejudices against Scots seem to shrink into small dimensions by the side of Buckle's, the meeting might easily have proved brief and uncordial.* Why Buckle invited this opinionated, humourless man to join his party it is difficult to say. He may have been driven by loneliness to welcome anybody who had the time and money to make the journey, or possibly Glennie was less tedious to know than his writings suggest. Huth, whose dislike of Glennie is infectious, subscribes to the former theory. "Mr. Buckle," he says, "feeling his health improve, and his love of conversation revive, sought a companion for the remainder of his journey, and, failing the company of anyone else, secured that of Mr. Glennie."[19]

Glennie was a lawyer, who after dabbling in medicine and surgery, was called to the bar in 1853. One episode of his later life is worth mentioning here for the light it throws on his character. In 1876 he went to Serbia to report on the war with Turkey and, in order to get to the front, seems to have posed as a peer. Archibald Forbes, the Correspondent of *The Daily News*, the first paper to give an account of the atrocities of the Bashi-Bazouks, published an attack on Glennie, who was disposed to defend the Turks, and who claimed to be "rather favourably impressed than otherwise by all he saw and heard of their behaviour".[20] Forbes, among other charges, accused Glennie of fraudulently obtaining permission to get to the front, and Glennie, to vindicate his character, knocked Forbes down. A duel nearly ensued,† but the Correspondent of *The Daily News* who had issued the challenge, failed to turn up.[21]

A man who was to get to the Serbian front with such agility, had little difficulty in introducing himself to Buckle. The news of the Prince Consort's death gave him the opportunity he desired. The

* A. H. Sayce in his *Reminiscences*, maintains that Buckle's prejudice against the Scots and the Clergy partly accounts for the vigorous criticism his writing provoked. Sayce, who came to know Glennie in his "later and somewhat impecunious days", says, "his friends unfortunately found him a bore", p. 33. This statement, coming from a professor of Assyriology, carries conviction.

† Forbes was not alone in thinking that Glennie had behaved badly. The Reverend Malcolm MacColl, having seen the bodies of prisoners impaled on spikes, and having published an account of it, was furious to hear Glennie quoted as chief witness for the defence of the Turkish miscreant. "Mr. Stuart Glennie," wrote the indignant clergyman, "has heard nothing of the atrocities. He has also heard nothing of either Dr. Liddon or myself in Serbia. Dr. Liddon and I were in Serbia for all that; and what is more, we heard a good deal of Mr. Stuart Glennie then, and how he reached Deligrad and left it." (Reverend Malcolm MacColl to the Editor, *The Daily News*, 21st October, 1876.)

story of the meeting is, however, best told in his own infelicitous words. "It was not till the 9th, that, lunching with some friends who had got up before us, I chanced to hear that the occupant of the only *dahabeeyah* that was downward-bound was Mr. Buckle, and that already all his preparations were made for departure. I called, therefore, that afternoon, having great political news to communicate which a wealthy countryman of mine, much favoured by the Viceroy, and who had come up in one of his steamers, had brought us the previous evening. So—through the throng of Arabs, Copts, and Nubians, vendors of ostrich eggs and other wares and curiosities; dancing-girls, Abyssinian and Ghawazee, handsome, gold-bedecked Hamdas and Lateefehs; and, less venal than these, divinely-shaped, speaking-eyed Baccheetas, from the Nubian island of Elephantine opposite, fitly called the 'Isle of Flowers'—I, with some difficulty, made my way, and crossed the plank from the sands to the lower deck of Mr. Buckle's *dehabeeyah*. Thence, I was ushered into the little saloon-cabin under the quarter-deck and was first of all struck by the change in Mr. Buckle from what I remembered him, on the only occasion on which I had previously seen him, when delivering at the Royal Institution, with the fluency and eloquence of the most accustomed and accomplished speaker, his lecture 'On the Influence of Women'—his first, and unfortunately his last, public address. Yet perhaps it was the beard he now wore, and his negligent dress, that chiefly made it difficult for me to recognize, in the worn-out student, the successful author, and lion of a London season. . . . The news I had to give was the death of the Prince Consort, and, in consequence of the Trent affair, the threatened war with America. The latter, Mr. Buckle, as I, most heartily wished might never occur. The former event, however much to be regretted for the Queen's sake, neither he nor I could see any important political results from, except so far as, in its indirect effects, it would probably be one of many causes working to the Republican transformation of Constitutional Monarchy."[22] The record of this meeting continues with a long account of a conversation about spiritualism. Unfortunately Buckle's views seem to be given merely as a text for a sermon from Glennie, and differ completely from those he had expressed to Longmore not many days before.[23] Glennie's book is not, however, of great value to those who are interested in Buckle. Huth discovered so many absurdities and inaccuracies in the work that it is difficult to credit anything it contains.*

* See Appendix I.

After arranging to meet again in Cairo, Glennie sailed down to the first cataract, and Buckle, despite a contrary wind, began the journey back to Thebes, which he reached on the evening of 14th January. Here, he and the boys found a pile of letters from England, the first they had received since leaving Cairo. Mrs. Huth's letters to her sons were sprinkled with messages to Buckle. "Don't you think we are very happy," she says in one, "to have such a friend as Mr. Buckle, and don't you think that he is a very rich man to have it in his power to bestow so much happiness? Do tell me what you think of Mr. B. now, and he need not see it, for we will make it a practice never to let him see our letters when we speak ill of him. I will put always at the top of mine 'don't show' and that will mean I am going to speak of the wicked man as he deserves."[24] "Be happy my dear boys," she says in another letter, "and do what you can to contribute to the man's happiness who is with you. Bless him, bless him a thousand times, and may his life be studded with pleasures as much above those of the human kind, as he is above us all. . . . This morning when papa came into the nursery, Dalsy* said 'O Papa, I wish you would buy me a bookcase.' So he asked why, upon which she showed him three or four picture books. We are getting old before our time, for there are the boys travelling in the Orient, and the baby wants a bookcase. . . . Last night I dreamt of my Egyptian letters, that I had received before going to bed . . . and Dicky* dreamt of Mr. Buckle. So you see what the family is doing here. Whilst you *live*, we only *dream*. . . . Annie Walters is anxious lest dear George (the gentleman that she is engaged to) should not be able to enter into Bucklean ideas. . . . I crammed Dicky that as Mr. B. could not get a European servant, he engaged an Egyptianess as nurse for you, and that now you are always washed and bathed by a black woman and that you cry out 'Egyptianess I want my boots blacked.' "[25] In another of her letters Mrs. Huth says: "Dalsy and I have got woollen over-boots, something like those that we used to call the great B.'s 'elephant boots', of course only when his back was turned, for we would not have him know this piece of rudeness for the world."[26]

Buckle stayed at Thebes for six days and spent much of the time collecting antiquities with which he proposed to form a museum in the stable at the back of 59 Oxford Terrace. He carefully catalogued everything he bought[27] and his purchases were both varied and extensive. When he later returned to Cairo he greatly increased his col-

* Dalsy was Mrs. Huth's daughter. Dicky was was her youngest son.

lection, buying chiefly from a Museum called the Odelschachi. Some idea of the amount of curiosities he bought may be obtained from the instructions he gave Huth about unpacking the cases in which they were to be sent back to England. "I shall send my antiquities and those of the boys to Briggs at Alexandria tomorrow, requesting them to send them by the first opportunity *direct* to London. Some of them are of considerable value, and being also very brittle and most carefully packed, I don't like to trust them to strangers at Southampton. I therefore send them addressed to you . . . feeling assured that you won't mind the trouble of being yourself present at the London Custom House and having with you some experienced packer. The cases contain *nothing* but antiquities, curiosities and clothes—on none of which is there any duty. There are in all six cases. . . . I do hope that the Custom House officers will be gentle with my antiquities, some of which are of wood and 4,000 years old, and consequently of extreme fragility. . . . Among my collection are two ancient Egyptian heads; one for myself and one which I bought as a present for Dicky. Give him it with my love."[28]

While at Thebes Buckle wrote a letter to a widow, Mrs. Faunch, whom he had known in London, inviting her to join him in Egypt. "My dearest Lizzy," it began, "only half an hour ago I heard that a Turkish Officer who is going along the hill as far as Cairo, would take charge of any letters for me and post them in Cairo. I therefore take the opportunity of writing a few lines to you to tell you that I have been and still am quite well, in spite of the heat of the weather; for I am now in the tropics, being, as you will see by the map, to the South of Egypt. The mornings and evenings are beautiful, but the sun in the middle of the day is intense. It hardly ever rains here; and often four or five years pass by without a single shower.

"Such favourable offers have been made to me, that it is very likely that I may settle here or in Egypt for a few years. Would you, dear, come out to me if I were to stay here? In such case I should of course make myself responsible for the rent of your house and for every other expense you incurred, either directly or indirectly.

"Communications from here to Europe are very rare and I do not know how long it may be before I have another opportunity of writing, but if you could make up your mind to come to me, I would employ a trustworthy person to bring you and make every arrangement for your comfort. . . .

"I have many letters to write by this opportunity and only two or three hours in which to write them, so must conclude with the best love of your very affectionate Harry."[29]

It is difficult to discover much about Mrs. Faunch since some of the evidence was purposely destroyed and everybody who knew about her, including Buckle himself, was naturally reticent on the subject. She was born at Hammersmith in 1826, the daughter of William Cannon, a blacksmith. When she was twenty she married a local carpenter, William Faunch. The young couple lived in a cottage at Kew, near William's parents, which they shared with two other tenants. In 1857 William Faunch died. Somehow Lizzy seems to have been better provided for as a widow than as a married woman, for three years after her husband's death she was installed in 37 Wyndham Street, and had a servant to look after her. By 1865 she was living in more exalted circumstances still, at 1 Lodge Place, Regent's Park. Some time later she moved to a fashionable block of flats in Victoria Street, and even figured in the exclusive "Royal Red Book and Court Register". She died of consumption in 1905 in an Asylum at Tooting Bec.[30]

The rest, unfortunately, is silence, and the omissions in Mrs. Faunch's biography can only be supplied by conjecture. The most obvious and likely explanation of her rise from obscurity to eminence and her sad decline, ending in a pauper's grave, is that she was a woman of some beauty, who contrived to capitalize her charms. From the little evidence that we have, it seems very likely that Buckle was the first to assist her in her ascent to fortune, and that after his death she found some rich and influential friend who helped her to rise further in the world. If the novelists and gossip-writers of the period are to be believed, many ladies living in St. John's Wood did so at the expense of their lovers. Ouida's magnificent Guardsmen kept such establishments. Certainly no other supposition explains so convincingly how the carpenter's widow achieved such heights.

After nearly a week at Thebes, Buckle set sail for Cairo, stopping on the way to visit the Pyramids. "Today we have been to the top of the Pyramid of Cheops," Eddy told his mother. "We started this morning directly after breakfast for Gizeh, where the pyramids are, on jolly spirited donkeys, such as we had not had up the Nile for a long time. . . . The first thing we did when we got to the Pyramids was to look at the Sphinx, it is so buried in the sand that only its head and back is visible. It measures 143 feet from its head to the end of its back. . . . We broke a bit off its neck to take home with us, as everyone else does, and then walked on to the Pyramid of Cheops and prepared to go up. I and Alfred each had two Arabs (who were very talkative and kept asking for 'bakshish' all the way up) to help us, or rather pull us up. We did it in ten minutes. . . . It took Mr. Buckle twenty-five, so I think I and Alfred got up pretty quickly. We had a longish rest at the top, and Mr. B. smoked a cigar and then we came down again."[31] The boys afterwards explored the interior of the Pyramid while Buckle waited for them outside.

When *El Ableh* reached Boulak, Buckle decided to live on board rather than transfer to an hotel in Cairo. At Boulak there was another bunch of letters from England. It became clear from them that the post from the Nile was very slow and Mrs. Huth was growing anxious. Buckle at once wrote to reassure her. "I do not wonder at your anxiety in being so long without intelligence; but I have done all in my power, and have never, since we left England, allowed a post to go by without writing. Your picture of your imagination of my hanging over the bed of a sick boy, and bringing you back a child the less, has gone to my very heart, and made me feel quite miserable, since I know what must have passed through your mind, and what you must have suffered, before you would write this. But why, dear Mrs. Huth, why will you allow your judgment to be led captive by such dark imaginings? I never begin any considerable enterprise without well weighing the objections against it. In taking your children where I have taken them, and where they are about to go, I have estimated all the difficulties—or, if you will, all the dangers, and I *know* that I am able to meet them. I say that I KNOW it. And I am too deeply conscious of my own responsibility to write such a word loosely or rashly. . . . It is my deliberate opinion, that until you see your boys again they will run no risk greater than they would have run had they spent the same time under your roof . . . though you of course love your children better than I do, and better indeed than anyone does—for who knows so well as I that no love can equal the love of a mother?—still, even you could not watch them more carefully than I do; and, as you would be the first to acknowledge, you would watch them with less knowledge both of what should be guarded against and what should be done. The boys are, and have been all along, in perfect health. Eddy is gaining flesh and losing that anxious, worn, and sort of old-mannish look about the lines of the mouth which for many reasons I never like to see in children. As to Alf he is the picture of impudent health, saucy, joyous and buoyant. As the boys were vaccinated three years ago there is no occasion to repeat the operation. The protection is complete. There *are* instances of persons having the smallpox who have been so recently vaccinated, just as there are instances of persons having the smallpox twice. But there are also instances of people being killed on the railroad; and as there are no railroads in Palestine or Syria, we may fairly put one danger against the other, both being about equal. . . . Meanwhile, do not be uneasy; I pray you, do not be uneasy. I know well what I am doing, and I know how much depends on my doing it properly. Besides, if you give way to anxiety you will make yourself ill; and if you get ill, my excellent friend Huth will hate me as the cause, and maybe, will poison me in my food when I come home. So be of good cheer. . . .

"We have anchored one and a half miles from Cairo, as I think living on the Nile more healthy than being in an hotel. I shall therefore keep on the boat, and all my establishment, including my virtuous and noble-minded cook, until we start for the desert. As to cookey, please God! he and I will never part till the Asiatic part of the journey is ended. . . .

"I make no doubt that we can reach Vienna by June; but to hurry ourselves would spoil all, and be too fatiguing, as for about three months all our travelling will be on camels and horseback. How long do you think of staying at Vienna? and would it matter if we did not arrive there till the first week in July? I suppose you will remain at least a month; and I shall be glad of a little rest to push on the boys in their knowledge, so that they may return to England with everything gathered up and thoroughly digested.

"Good-bye! keep up your spirits, and look to the future with confidence. All will go well."[32]

At Boulak Buckle began to plan the next stage of his journey. "About the 19th or 20th," he writes to Henry Huth, "we shall, I hope, cross the desert to Sinai, and if possible go from Sinai through Petra to Jerusalem. If, as constantly happens, Petra should be unsafe, we shall return to Cairo, after seeing Sinai; and from Cairo cross the desert, at the north by El Arish, to Gaza and Hebron. Directly we get to Cairo I shall begin to make preparations, and buy the tents, furniture, &c. In Palestine and Syria I do not intend to go into hotels anywhere, nor even at Jerusalem. They are often damp and dirty, and I am satisfied that tent-life, with proper precautions, may be made extremely healthy. . . . I shall buy at Cairo iron bedsteads and good thick blankets; and looking at these and other appliances, my dragoman calculates that we shall need eighteen or twenty camels. At present we have three servants—our dragoman (i.e. Hassan), an excellent cook, and a boy about eighteen or nineteen; the boy is dull and inefficient, so I shall get rid of him at Cairo, but the other two I shall take on with me. Instead, therefore, of the badly-cooked, indigestible stuff which most Eastern travellers eat at the khans, or in large towns at the hotels, we shall be well fed; and if I can succeed in keeping the boys' digestive functions in complete order, I have not the smallest fear of the fatigue and exposure hurting them. I shall supply my servants well with fire-arms, and have the best escort that can be procured. . . .

"This will be a very expensive journey; but looking at the objects to be attained by it, I shall not grudge the cost, and (unless I am greatly mistaken in your views concerning the boys) you will not grudge it either. At all events, it is clear that if the journey is to be made by boys not very strong, and by a man not much stronger, it would be madness to spare money, when money will increase the chance of impunity."[33]

Every day Buckle's health improved and he felt better and stronger than he had done for years. Indeed it is difficult to believe that he would have arranged so strenuous an expedition into Palestine and Southern Syria if he had not recovered much of his old vigour. He stayed nearly a month in Cairo, his departure being postponed because of his decision to await the arrival from England of Josephus's *Antiquities of the Jews*, without which he felt the educational value of the journey would be seriously diminished for the boys. Possibly this was not the real or only reason for the delay. "Mr. B.," says Eddy, "was very disappointed in not having any letters by the last Mail."[34] It may be that he was expecting Mrs. Faunch's reply as well as Josephus's history.

Buckle had several introductions to people at Cairo and consequently dined out frequently. Janet Ross,* who first met him at Alexandria, introduced him to Hekekyan Bey, an Armenian, ex-minister of Education, and the future author of *A Treatise on the Chronology of the Siriadic Monuments*. The meeting was rather a fiasco. Hekekyan "quoted the Bible in English apropos of something

* Janet Ross was the daughter of Lady Duff Gordon, and granddaughter of Mrs. Austin. Her husband was the manager in Egypt of the banking-house of Briggs and Company.

Egyptian; whereupon Buckle stuck out his chin and scornfully repeated the verse in Hebrew, giving his own translation and remarking that when people cited an authority they should do so properly".[35] Janet Ross was hardly more successful in teaching the historian to load and fire a pistol. When she advised him to make use of his newly acquired accomplishment only in desperate extremity, he was not amused. Mrs. Huth, in one of her letters to the boys, shows the same lack of confidence in his prowess with a revolver. "I should not much mind his aiming it at me," she says, "for I think that would not prevent my living a long life after it." Although Buckle gave Mrs. Ross "the idea that he considered himself, as he was, very superior, and that he talked a little for effect", nevertheless she found listening to him extremely refreshing "after hearing about cotton-seed and grain, varied by small scandals, the staple conversation at Alexandria".[36]

An American gentleman, Charles Hale, frequently met Buckle in Cairo, particularly at the parties of the American Consul, Mr. Thayer, who was exceedingly kind and helpful to the English travellers. Hale's reminiscences of Buckle at Cairo give a better idea of his table talk than anything Glennie records.

"I must tell you of my dining yesterday with Mrs. Ross to meet Mr. Buckle, the author of the *History of Civilization*, who has just returned from his two or three months' voyage up the Nile, in which he pushed as far as Nubia. He is now staying for a little while in Cairo, or rather in his *dahabeeyah* or boat (which he says is more comfortable than any hotel), moored in the river at Boolak, the port of the town. . . .

"The dinner was at an hotel called the 'Restaurant d'Auric'. We assembled in Mrs. R.'s drawing-room, an apartment in the banking-house at a little distance, and walked to the hotel. . . . I happened to walk with Mr. Buckle, so that I had a brief talk with him in the street before the general conversation began at the table. He remarked upon the extraordinary devotion exhibited by Delane of the London *Times* to the interests and politics of Lord Palmerston. . . .

"Buckle, of course, was the card. He talked with a velocity and fulness of facts that was wonderful. The rest of us could do little but listen and ask questions. And yet he did not seem to be lecturing us; the stream of his conversation flowed along easily and naturally. Nor was it didactic; Buckle's range of reading has covered everything in elegant literature, as well as the ponderous works whose titles make so formidable a list at the beginning of his History, and, as he remembers everything he has read, he can produce his stores upon the moment for the illustration of whatever subject happens to come up.

"In the first place, let me say how delightful it was to discover his cordial interest in our own country. He expresses a strong hope that England will take no part against us, and do nothing to break the blockade. He is going to write about America; indeed, his next volume, besides containing a complete view of the German philosophy, will treat of the United States. But he will visit us before he writes. Although appreciating the great work of De Tocqueville, he complains of the general inadequacy of European criticism upon America. . . . For his own part, he considers the subject too vast, he says, and the testimony too conflicting, to permit him to write upon it before he has seen the country; and meanwhile he scrupulously refrains from forming any conclusive opinions. . . . The common people in England, he said, are by far the most useful class of society. He had been especially pleased by the numerous letters he had received from working-men who had read his book. These letters often surprised him by the acuteness and capacity displayed by their writers. The nobility would perish utterly, if it were not constantly recruited from commoners. Lord Brougham was the first member of the secular peerage who continued after his elevation to sign his name in full, 'H. Brougham', which he did to show his sympathy with the class from which he sprang. Buckle remarked that the history of the peasantry of no European country has ever been written, or ever can be written, and without it the record of the doings of kings and nobles is mere chaff. . . .

"Mr. Thayer asked him if in England he had been subjected to personal hostility for his opinions, or to anything like social ostracism. He said, generally not. A letter from a clergyman to an acquaintance in England, expressing intense antipathy to him, although he had never seen the writer, was the only evidence of this kind of opposition. 'In fact,' said he, naively, 'the people of England have such an admiration of any kind of *intellectual splendour* that they will forgive for its sake the most objectionable doctrines.'

". . . After dinner we returned to Mrs. R.'s apartments, where we had tea. Buckle and Hekekyan now got into an animated discussion upon the ancient Egyptian civilization, which scarcely gave the rest of us a chance to put in a single word. It was, however, exceedingly interesting to sit and listen. Indeed, although there was nothing awful about Buckle, one felt a little abashed to intrude one's own remarks in such a presence. . . . We stayed until nearly midnight, and then, taking our leave, Buckle accompanied Thayer and myself as far as the door of our hotel. Buckle received most kindly all suggestions made to him of books to be read upon American affairs, and people to be seen in the United States. . . .

"*February* 15.—This day we had an excursion to the Petrified Forest. Mr. Buckle was determined to go in a thing called a *mazetta*, a sort of huge bedstead with curtains, borne on the back of a camel, big enough to carry a small family, in which he expected to find room for himself and the two boys travelling with him. . . . To begin with, it was not thought prudent that Mr. Buckle should use the *mazetta* until the procession had got beyond the narrow streets of Cairo, lest the camel bearing it should take fright and knock the whole thing to pieces against the wall of a house. Accordingly, he and his charges took donkeys, and I rode off with them, at the head of the column. By-and-by Mr. Buckle changed to the conveyance originally proposed, but a very short experiment (literally, I suspect) sickened him of the *mazetta*, whose motion is precisely that of a ship in a storm, and he sent back to the town for donkeys. At the next halt the ladies took him into the carriage, where he found himself, as he said, 'in clover', and that was the end of his greatness in camel-riding. This remark, by the way, suggested a name ('Clover') for our boat in our voyage up the Nile just afterwards; but patriotism prevailed, and we named her 'Union'.

"The journey to the forest, about ten miles, was safely accomplished. We found the petrifactions duly wonderful. An excellent luncheon was laid out, after which we had an hour and a half of very entertaining conversation, in which Mr. Buckle and the Reverend Mr. S. held the leading parts—all around us as desolate and silent as one could imagine. It was interesting to observe the manner in which Buckle estimated eminent names, grouping them in some instances by threes, a favourite conceit with him. John Stuart Mill, of all living men, he considers as possessing the greatest mind in the world. Aristotle, Newton, and Shakespeare are the greatest the world has produced in past times. Homer, Dante, and Shakespeare are the only three great poets. Johnson, Gibbon, and Parr are the three writers who have done the greatest harm to the English language. Of Hallam he has a strong admiration. He spoke of

Sydney Smith as the greatest English wit, and of Selwyn as next to him, and described Macaulay's memory as unequalled in conversation.*

"*February* 16.—The morning was gratefully devoted to rest. In the afternoon, attended service at the Mission, where the Reverend Mr. S. preached an interesting discourse from John XV. 1–4. On the way home met Mr. Buckle, who came in, and was persuaded to stay to dinner. In speaking of religion, he said that there is no doctrine or truth in Christianity that had not been announced before, but that Christianity is by far the noblest religion in existence. The chief point of its superiority is the prominence it gives to the humane and philanthropic element; and in giving this prominence lies its originality. He believes in a Great First Cause, but does not arrive at his belief by any process of reasoning satisfactory to himself. Paley's argument, from the evidence of design, he regards as futile: if the beauty of this world indicates a creating cause, the beauty of that great cause would suggest another, and so on. He believes in a Future State, and declared most impressively that life would be insupportable to him, if he thought he were for ever to be separated from one person—alluding, it is probable, to his mother, to whose memory he dedicates the second volume of his book. He has no doubt that in the Future State we shall recognize one another."[37]

Buckle's preparations for the next stage of his journey were meticulous and unconventional. Hassan and the cook were to accompany the party, and camel-leaders, an armed guard and two influential Sheiks were also engaged. "We are going to have *four* tents," Eddy writes to his mother, "one to sleep and dine in, one little one to put up in the middle of the day to lunch in, one for the servants, and one diminutive one fitted up as a Water Closet. We believe ourselves to be the first party of gentlemen who have had that luxury. Mr. B. is just now numbering his antiquities and saying, 'Oh Lord deliver us from the snares of the devil.' "[38] The rest of the furniture which they took with them was almost as remarkable. "We have got iron bedsteads that fold up and put into a bag like my fishing-rod, only thicker; we have got four camp-stools, and little Bucky is going to have an iron chair with a back to it, that folds up, and a camp-stool to put his legs on. We have got prepared milk in tin cases so that we shall not have to go without milk as so many people do; and we have got

* Buckle met Macaulay at a dinner given by William Wood (Lord Hatherley), 19th June, 1852.

preserved tongue in tin cases, and boiled beef, and I don't know what; so we won't starve. . . . We are very busy today packing up. Mr. B. is packing now, and directly I have finished this letter I am going to pack—so we won't be able to read much today. Mr. B. has put a little blistering-plaster on my forehead for his own amusement, and won't let me take it off again. I have got a very small mummied crocodile; it is such a darling little thing that I know you won't mind it."[39] Alfred, who wrote home at the same time as his brother, had little to add, except that "Mr. Glennie is going with us and Mr. Buckle says he is a very clever man". The letter is signed: Alfred Henry Huth esq., M.P., F.R.S., D.D., LL.D.

On 4th March Buckle and the boys took the train for Suez. The next day, the party, which now included Glennie, crossed by boat to the opposite shore and rode on camels to the oasis surrounding Moses' well, where they encamped for the night. Here they met the Reverend St. John Tyrwhitt, Vicar of St. Mary's, Oxford. "Nothing can have been more delightful," he records, "than Buckle's conversation for the half-hour I passed in his company; and he was full of life and energy of mind. But his whole frame seemed slight and worn to a degree, and I thought he was taking mistaken precautions against heat. . . ."[40]

Buckle must have looked a ludicrous figure in the desert of Sinai. He wore a red and black tartan shirt of flannel, the sleeves of which were too long and protruded from a swallow-tailed black coat, which, he himself admitted, his valet would have scorned to wear. To protect his head from the sun he carried a white umbrella.[41] When Glennie suggested that his dress was unsuitable for desert life, Buckle pointed out that great Arab Chiefs wore voluminous robes, and that protection from heat is as much assured by flannel as protection from cold. Convention he regarded as a form of slavery whose oppressive laws smothered experiment and progress, and consequently he was eccentric on principle, living in fearless rebellion against the exacting tyranny of custom. On the Nile he refused to fire salutes and in the desert he would not carry a flag. Once when one of the boys put a bottle in the middle of the table, Glennie told him to move it to the corner. "Leave it where it is," said Buckle, "I hate to see things always done in the same way."

He found the motion of a camel so "insufferable" that he crossed the desert on a donkey, which he called "Lucius". "Lucius" was probably the first donkey to traverse the desert, for a special camel had to be provided to carry the water he required. Buckle's plan was to visit Mount Sinai and then to make his way to Petra and thence to travel northwards. At eight in the morning on 6th March, the party set out, following the legendary track of the Israelites, and an incongruous collection they were: Arab servants, two small English boys, Glennie, for ever deriding the belief that the country he traversed was sacred, and Buckle whose pilgrimage was soon to end for ever at Damascus with his life's work half done.

CHAPTER IV

THE LAST JOURNEY

THE first part of the journey in Sinai lay through desert and provoked Glennie to deliver himself of the following soliloquy. "Nay, that men—not at home, and following as in a dream, where everything is possible, the Forty-years-wanderings of the Israelites, but following through actual deserts the very track of these wanderings, as—so far at least as Sinai—we so probably do—that men should in these days, and here, literally and truly believe that the Israelites had such other day-guidance and night-illumination as is affirmed in the book of 'Exodus', seemed almost incredibly marvellous; and that, not believing that the Israelites had such supernatural day-guidance and night-illumination, they should pretend to believe it, or, refraining from not distinctly saying that they do *not* believe it, should permit it to be understood that they do believe it, seemed—ah, men otherwise truthful, manly, and honourable, do permit this to be understood, and, as it should certainly seem, falsely understood; and it would appear wiser, therefore, to endeavour to explain this to oneself by the complexity of human motives and character, than to give vent to expressions, however apparently justifiable, of indignation, and contempt."[1]

Few books are more stuffed with nonsense than Glennie's *Pilgrim Memories*, and the impudent presumption of its author appears the more gross when he exposes, as he cannot constantly help doing, the emptiness of his pretensions. It is very hard to understand how Buckle could have endured his companionship, and listened with patience while he was told that the true Bible of educated Europeans was Shakespeare's Plays, or that "the root of all tragedy was the fatal condition of felt lovelessness and loneliness". Glennie was not only a bore but a crank, who devoted most of his waking energy to laying down the law on subjects about which he knew little, at a length which would have dismayed the elders of the Kirk.

The travellers' routine was arranged by Buckle. They got up at six o'clock and breakfasted half an hour later in the shade of the largest tent. Tea, eggs, rice, camel's milk, and marmalade were the normal fare. A little before eight, while the tents were being struck and the baggage camels prepared, the party set out, riding most of the way, but walking for part of the time. At eleven they rested for a few moments and refreshed themselves with Carr's biscuits helped down with lukewarm water. Lunch, consisting of figs and more biscuits, they ate on the march, usually at about twelve o'clock. Then during the hottest part of the day they rested, sometimes pitching a tent if they could find no other shade. At six they generally reached their encampment for the night, and ate their principal meal. At nine Buckle retired with a cigar and read the Bible, or Josephus, before going to sleep. Glennie was the last to bed, his time being occupied in thinking great thoughts about Mosaic miracles, or the stars in the firmament.

When the track to Mount Sinai began to follow the sea-shore, Glennie decided to bathe, although Buckle attempted to dissuade him because of the danger from sharks. After floating for a time in "entranced enjoyment", he noticed a long dark object under the water. "Whatever it was," he says, "it occurred to me that I had been just about my usual time in the water. So, I cannot positively say whether it was a shark or not."[2] One is given to understand from this account that if Glennie's time had not so abruptly run out, he would not have hesitated to investigate further. Indeed he was seldom reluctant either to impute cowardice to others, or to imply that he himself had the courage of a lion. His description of his descent of the First Cataract is very characteristic. "Still grander, however, was the shooting of this First Cataract. . . . Some travellers do not risk it; nor, I believe, did Mr. Buckle; but I found it one of the most glorious sensations I ever experienced."[3] This heroic feat, as Huth was quick to see, strangely recalls Pepys' anecdote of the passage of a Frenchman through London Bridge, "where, when he saw the great fall, he began to cross himself and say his prayers in the greatest fear in the world, and, soon as he was over, he swore '*Morbleu! C'est le plus grand plaisir du monde*'."

After seven days of travelling they came to the copper mines of Maghâra, which are over 4,000 years old. A Scotsman, Major Macdonald, had built himself a house nearby, taken possession of the Turquoise mines, and, without being able to speak a word of Arabic, had made himself undisputed master of all he surveyed, the "uncrowned King of the Desert". Major Macdonald's mining venture in the end proved unsuccessful, for most of the turquoises were of an inferior kind. The Major was exceedingly hospitable and was delighted to meet Buckle whose book he had read. "As for myself," says Glennie, "a Scotsman seldom needs any other introduction than his name to a countryman abroad." After a breakfast of Capricorn Cutlets washed down with whisky, "the dew of his native mountains", as our Boswell calls it, the party visited the mines and examined the inscriptions, some dating back to Snefru, the first king of the fourth Dynasty.

Having stayed the night with Major Macdonald, they made the journey next day to Wadi Firan, the most fertile oasis of the whole peninsula and the site of an early Christian monastery. Two days later, on 14th March, they reached Mount Sinai. Buckle examined the guest rooms of the Monastery of St. Catherine, but preferred to sleep in his tent. After a deafening thunderstorm, which raged most of the night, the English party climbed to the top of Mount Sinai next morning. On the way up they looked into the Chapel of St. Mary, which Baedeker explains was erected by the Monks in gratitude for their deliverance by the Virgin from a plague of vermin. "The traveller," he adds, "will have abundant opportunity of observing that this miracle needs renewing." At the top of the mountain, where Moses received the Ten Commandments, stand a chapel and a mosque. "The Mosque," said Alfred in one of his letters, "is all hung with rags and the chapel is full of dirty prints of the Virgin Mary and lots of other saints. We stopped on the top a little time and had lunch and some water from Moses' Well, which Mr. Buckle said was the best he had tasted since he left England."[4]

From Mount Sinai Buckle wrote to Mrs. Huth telling her of his future plans. "As I know how anxious you must be," he says, "to have the latest possible news of the desert travellers, I have arranged to send a Bedouin express on a fleet dromedary this evening to Suez. He will reach Suez in about three days with this letter.

"We are all quite well—very tired every evening, but waking up quite fresh and vigorous every morning. Our average day's journey is seven hours of actual riding, and we rest about three hours during the day. I hope that we shall succeed in getting to Akaba, then to Petra, and from Petra through Hebron to Jerusalem.

"But as there are rumours at Sinai of war among the tribes, I have sent a Bedouin to Akaba to learn the actual state of things before I venture to start; and I shall take a similar precaution at Akaba in regard to Petra. An American party leave here tomorrow, without taking any steps to procure information, and much wish us to go with them. But I do not like to run the risk, as with, I believe, one exception, no one has been to Petra during the last five years. I have sent for the head sheik, Hussein, and if he will accompany us with an escort, we will go—if not, not. So, as the Irishman said, 'Be aisy, now'.

"I am too tired to write more. The excitement and exquisite interest of the life we are leading are indescribable, but unfit me for every other exertion.

"Our encampment here is 5,500 feet above the level of the sea—the mid-day sun intensely hot, but the mornings bitterly cold."[5]

On 18th March the travellers set out for Akaba, along a route most of the time following the sea-shore. One morning, while deep in conversation with Glennie, Buckle narrowly escaped the spring of a cobra which "Lucius" had disturbed. He made a joke of the incident by inveighing against the blindness of fate through which the career of a great philosopher might have been ended by the merest accident. After six days on the march, the party encamped by the palm-groves of Akaba, under the walls of the old Turkish fortress, and here they joined forces with some English and American travellers who also proposed to visit Petra.

While waiting at Akaba, Buckle met a Scottish Catholic, Alexander Gray, whom he had previously encountered at Sinai. Gray, though disagreeing with most of Buckle's views, was deeply impressed by his conversational powers and fascinated by his company. "I remember, because it struck me very forcibly," Gray wrote later, "that one day when the German* was defending some point of religious doctrine, Buckle pointed out that he had omitted one or two stronger arguments in his favour, which he proceeded to give. It was quite evident to me that few priests or parsons existed who were qualified to defend their respective creeds better than was Mr. Buckle himself any one of them. . . . My asking him one day what in his opinion were the strong and what the weak points of Catholicism and of Protestantism, led up to the following, to me, memorable remarks:—'I understand that the Catholic Church is making great progress in America; but it must do so, for what has it to contend against there? Only Protestantism, which is inconsistency itself. I,

* There was a German Lutheran clergyman in one of the parties which Buckle joined at Akaba.

too, was brought up a Protestant, and was taught to regard my private judgment as my birthright, of which no one could rob me. But when, in making use of my private judgment, I was led to reject Christianity, an outcry was at once raised against me for exercising this very undoubted right.' Then turning towards me, he said: 'Your Church at least is consistent, for it does not profess to allow the right of private judgment. But then it starts from false premises, for it assumes that Christ was the Son of God. Prove to me that Christ was the Son of God, and I too at once become a Catholic.' "[6]

For the past five years the Arabs had been fighting among themselves for possession of Petra and the country around. The position was so unsettled that travellers to Jerusalem normally went by Jaffa. The last party to attempt the journey from Akaba had been attacked, and one person had been killed and another had died of fright. But by 1862 the 'Alawin tribe had sufficiently mastered their opponents to be able to offer the English and American parties an escort and safe conduct. Negotiations with Sheik Mohammed, the powerful leader of the 'Alawins, were eventually completed, and the caravan which set out on 20th March numbered a hundred and ten well-armed men.

The journey to Petra was not without difficulties. As soon as the tents were struck some of the camels, venting their customary spite, threw their loads into the sea. Owing to the danger of attack, the caravan had to advance in warlike array, with scouts on the flanks, and there was no longer any question of sending on tents and baggage in advance. Soon the Arab escort alleged that they had discovered a new danger which only more money could avert. Then Buckle's cook took fright and swore that nothing would persuade him to go on. Only after being threatened with prison for breaking his contract did he change his mind. On 4th April the party climbed Mount Hor. When Buckle, hot and exhausted, arrived at the summit, after an hour and a half's climb, he exclaimed: "No wonder poor old Aaron died when they dragged him up here!" During the descent he was forced to threaten his Arab escort with his revolver, because the man kept pushing him to make him go faster. That afternoon the tents were pitched in Petra. "We had nice companions in the desert," Eddy reassures his mother, "Cobras and Scorpions. Our Arabs killed four Cobras in one day, and one party found a scorpion on their towel once."[7]

After three days at Petra the Caravan started out for Hebron and, despite several alarms, reached the town safely. Here they left their escort and, after visiting Bethlehem, reached Jerusalem late in the afternoon of 16th April. "We arrived here," Buckle wrote to Mrs. Huth, "after a most fatiguing and arduous journey through the *whole* desert of Sinai and of Edom. We have traversed a deeply interesting country, visited by few Europeans—and by none during the last five years, so dangerous was the latter part of the journey reputed to be. But I had taken my measures before venturing to go beyond Sinai, and gradually feeling my way, secured, as I went on, the protection of every leading sheik, having studied at Cairo their relative power and position. Having an ample stock of provisions, I was prepared at any moment to fall back and return if need be to Egypt. Three other parties, chiefly Americans, joined us at Sinai, each having their separate establishment arranged, with their own dragoman, but all, for greater safety, keeping together till we reached Hebron. We were in all fifteen persons, and with our servants and escort we numbered 110 armed men. . . . There were several alarms, and there was undoubted danger; but in my deliberate judgment the danger was not greater than would be encountered in a rough sea with a good vessel and a skilful captain. Some of our fellow-travellers were in great fear two or three times, and assured me that they had no sleep on those occasions. For my own part, I never was kept awake ten minutes. The boys behaved exceedingly well. Once Eddy woke me by screaming out in his sleep that robbers were coming, but I took no notice and to this day he does not know it. I told them always to keep close to me in the caravan; they always slept in my tent; and, without concealing from them the real state of affairs, I simply assured them that whatever happened to them should also happen to me. They believed me. They were satisfied that I meant what I said; and I am more than repaid by their confidence and affection.

"The result is that we have seen Petra—as wonderful, and far more beautiful, than anything in Egypt. Burckhardt, about forty years ago, was the first European who ever set foot there; and since then, not more probably than 100 persons have seen it; that is to say, have really *seen* it as we did, at leisure, and spending three whole days there. Occasionally gentlemen without tents, and with no food but what they can carry on their own horse, gallop from Hebron to Petra (about 120 miles) in two days and a half, reaching Petra in the evening, seeing it by moonlight, and then gallop back before the Bedouins and Fellahin are aware of their presence. The English and other Consuls, and the Governor of Cairo with other persons of influence, all declared that this was the only way I could see Petra; but the hardship of the journey, and the risk of sleeping in the open air, prevented me from thinking for a moment of such a plan. Among the English here our journey has created quite a sensation; and the result is one of many proofs which have convinced me of the profound ignorance of officials in the East of everything which their own eyes do not see. I had to collect all my facts through an interpreter, but I analysed and compared them with something more than official care and precision. Having done so, I acted; and I really look back to this passage through Petra from Egypt as by far the greatest practical achievement of my life. I believe that you are both laughing, and I am almost inclined to laugh myself. But I am conceited about it, and I think I have reason to be so; for I must, moreover, tell you that nearly all our party were more or less ill with fatigue, anxiety, and the extraordinary vicissitudes of temperature. At 3.30 p.m. the heat was on one occasion 119° Fah., and before sunrise the next morning the thermometer had fallen *in the tent* (and our tent was by far the thickest and warmest of all) to 42°. Headaches, sickness, bleeding at the nose, and bowel complaints were very common; but we three had not even pain or inconvenience of any kind. . . . The dear little kids are now the picture of health, and we are all as brown as Arabs. . . .

"The truth is that we were the only ones who had proper food and were properly clothed. We had plenty of green vegetables preserved; also preserved meats of every kind, and excellent preserved Julien soup; while others, day after day, lived upon fowls, tasteless mutton, and hard biscuits. They also, in spite of my warning, committed the enormous but very tempting mistake of wearing summer clothes in hot weather. On the other hand, I and the boys had on complete winter clothing, which was never to be changed till going to bed, when I always saw myself that the boys had two good blankets over them, however warm they might be. Poor Eddy often complained of the heat when he went to bed; but I was inflexible as to the blankets, being satisfied that a free and constant action of the skin is the only safety valve in this dangerous climate. Others thought differently, and, strong and vigorous young men as most of them were, they fared differently—being constantly unwell, and always ascribing their complaints to the wrong cause. . . . I must tell you that I am far stronger both in mind and body than I have been since you knew me, and I feel fit to go on at once with my work. But I neither read nor write. I think; I see; and I talk. Especially I study the state of society and habits of the people. We shall stay here to the end of this week, and then go to Jericho, the Jordan, Dead Sea, and Bethlehem, and thence northward for Nazareth, the Sea of Galilee, Damascus, Baalbec, &c. I feel boyish enough for anything, and fancy myself growing younger; yet I am old, very old—forty on the 24th of last November. It's a great age."[8]

The day after his arrival in Jerusalem, Buckle tried to find a house to live in, but it was Holy Week and the town was crowded, so he was forced to remain in an hotel. Buckle and the boys visited the Garden of Gethsemane and the Church of the Holy Sepulchre. "We have been to see the Church of the Sepulchre," Eddy wrote home, "it is as I expected it to be, very gaudy and very ugly. On Thursday we are going to see the ceremony of the washing of the feet, and on Saturday the Greek holy fire, which perhaps you know is a wonderful miracle. The bishop goes into a little cupboard with a match and a piece of wood and comes out again with the bit of wood lited which the people suppose is lited from heaven."[9]

After watching the miracle, Buckle returned to his hotel and the discussion at dinner turned to religion. His refusal to accept the supposition that Jonah lived three days in a whale's belly provoked a clergyman present to leave the table. When dinner was over, Buckle again talked about Christianity and said that he believed in the New Testament, after eliminating the supernatural. Christ, he said, was the greatest teacher and civilizer of mankind that ever lived, whose teaching it was impossible to explain except on the assumption that it was divinely inspired.

Before leaving Jerusalem, Buckle again visited Bethlehem, and then rode on to the Dead Sea, the water of which Eddy described as "tasting worse than rhubarb and magnesia and senna". All the time the English party travelled in this desolate region they were accompanied by thieves as a sign that blackmail had already been levied. A gentleman and his wife who took the same road a few years later, refused to pay, as Buckle himself might easily have done. They were robbed, stripped of all their clothes, and left with nothing but *The Times* newspaper. The disconsolate couple returned to Jerusalem, the man draped in the agony column and his wife in the Supplement.

From the Dead Sea Buckle travelled north to Jericho and from thence back to Jerusalem. On 24th April the party set out for Nazareth, a four-day journey, and here Buckle fell ill, partly no doubt as a result of fatigue. Everybody found that riding all day in extremely hot weather was exhausting, and it must have been particularly so for a man unaccustomed to exertion and weakened by previous ill-health. The first night he encamped at Nazareth there was a tremendous storm and the tents were all flooded. Buckle awoke with a severe sore throat and decided to sleep in the Latin Monastery. There, in fact, he spent a week in bed, attended first by a Spanish monk and then by an Armenian Protestant doctor. Neither realized what was wrong and both suggested different treatments. As the patient himself also prescribed his own remedies, the medicines he took did more harm than good. "A restless night," he wrote in his diary, "with great prostration, amounting almost to wandering, confirmed my opinion that I am being badly treated. When, therefore, the doctor came, at 8 a.m., I persuaded him to send me some muriate of iron, of which I took ten drops in a wine-glassful of water. I further ordered strong mutton-broth to be made; for since Tuesday I have had nothing stronger than rice-water and milk; and at 10 a.m. I got up, and am now writing my journal (11.15) with the window open. The throat is very painful when I swallow, but I feel better in all other respects. I would not let the doctor meddle with my throat this morning, as I wish the ulcer to reach its full size and then be lanced." The next day he writes, "Much better, but appetite being bad, and tongue covered with a coat like white cream, I took at 6.30 a.m. two of Mr. Morgan's pills, containing grey powder. Rose at 7.30. Ate no breakfast. Walked half an hour; the first time I have been out. In afternoon played backgammon. The only nourishment I can take is mutton broth with toast, and occasionally a little milk. But at 6.30 I took half a wine-glass of brandy in two tumblers of water, and felt better after it."[10]

After more than a week in bed, Buckle, feeling somewhat better, decided to make a move. The fever made him restless, and, although it would have been wiser to have stayed where he was, he was anxious not to delay Glennie and waste more of his time and money. The remainder of Buckle's journey is simply the story of his courageous fight with illness and exhaustion. On 7th May he travelled from Nazareth to Acre and although he had been over five hours on the march, he walked round the town after a short rest. The next day his sore throat became worse but he refused to postpone his visit to Tyre. On the way there he passed the Prince of Wales who was making a tour of the Holy Land with Dean Stanley as his guide.

From Tyre Buckle travelled to Sidon, where he consulted a doctor who told him he needed rest. After two days, he felt better again and so pushed on for Beyrout, from whence he sent Mrs. Huth the last letter he ever wrote. "We have arrived here," he says, "all well, after a journey from Jerusalem, interesting beyond all description. . . . We saw Tyre and Sidon, and got much valuable information respecting the excavations conducted there for the last eighteen months by the French Government. . . . Tomorrow we shall see the Assyrian remains near here; the next day start for Damascus, and Baalbek, and return to Beyrout by the Cedars of Lebanon, the oldest and grandest trees in the world.

"I have most reluctantly abandoned Constantinople. . . . The only other route to Vienna is by Trieste. We must, therefore, take the steamer from here to Smyrna, Syra, and Athens, but shall see little or nothing of Greece, as the weather will be too hot. . . .

"I expect to be at Trieste about the middle of June; and as you said that the end of July would suit you to reach Vienna, this leaves me a clear month, which I purpose spending at Gratz or Grätz in Styria, on the railroad between Trieste and Vienna."[11]

Although he said nothing about his health to Mrs. Huth he was so ill that a stranger, staying at the same hotel in Beyrout, begged him to return to Europe and recruit his strength. But having come so far, Buckle would not abandon the journey to Damascus and set out for the city on 16th May, although fatigue forced him to rest constantly. One of his last conversations took place at the foot of the ascent of the Anti-Libanus, when he told Glennie that he had enjoyed twenty years of almost uninterrupted happiness. His mother's death had broken the spell, but there were still many pleasures left to him, not the least of which was his work.

When at last Damascus, the vision which had filled his childhood dreams as he read and reread the *Arabian Nights*, came into sight, he was deeply moved. After a moment's silence he declared: "This is worth all that it has cost me!" At nightfall Buckle, Glennie and the boys rode through the city gates and down interminable, winding streets. "Utterly prostrated," the invalid sent for Dr. Nicora, a Frenchman, and the only qualified man in the place. He prescribed opium among other medicines. After a restless night, Buckle was able to visit the bazaars for half an hour, leaning on the arm of a servant, but at dinner that evening, a combination of fever and drugs made him delirious and he suddenly startled the company by exclaiming: "*Oh mon Dieu, je deviens fou!*" Glennie assisted him to bed and was greatly distressed by his incoherent utterances. "Oh my book, my book!" he moaned. "I shall never finish my book."* Then later he burst into tears and said: "I know I am talking nonsense, but I cannot help it."[12]

As he had done before, Buckle treated himself from the medicine-chest he had brought with him from England, and only when he was too weak to resist could he be persuaded to follow Dr. Nicora's treatment. "He rarely followed my prescriptions," complained the Frenchman; "more often than not he did exactly the opposite to what I told him." Since the doctor believed bleeding to be the treatment for typhoid, the patient in fact knew better, and although he would probably have died anyway, it is difficult to resist the conclusion that his physician hastened his death. On 22nd May, Glennie, who had arranged to travel on to Baalbek, called on Mr. Sandwith, the British Acting Consul, to tell him of his departure, and to say that he considered Buckle sufficiently recovered to leave him. "Relieved at hearing a better account," says Sandwith, "I ventured as soon as Mr. Glennie had left, to call at the hotel which is situated in the street identified by antiquarians with that called in the New Testament 'Straight', where Paul lodged. I found Mr. Buckle in bed with a worn and anxious look, and sitting by his bedside, I talked with him for about a quarter of an hour."[13] Buckle spoke about his travels with considerable animation, mentioning, among other things, the name of Dean Stanley whom he greatly admired for his intellectual power and independence, and whose book on Sinai and Palestine he had taken on his travels.

On Monday, 26th May, the Consul called with the Reverend Smylie Robson, a missionary of the Irish Presbyterian Church, and found Buckle worse. "Up to Monday afternoon," wrote Sandwith, "neither Mr. Robson nor myself had at all despaired of the deceased's

* Ruskin, mistakenly believing that these were Buckle's last words, wrote: "Some years ago I remember reading with contempt—which I was forced to conceal, because everybody called me a monster for experiencing it—of the grief felt by an Eastern traveller struck by fatal illness, not that he was leaving this pleasant world, but that he should never finish his book." Notes for lectures on "Modern Painters", *The Works of Ruskin*, Ed. Cook and Wedderburn, Vol. XXII, p. 523. J. A. Froude, who also believed that these were Buckle's last words, comments as follows: "He went away as he had lived, nobly careless of himself, and thinking only of the thing which he had undertaken to do." J. A. Froude, *Short Studies on Great Subjects*, Vol. I, p. 3.

recovery, but when on that afternoon we found the symptoms become more grave and the patient's mind to begin to wander, we immediately telegraphed for Dr. Barclay, an American physician of Beyrout."[14] The message was delayed for a day through the negligence of the telegraph clerks, and by the time Barclay arrived, Buckle was unconscious. For the last three days of his life, Sandwith, Robson and a maid of Lady Ellenborough's who had once been a nurse, kept continuous watch by the bedside. Sandwith "consulted with Mr. Robson about the propriety of asking Mr. Buckle if he had any final testament to make, but we found he was not sufficiently himself to respond pertinently to our questions."[15]

When Dr. Barclay arrived on the afternoon of the the 28th he pronounced the case almost hopeless, but did what he could to reverse Dr. Nicora's treatment and to stimulate rather than lower the patient. At eight that evening Buckle became more lucid and asked to see Eddy and Alfred. He embraced them, murmuring, "Poor little boys!" At six next morning a change for the worse became evident and at a quarter past ten he died with a wave of the hand. "I shall never forget," wrote Sandwith, "the look of intellectual majesty as well as of sweet dignity which Death had stamped on his features."

Buckle was buried the same evening, in the Protestant cemetery at Damascus, which fanatical Moslems had recently desecrated. The Anglican Service was read by Mr. Robson and was attended by the Vice-Consul and the two little Huth boys, "who were heart-broken at the sudden loss of their noble-minded companion and friend".[16] On the gravestone is inscribed in Arabic: "The writer is resting under the earth, but his works endure."

Glennie, who had arrived at Beyrout on 31st May after his excursion to Baalbek, learned at the Consulate of his travelling-companion's death, and immediately wrote to *The Times* to report the sad news. The Huth boys were escorted back to Beyrout by Dr. Barclay, and after travelling with Glennie as far as Trieste, were met and taken home.

Alfred Huth in the appendix of his biography, refers to Glennie as being "unwilling to waste his time in attendance on his dying companion".[17] This statement led to a ferocious controversy conducted in the pages of *The Athenaeum*.[18] The crux of the argument was the extent to which Glennie appreciated the seriousness of Buckle's illness when he left for Baalbek. Dr. Nicora recognized the fever as typhoid two days before Glennie left, and Buckle died a week after his departure. Glennie must therefore have known that his friend's illness was serious. On the other hand Sandwith only realized that there was little hope of recovery as late as the 26th, and in Glennie's favour it may be argued that Buckle was in the Consul's care and there was little that he could have done if he had stayed.

Buckle's grave in the Protestant cemetery at Damascus remained unmarked for several years. One of his most intimate friends, John Dickinson,* wrote a letter to Henry Huth saying, "considering the fortune left to his family by my late friend . . . I had reason to be deeply shocked, before this last affair of the unmarked grave, at the neglect with which poor Buckle's literary remains and strongest wishes had been treated by his family; who ought to feel so proud of him and who seem to feel the very reverse."[19] The fact that the grave was unmarked was brought to the notice of Major Evans Bell, an admirer of Buckle's writing, and a friend of Mary Rogers, sister of the British Consul at Damascus. In 1866 Mary wrote to her mother telling her that no orders had been given for a stone to mark Buckle's resting-place. Mrs. Rogers forwarded this letter to Evans Bell, who at once communicated with Dickinson and Henry Huth. "I was astonished," Bell wrote to Mary Rogers, "to see it mentioned in one of your letters that there was not a stone to mark the place of Henry Buckle's remains, and at once took an extract from your letter and communicated with two of Buckle's most intimate friends, Mr. John Dickinson and Mr. Henry Huth. Both of them were surprised and shocked to hear of such neglect, and at first both of them felt great repugnance to appeal on the subject to Mrs. Allatt, who from religious prejudices has never had the slightest sympathy or pride in her brother's fame, and who in fact has since his death thrown every obstacle in the way of publishing his literary remains. . . . However Mr. Huth decided that it would be hardly decent to do anything without consulting her, and she at once wrote in reply saying that she had no idea that all these usual forms had not been observed. . . ."[20] In her letter Mrs. Allatt enclosed an epitaph for the gravestone. After the briefest recital of Buckle's parentage and dates of birth and death, it concluded, "I know that he shall rise again." Not one word did it say of the *History of Civilization*. It was Miss Rogers who added the

* Dickinson's father had patented a process of manufacturing paper of an indefinite length, thereby meeting the increasing demands of newspapers. John Dickinson was born in 1815 and educated at Eton. In 1861 he succeeded John Bright as Chairman of the India Reform Society, and on his father's death inherited a large fortune. He died suddenly in 1876.

Arabic inscription contrasting the brief existence of an author with the enduring life of his work.*

Despite Mrs. Allatt's obstruction, many of Buckle's friends thought that his Common Place Books ought to be published and Capel proposed the idea to John Stuart Mill. "I wish to enquire," he wrote, "whether you would not think it advisable that his (Buckle's) Common Place Books should be given to the world, and I have no doubt that Longman's would be glad to publish them on reasonable conditions. I was pretty well acquainted with them and I cannot but feel that the very variety and extent of matter they contain would be of the greatest service. I know too that it was his intention to publish them himself, in the event of his being unable, through failure of health, to carry on his work."[21] Mill, who had already been sent Buckle's papers with a view to their publication, thought the idea a good one. Too busy to edit the remains himself, he left most of the work to his stepdaughter, Helen Taylor.†

Mrs. Huth strongly approved of the plan and was anxious that the Common Place Books should be printed in their entirety, but Longman, although prepared to publish some of the remains, was unwilling to accept the financial risk of bringing out all that Buckle had left.[22] Mr. and Mrs. Huth, however, generously offered to defray the cost.[23] Helen Taylor, even more generously, said that she would be willing to do the work for nothing.[24] "I am now advancing pretty well with the Fragments," she wrote to Mrs. Huth in June 1869, "and have been able to show two considerable portions of them to Mr. Mill who agrees with me in thinking them extremely interesting, and likely to be generally thought so, when published."[25] In her next letter she says, "I am sure your wish to publish is wise; both with a view to Mr. Buckle's reputation; and with a view to their real literary value. In fact no memoir, however good, could give so good an idea of the workings of his mind."[26]

Before Helen Taylor undertook the work, there had been some talk of Capel doing it, but the suggestion was regarded unfavourably

* See Appendix II for a dispute between Glennie and Alfred Huth over Buckle's tombstone.

† Helen Taylor was born in 1831. Two years after her father's death in 1849, her mother, Harriet, married John Stuart Mill. When Harriet died in 1858, Mill bought a house at Avignon in order to be near her grave. There he lived with Helen, who helped him with his letters and work. She was an advanced Radical, and advocate of women's rights, socialism and female suffrage. On her tombstone, at Torquay, is inscribed: "She fought for the People".

by those who knew him best. "As to the Common Place Books, Mr. and Mrs. Huth, and Mrs. Grey, say they are sure they are expressing the views of all Mr. Buckle's friends when they say that they have the greatest objection to Mr. Capel as an Editor of any of Mr. Buckle's works. . . . It is quite true that Mr. Capel was a friend of Mr. Buckle's during his lifetime, and it is also true that he is a man of a great deal of intellectual power, but those who have known him for years, say that he seems to have some strange weakness which prevents him ever finishing any work he begins. Mrs. Huth has asked me to tell you that during the eighteen years she has known him, he has never finished one work or article, though he has begun a great many; and he has several times proposed to deliver lectures at the Royal Institution and elsewhere, but even after the day was settled and everything arranged, he has not been able to carry out his intention. But this is not the only reason why Mr. Buckle's friends object to him as an editor—he has lately been in the habit of expressing himself about Mr. Buckle in a very depreciating and perfectly unjust manner, so much so that he has given his friends great offence: and they are quite unable to understand the reason of this strange conduct, as Mr. Capel was one of Mr. Buckle's most ardent and enthusiastic personal admirers during his lifetime."[27]

Capel's apparently strange behaviour was possibly caused by his discovery of Buckle's friendship with Mrs. Faunch. Certainly he claimed in a letter to Mill that he was Buckle's "most intimate, and withal the most useful friend he ever had. . . . I was his ready and untiring co-operator in everything in which he could receive aid."[28] In an earlier letter he tells Mill how he had "associated with Mr. Buckle on the most intimate terms for more than half-a-score years, travelling and staying with him, procuring information and reading up matter for him, particularly while he was composing his second volume: a good deal of which was written at my house. . . ."[29] Capel's estimate of his importance to Buckle was perhaps a little over generous; indeed at times he got on his friend's nerves. "His restlessness," wrote Buckle of Capel, "and irritability are, I fear, the result of disease. Poor fellow! It is sad under any circumstances to feel the brain impaired; but how infinitely sad when there is nothing to compensate the mischief—nothing, if I may so say, to justify it."[30]

When Helen Taylor agreed to edit the Common Place Books, to which Miss Shirreff was to prefix a biographical Memoir, she received a very discouraging letter from John Buckle. "I don't think," he says, "incidents of my cousin's life would be interesting to the public. . . . No one probably was so well acquainted with his character as myself and I send you a sketch intended for your own eye. He was weak in body from childhood and his education was very much neglected on that account. . . . For many years I lost sight of him. He went abroad, and on his return he spent some time at my father's house, where I found that he had acquired a good knowledge of French, familiarity with German, and Italian fairly. He afterwards acquired some knowledge of Spanish and Dutch and a smattering of Danish. His mind was now in full activity and free from all illiberality of opinion. He had become a great Chess player, and was very quick and expert at all games of chance and combination. . . . Though very fond of money, he could lose at games of skill without losing his temper for a moment. Indeed I never saw him out of temper after he grew to manhood. . . . He began to collect books and read greedily. His industry . . . was prodigious, and he only lived to read, extract and analyse books, exercising his memory at the same time in schoolboy fashion and learning by heart long passages, especially from Burke. He soon fixed upon a subject for authorship. It was the reign of Elizabeth. Expanding his ideas he determined to write a history of the sixteenth century, which I fully approved, and in the end he regretted that he had not confined himself to that period. . . . He was a very patient listener, and very patient of contradiction and irony, and very candid. His love of Truth was sincere and ardent. But he had a great notion of originality and generally stuck to his own opinions. On abstract questions I thought them often crude which I attributed to his neglect of the exact sciences. He was ignorant of them all, and he appeared to be very slightly acquainted with original histories, and to have very little taste for them. . . . Cricket and other manly games were unknown to him. He could not drive nor ride, nor even dance at any period of his life. He had no taste for music or painting, no eyes, no ear. I don't think he had ever read the great Italian poets, nor *Don Quixote* in the Spanish. He was ignorant of Greek and his knowledge of Latin was imperfect. . . . In Bibliography he was great, which gave strangers a notion of extensive reading. A glutton for books, he taxed his digestive powers overmuch. . . . Very ambitious of fame and latterly too fond of display before incompetent judges, he had been too much petted by ladies, and having a good memory he became too ostentatious of his reading. . . ."[31]

Mill and Helen Taylor obtained John Buckle's permission to show this letter to Miss Shirreff, who was rightly indignant at the accusations it contained, most of which she refuted at length. "I have been constantly moving," she tells Helen, "and frequently not well since I saw you or I should have written before to tell you how much I have been distressed by that letter of Mr. J. Buckle which Mr. Mill gave to me. I had long ago had reason to think that the warm feeling of affection and respect with which our poor friend regarded his cousin was ill responded to. Sayings of his at the club had been repeated to us, but I could not have believed that he would have written such a letter as this, so calculated to lower Henry Buckle in the estimation of Mr. Mill with whom of all men he would himself have wished to stand well as his cousin must well have known. . . . I deny the love of display for his conversation was as rich and full for a home circle, for his mother and me alone, as for a large party. . . ." Miss Shirreff goes on to point out that "he had read far more Greek than many better scholars", although he did not value scholarship as an end in itself. He merely "wanted the dead as the living languages for the treasure contained in them. That he had read the great Italian poets I know, though his cousin doubts it, many a passage have we discussed together. . . . Whether saying that Mr. Buckle was 'too much petted by ladies' is meant as a sneer at *him* or at *them*, I know not; but the ladies need I think take no shame to themselves for having recognized and loved the high qualities of the Man, while they reverenced the Genius."[32]

For some months Miss Shirreff collected material for her Memoir, while Miss Taylor supervised the copying of the Common Place Books. But in August 1869 she began to be "more uncertain about the probability of doing anything at all satisfactory".[33] On 2nd September the blow fell, and she wrote to Helen saying: "I am afraid my letter today will cause you some disappointment since its purport is to make known to you my final decision not to undertake the biographical sketch of Mr. Buckle. . . . No materials are forthcoming to enable anyone to construct such a biography as could be satisfactory to friends or interesting to the public. . . . After much hesitation and much pondering over all the journals reveal and much that they recall —a task which has been very trying to my own health—I am obliged to tell you that I cannot do what you wish."[34] Miss Shirreff concludes her letter by saying that her regret was lessened by the fact that Mrs. Allatt and the friends she applied to for letters or information, had all, except for Mrs. Huth, been averse to the idea of a biography.

Helen Taylor, who had been working hard at her part of the book for some time, was naturally distressed and perplexed by Miss Shirreff's withdrawal; and wrote at once to Mrs. Huth to tell her the sad news. "I was much pained," Mrs. Huth replied, "on getting Miss Shirreff's announcement of her having given up the idea of writing the biography. The material, though scanty, would at all events have enabled her to show that the moral character of Mr. Buckle was equal to his intellect, if it did not even surpass it. But poor Miss Shirreff's health seems so entirely shattered that, on that account, even I have not the heart to try and persuade her to reconsider the decision. Under the present circumstances I am very anxious to get as much of the materials which had been prepared for Miss Shirreff, as I can, and to put them in the care of my sons, so as to enable them, if the papers cannot be turned to better account, to correct at least by their aid, or refute, anything . . . which may perhaps be printed of Mr. Buckle at some future time."[35]

Helen Taylor, who was now confronted with having to write the life herself, was anxious to find out more about the material available, and to discover whether the reason Miss Shirreff gave for abandoning the work was the real one. Helen's suspicion that it was not, was confirmed by Miss Shirreff's reply to her enquiries. "It is almost amusing," Miss Shirreff writes, "to find myself classed with those who hold men in too high respect! My great danger in my youth lay in the opposite direction and if you had ever time to look at anything I have written on Education, or women's position, I think you would find no blindness to wrongs committed and endured respectively. But I have owed too much to the friendship of men . . . not to feel considerable deference to their judgement and especially on questions regarding knowledge of the world which few women possess. . . . The silence of all male friends in a man's biography might and probably would be interpreted greatly to the disadvantage of the person concerned. . . . We cannot expect that the public will accept women as equally good judges with men of a Man's character. . . . Intimately as I knew our poor friend for some years, I felt while I was writing that after all I was groping in the dark and enquiry has proved my misgiving to be just. . . . I think it better to confess to you in confidence that there are reasons beyond the scantiness of the material which would prevent me now or ever attempting this biography and I am induced to make this painful admission to you, in the hope that you will take my assurance on trust that what I abandon had better not be taken up by any others. I have given it up principally because I felt that enemies' hands—and there are many—might take occasion of my words to asperse the memory I would guard sacredly at any cost but that of Truth. I trust that nothing in your own experience may enable you to measure the suffering I have gone through before coming to this conclusion. Many a cherished recollection is embittered, many a letter, once a treasured possession, never can bear the same meaning again. I hope to save Mrs. Huth and other friends the pain I have endured; accordingly in telling her that I had given up the biography I spoke of nothing but the scantiness of materials. . . . Unless she forces it from me, she shall not be pained with the sad result of the enquiries I earnestly wish I had never been forced myself to make."[36]

The vague but alarming hints contained in this letter led Helen Taylor to ask for more precise information, which, "after long and painful consideration", Miss Shirreff decided to give. "I had hoped to spare myself this and never actually to have given expression to the blame which even now seems almost like treason to the old friendship. Having thought it necessary in the first instance to tell you that I had a reason beyond that of the scantiness of materials, I now see that I have caused a false impression and it will only be removed by a frank statement made in *strict confidence* to yourself and Mr. Mill. When I began to make enquiry I got very painful statements made to me." These, as Miss Shirreff goes on to explain, came from a source difficult to dispute. "Mr. Capel, whom you suppose I have been influenced by, said nothing to me till long after. . . . I resolved however to be guided by the Journal . . . for his integrity and perfect truthfulness I trusted most entirely, and it was this very trust that the journals themselves broke down. . . . The discrepancies between that daily record and the letters written at the same time and conversations . . . were such as to make me feel bereft at once of all ground upon which to rest any assertions concerning him or any contradiction of what others might assert." Miss Shirreff admitted that what to her was proof, "might have escaped the eyes of any but an intimate friend", and it is therefore difficult now to refute her; but certainly internal evidence suggests that she was over suspicious, despite her sincere reluctance to think ill of her friend. Neither Mill nor Helen Taylor appear to have been convinced that the charges against Buckle had been established, and were inclined to think that even if he was guilty of duplicity, Miss Shirreff perhaps exaggerated the extent of his fault.

To show that she was not allowing disappointed feeling to blind her judgement, Miss Shirreff gave two examples of Buckle's behaviour which had disillusioned her. Buckle's friends were led to believe that he had spoken extempore when he had delivered his lecture on "The Influence of Women" at the Royal Institution. ". . . It was partly as being the first effort of public speaking that it was so much admired and the eloquent flow of language and arrangement of thought was regarded as denoting hitherto unknown powers in one but lately known as a writer. The lecture was to be printed in *Fraser's* and he asked us and others to assist him with notes to enable him to write it out for the press. I did so, and my sister also contributed, and now if you turn to the journal you will see that the lecture was carefully written, learnt off by heart and even prepared for the press (in part if not wholly) before it was delivered! The pitiful vanity that could care for such a triumph sinks to insignificance beside the want of Truth, and yet that one so gifted, one seemingly so great should have stooped so far to win applause is sorrowful enough."[37]

Helen Taylor did her best to reassure Miss Shirreff. "When I read the Diary with no prepossession on the subject," she wrote, "it left upon my mind the impression that the lecture was spoken extempore." Helen moreover talked the matter over with Mill and, as she wrote to Miss Shirreff, he "thinks that many speakers write their speeches beforehand and yet may be said to speak them extempore, because they do not learn them by rote. In these cases they can never be sure either that they will speak all that they have written or exactly how they have written it, or that in the excitement of speaking they may not throw out new ideas and illustrations or express themselves with greater felicity than they have done in writing."[38] Mill, in fact, seems to have appreciated the situation very clearly, for Buckle constantly changed his mind. At one moment he decided not to write any part of the lecture beforehand, and told Parker, who wanted an advanced copy to facilitate printing the lecture in *Fraser's*, "I cannot make up my mind to write the lecture, because, if I were to do so, I am sure that new views or expressions would open themselves to me in speaking, and I should deliver something quite different from what I had written."[39] It may well have been at this stage that he asked Miss Shirreff to take notes. In the end he did write out the lecture, but since it took an hour and forty minutes to deliver, and since he only had a week to write it out, he presumably left much to improvisation. The version of the lecture he sent to *Fraser's* cost him considerable effort. "I have by sitting up very late last night," he told Parker, "and working hard today, succeeded in writing out the lecture. I am really so tired that I can't read it over. . . ."[40] The fact that the draft he sent to *Fraser's* was written *after* the lecture, suggests that what he said on the day differed from what he had previously written.

Pained as Miss Shirreff was by what she regarded as Buckle's duplicity over the lecture, she was even more grieved and shocked to discover about Mrs. Faunch. That she should be offended by the impropriety of the connexion was only to be expected, but often she writes as if the secrecy of the arrangement was what made it so particularly immoral. Inclined as we may be to join with Miss Shirreff in censuring Buckle, it must be admitted that his failure to broadcast details of the liaison may be attributed equally to dishonesty or discretion. "I was told on authority difficult to doubt," writes Miss Shirreff, "that when going abroad with the Huths' two boys, whom he volunteered to take charge of, he told a friend that he intended having a Nubian mistress when he got to Egypt, against his friend's earnest remonstrance.* The person who wrote this did not know what had been done later but related another dark fact, namely that Mr. Buckle had written from the East to the woman so often referred to in the journals (the name is generally erased) begging her to join him, which she refused to do. My informant professed to have heard this story from both Mr. Buckle's sisters separately and that they had refused an application for money from that woman on the ground that she had declined to join him. Still I tried to think there might be a mistake or over-statement. That he should have deliberately purposed renewing such a connexion while travelling with his friend's children seemed impossible." The evidence compelled Miss Shirreff reluctantly to accept the disagreeable truth, since her sister, Mrs. Grey, saw a copy of the letter which Buckle had written to Mrs. Faunch. "I need not dwell upon any more details of what is exquisitely painful to mention," concludes Miss Shirreff's letter. "Much more I heard and though nothing else admitted of proof I felt only too deeply that I no longer dared to contradict anything. . . ."[41]

Helen Taylor attempted to comfort Miss Shirreff by saying:

* The fact that the remonstrance was so earnest gives one cause to suspect that it encouraged Buckle in what sounds suspiciously like a joke, although obviously not one to Miss Shirreff's taste. Her upbringing gave her rather limited experience of this sort of humour.

"Both Mr. Mill and I have a vague idea of having heard it said or of having read, that it was intended originally for him (Buckle) to part with the two sons of Mrs. Huth at some point in his journey. . . . He may have written to the person you mention to join him at the point where he intended to part company with the two lads."[42] But Miss Shirreff was not to be consoled, and she replied that she had never heard of any such meeting-place and that "it had always been intended that he should restore the boys to their mother at Vienna. In the meantime the letter to *that* woman speaks of intending to remain in the East for two or three years which is supposed to have been said because she had taken a journey with him before and extremely disliked travelling. It is a miserable net-work of deception!"[43] Miss Shirreff was quite right in thinking that the plan was for the Huth family to be reunited in Vienna. But since the letter to Mrs. Faunch was written in the middle of January 1862, even if she had decided to accept Buckle's invitation, which he must have known to be improbable, there would have been plenty of time for him to have gone to Vienna and to have joined her afterwards. Besides, if she had really decided to stay in the East for some years, she would have wanted time to make her arrangements, and even if she had been prepared to take the very next boat for Egypt, it is unlikely that Buckle would have agreed to her doing so. His letter to Mrs. Faunch certainly showed that he had thoughts of settling abroad, but this idea was neither new nor secret. Before he left England he told Mrs. Grote: "Sometimes I fear that I have permanently hurt myself, and form plans of leaving London altogether—but time will show!"[44]

Mill and Helen Taylor, although anxious to suggest mitigating circumstances, thought that Mrs. Huth should be told of the charges brought against her friend. "She is bringing up her sons," writes Helen to Miss Shirreff, "in a strong reverence for Mr. Buckle and it seems only right that she should know something that concerns herself and them."[45] Miss Shirreff, however, thought that it was unnecessary to pain Mrs. Huth by such revelations, and moreover she believed that as the material collected was insufficient, "the idea of some future biography to be written by them (Edward or Alfred Huth) is a harmless vision to indulge in, which pleases her and which her sons will drop."[46] Only if there seemed to be a serious threat that the Life would really be written, did Miss Shirreff think it would become necessary to reveal what she had discovered. Presumably when Alfred Huth began to write Buckle's life, Miss Shirreff made her disclosure. Whether

Mrs. Huth herself ever found out that her hero had feet of clay, whether she saw Capel's copy of Buckle's letter to Mrs. Faunch,* whether Alfred obtained it before or after he wrote the biography, it is impossible to say, but it seems probable that he knew a great deal more than is to be found in his book.

In 1869 Miss Shirreff wrote: "His book was his real life—it was his last thought in death—let his memory then live in that. The world knew him but little as an individual. He did little more than flit over its stage. It seems fittest in every way that he should be known in future by the recorded utterances of his genius only."[47] Three years later, however, she sent her Memoir to Helen Taylor, and some time after that helped Huth with his biography as he acknowledges in his Preface, so it seems that she recovered her sense of proportion.

It is clear from many of Miss Shirreff's letters that part of her reluctance to write the biographical sketch derived from her fear of Glennie. "We have to deal," she says of him, "with an unscrupulous man, who out of spite might bring forward stories that we *cannot* contradict with authority and yet that it would look ill not to notice."[48] Mrs. Huth felt the same. "As he is not very scrupulous as to truth and has had hours of talk with Mr. Buckle, he can put things into his mouth which no one will be able to prove as false. . . . Mr. Glennie's only object in writing seems to be, to make himself as interesting as possible. He will therefore only put in that amount of evil, which according to him, will seem requisite to make the book 'piquant'. . . ."[49] The Memoir Glennie wrote on his return from the East in 1863, gave little grounds for confidence in his reticence. "Truth," he then said, "compels me to say that, during these months of intimate acquaintance as fellow-travellers, there were instances in which my indignation was roused, not only against what appeared to me distorted moral views, but against acts wanting in generosity, if not in justice. Out of regard, not only to the feelings of his friends, but to the reticence which I conceive imposed on myself by the intimacy even of an accidental acquaintanceship, and still more by his death, I have in these pages suppressed all allusion to those particular views and acts to which I thus generally refer."[50] Although *Pilgrim Memories* contained some disagreeable hints, it made no specific disclosures; and so during the lifetime of Buckle's friends and relations nothing appeared in print to embarrass them.

* See Chapter III, Note 31.

Certainly there was a scandal in Buckle's life, and Capel, Miss Shirreff and his cousin, John, revised their opinion of him. Yet Miss Shirreff did, in the end, send Helen Taylor a short Memoir to include in her biography; Alfred Huth did write Buckle's Life, almost certainly knowing about Mrs. Faunch; and John Stuart Mill, who had heard all the accusations, nevertheless encouraged his stepdaughter to finish her work. These people, whose integrity is above suspicion, must have decided that the discovery of particular moral defects did not imply complete depravity, a conclusion with which it would be uncharitable to disagree.

CHAPTER V

THE HISTORY OF CIVILIZATION

THE *History of Civilization in England* was inspired by Buckle's profound dissatisfaction with the writings of his predecessors. These he regarded as excessively specialized. "The unfortunate peculiarity of the history of man," he says in his opening chapter, "is, that although its separate parts have been examined with considerable ability, hardly anyone has attempted to combine them into a whole, and ascertain the way in which they are connected with each other. In all the other great fields of inquiry, the necessity of generalization is universally admitted. . . . So far, however, is this from being the usual course of historians, that among them a strange idea prevails, that their business is merely to relate events, which they may occasionally enliven by such moral and political reflections as seem likely to be useful. . . . Historians, taken as a body, have never recognized the necessity of such a wide and preliminary study as would enable them to grasp their subject in the whole of its natural relations. Hence the singular spectacle of one historian being ignorant of political economy; another knowing nothing of law; another nothing of ecclesiastical affairs and changes of opinion. . . . For all the higher purposes of human thought history is still miserably deficient."[1] By avoiding the pitfalls of specialization, Buckle hoped to contribute "something towards filling up that wide and dreary chasm, which, to the hindrance of our knowledge, separates subjects that are intimately related, and should never be disunited".[2]

He conceived historical study to have made little progress because, assuming events to be purely fortuitous, historians had failed to see the working of certain historical laws. They had noticed, as it were, an apparently haphazard heap of beads; but they had failed to observe the thread on which they were strung. Just as astronomers have found the principles determining the motion of the stars, so ultimately will historians discover the laws which govern mankind.* "I hope," says

* The views expressed in this Chapter are Buckle's and not mine. Many of them are criticized in Chapter VI. Reference to the index should enable the reader to find whether any particular theory is later discussed and, if so, where.

Buckle, "to accomplish for the history of man something equivalent, or at all events analogous, to what has been effected by other inquirers for the different branches of natural science."[3]

Buckle maintained that History would never be established as a Science while historians and theologians persisted in maintaining that God constantly intervened in human affairs. This belief persuaded writers to make absurd assertions: for example that battles are lost, "not because the army is ill supplied, not because the campaign is ill conceived, not because the general is incompetent; but because the people or their prince are wicked, and Providence seeks to punish them".[4] Man's behaviour is, in reality, unpredictable not because it is irregular, but because our knowledge of it is incomplete. Unfortunately, the great majority of people have a very different faith. "They believe that what is unexplained is inexplicable, and that what is inexplicable is supernatural. . . . Science has not yet explained the phenomena of history; consequently, the theological spirit lays hold of them, and presses them into its own service. In this way there has arisen that famous and ancient theory, which has received the name of the moral government of the world. It is a high-sounding title, and imposes on many, who, if they examined its pretensions, would never be duped by them. . . . For it is not only unscientific, but it is eminently irreligious. It is, in fact, an impeachment of one of the noblest attributes of the Deity. It is a slur on the Omniscience of God. It assumes that the fate of nations, instead of being the result of preceding and surrounding events, is specially subject to the control and interference of Providence. . . . Thus it is, that the very men who, at one moment, proclaim the Divine Omniscience, do, at the next moment, advocate a theory which reduces that Omniscience to nothing, since it imputes to an All-wise Being, that the scheme of human affairs, of which He must, from the beginning, have foreseen every issue and every consequence, is so weakly contrived as to be liable to be frustrated; that it has not turned out as He could have wished; that it has been baffled by His own creatures, and that, to preserve its integrity, its operations must be tampered with, and its disorders redressed. The great Architect of the universe, the Creator and Designer of all existing things, is likened to some clumsy mechanic, who knows his trade so ill, that he has to be called in to alter the working of his own machine, to supply its deficiencies, to fill up its flaws, and to rectify its errors. . . .

"The signs of the time are all around, and they who list may read.

The handwriting is on the wall; the fiat has gone forth; the ancient empire shall be subverted; the dominion of superstition, already decaying, shall break away, and crumble into dust; and new life being breathed into the confused and chaotic mass, it shall be clearly seen, that, from the beginning, there has been no discrepancy, no incongruity, no disorder, no interruption, no interference; but that all the events which surround us, even to the furthest limits of the material creation, are but different parts of a single scheme, which is permeated by one glorious principle of universal and undeviating regularity."[5]

So ends what Buckle lived to complete of his book. His belief in the regularity of historical events is, however, no afterthought, rather it is the dominant idea of the whole work. "It is this deep conviction that changing phenomena have unchanging laws," he says elsewhere, "and that there are principles of order to which all apparent disorder may be referred—it is this, which in the seventeenth century, guided in a limited field Bacon, Descartes, and Newton; which in the eighteenth century was applied to every part of the material universe; and which it is the business of the nineteenth century to extend to the history of the human intellect."[6] In human affairs he says again: "Nothing is anomalous; nothing is unnatural; nothing is strange. All is order, symmetry, and law. . . . Such, however, is still the backward condition of the human mind, and with so evil and jaundiced an eye do we approach the greatest problems, that not only common writers, but even men from whom better things might be hoped, are on this point involved in constant confusion, perplexing themselves and their readers by speaking of inconsistency, as if it were a quality belonging to the subject which they investigate, instead of being, as it really is, a measure of their own ignorance."[7]

Scientific history, as Buckle understood that term, is only feasible on the assumption that human behaviour is determined. Consequently he devoted considerable space to arguing that free will, as ordinarily understood, is an illusion. In the opening Chapter of the History he attacks those who argue that historical generalization is impossible. To do so is to take for granted the very question at issue. The universality of order is an article of faith among scientific men who expect to discover regularity in the midst of confusion. It is because historians have denied the existence of a similar uniformity in human affairs, claiming that the workings of a mysterious Providence exempt Mankind from the trammels of natural law, that historical study has made so little progress. The crucial problem which historians must answer if any advance is to be made is: "Are the actions of men, and therefore of societies, governed by fixed laws, or are they the result either of chance or of supernatural interference?"[8]

The belief that events are fortuitous, according to Buckle, comes naturally to primitive people, who live in a world they can neither control nor understand, and who depend upon the apparent caprice of Nature for their food. Agriculture first helped men to recognize uniformity of sequence. "What they sow, that likewise do they reap. . . . Thus it is that, in the ordinary march of society, an increasing perception of the regularity of nature destroys the doctrine of chance, and replaces it by that of necessary connexion."[9] If historians applied the same causal principles to human beings, instead of regarding Man as something distinct from the rest of creation, History could rightfully claim to be a Science. That human beings are subject to Law and that their conduct is therefore predictable, is shown both by experience and reason. Buckle's metaphysical argument for belief in determinism is that "when we perform an action, we perform it in consequence of some motive or motives; that those motives are the results of some antecedents; and that, therefore, if we were acquainted with the whole of the antecedents, and with all the laws of their movements, we could with unerring certainty predict the whole of their immediate results."[10] For empirical proof of the regularity of human behaviour, he relied on statistics, from which he maintained the most comprehensive inferences respecting the actions of men could be derived. In particular, he concentrated his attention on figures for crime, and found that murders and suicides, at first sight the most arbitrary of offences, are committed with the same regularity as tides ebb and flow. The fact that over a number of years about the same number of people commit suicide annually, seemed to him convincing proof that the behaviour of individuals is determined by the general state of society. "Among public and registered crimes there is none which seems so completely dependent on the individual as suicide. Attempts to murder or to rob may be, and constantly are, successfully resisted; baffled sometimes by the party attacked, sometimes by the officers of justice. But an attempt to commit suicide is much less liable to interruption. The man who is determined to kill himself is not prevented at the last moment by the struggles of an enemy; and, as he can easily guard against the interference of the civil power, his act becomes as it were isolated; it is cut off from foreign disturbances, and seems more clearly the product of his own volition than any other offence could possibly be. . . . It may, therefore, very naturally be thought impracticable to refer suicide to general principles, or to detect anything like regularity in an offence which is so eccentric, so solitary, so impossible to control by legislation, and which the most vigilant police can do nothing to diminish. . . .

"These being the peculiarities of this singular crime, it is surely an astonishing fact, that all the evidence we possess respecting it points to one great conclusion, and can leave no doubt on our minds that suicide is merely the product of the general condition of society, and that the individual felon only carries into effect what is a necessary consequence of preceding circumstances. In a given state of society, a certain number of persons must put an end to their own life. This is the general law; and the special question as to who shall commit the crime depends, of course, upon special laws; which, however, in their total action, must obey the large social law to which they are all subordinate. And the power of the larger law is so irresistible, that neither the love of life nor the fear of another world can avail anything towards even checking its operation. . . . In the different countries for which we have returns, we find year by year, the same proportion of persons putting an end to their own existence; so that, after making allowance for the impossibility of collecting complete evidence, we are able to predict, within a very small limit of error, the number of voluntary deaths for each ensuing period; supposing, of course, that the social circumstances do not undergo any marked change. Even in London, notwithstanding the vicissitudes incidental to the largest and most luxurious capital in the world, we find a regularity greater than could be expected by the most sanguine believer in social laws; since political excitement, mercantile excitement, and the misery produced by the dearness of food, are all causes of suicide, and are all constantly varying. Nevertheless, in this vast metropolis, about 240 persons every year make away with themselves; the annual suicides oscillating, from the pressure of temporary causes, between 266, the highest, and 213, the lowest. In 1846, which was the great year of excitement caused by the railway panic, the suicides in London were 266; in 1847 began a slight improvement, and they fell to 256; in 1848 they were 247; in 1849 they were 213; and in 1850 they were 229."[11]

Such statistical uniformity is not confined to men's criminal acts. "Even the number of Marriages annually contracted, is determined, not by the temper and wishes of individuals, but by large general facts, over which individuals can exercise no authority. It is now known that marriages bear a fixed and definite relation to the price of corn." What applies to marriage and suicide applies equally to aberrations of memory. Year after year the same proportion of letter-writers forget to address their envelopes. "To those who have a steady conception of the regularity of events, and have firmly seized the great truth that the actions of men, being guided by their antecedents, are in reality never inconsistent, but, however capricious they may appear, only form part of one vast scheme of universal order, of which we in the present state of knowledge can barely see the outline—to those who understand this, which is at once the key and the basis of history, the facts just adduced, so far from being strange, will be precisely what would have been expected and ought long since to have been known. Indeed, the progress of inquiry is becoming so rapid and so earnest, that I entertain little doubt that before another century has elapsed, the chain of evidence will be complete, and it will be as rare to find an historian who denies the undeviating regularity of the moral world, as it now is to find a philosopher who denies the regularity of the material world."[12]

It would be wrong then to suppose that the methods of physical science are inapplicable to historical study. The history of the human race shows how Climate, Food, Soil and the General Aspect of Nature,* have influenced civilization.[13] Among entirely ignorant people the physical peculiarities of the country they inhabit regulate the creation of wealth. In countries where the soil is particularly fertile and food is cheap and abundant, a leisured class, whose own wants are supplied by the labour of others and who are thereby freed from the struggle for survival, comes into existence. In North Africa the majority of people are doomed by the penury of Nature to barbarism, for the Sahara yields so pitiful a supply of food that none of the tribes who inhabit it have ever had the leisure to become civilized. But where the Nile irrigates the desert, covering the sand with a rich alluvial deposit, "in that spot, wealth was rapidly accumulated, the cultivation of knowledge quickly followed, and this narrow strip of land became the seat of Egyptian Civilization. . . ."[14]

The history of the Arabs illustrates the thesis that early civilizations depend on the fertility of the soil. "The Arabs in their own country have, owing to the extreme aridity of their soil, always been

* What Buckle meant by "Aspect of Nature" is explained below p. 122.

a rude and uncultivated people; for in their case, as in all others, great ignorance is the fruit of great poverty. But in the seventh century they conquered Persia; in the eighth century they conquered the best part of Spain; in the ninth century they conquered the Punjab, and eventually nearly the whole of India. Scarcely were they established in their fresh settlements, when their character seemed to undergo a great change. They, who in their original land were little else than roving savages, were now for the first time able to accumulate wealth, and, therefore, for the first time did they make some progress in the arts of civilization. In Arabia they had been a mere race of wandering shepherds; in their new abodes they became the founders of mighty empires—they built cities, endowed schools, collected libraries; and the traces of their power are still to be seen at Cordova, at Bagdad, and at Delhi."[15]

In the ancient world the fertility of the soil was the primary influence on civilization, but in modern Europe climate has been the most powerful factor. Very hot weather indisposes men to work, whereas a milder and more invigorating climate encourages industry. The very bounty of Nature in certain parts of the world, where food can be obtained effortlessly, has had a detrimental effect on national Character. People who live in hot countries are encouraged by the Climate to be indolent. Because they need less to eat, and because food is easy to acquire, they are placid and unenterprising. In northern climates, where people have to eat more because of the cold, food is much harder to procure. Instead of vegetables, thrown up by the soil, men are forced to incur great risk and expend great labour pursuing "powerful and ferocious animals". Consequently Northern Nations have for the most part "displayed, even in the infancy of society, a bolder and more adventurous character" than those whose food is supplied "gratuitously and without a struggle".[16]

If the creation of wealth, and thus leisure, is a necessary preliminary to the development of a civilized state, the way in which such wealth is distributed determines the type of civilization established. "It may, I think," writes Buckle, "be proved that the distribution of wealth is, like its creation, governed entirely by physical laws; and that those laws are moreover so active as to have invariably kept a vast majority of the inhabitants of the fairest portion of the globe in a condition of constant and inextricable poverty. If this can be demonstrated, the immense importance of such laws is manifest. For since wealth is an undoubted source of power, it is evident that, supposing other things equal, an inquiry into the distribution of wealth is an inquiry into the distribution of power, and as such, will throw great light on the origin of those social and political inequalities, the play and opposition of which form a considerable part of the history of every civilized country."

As the rate of wages paid at a given time in a particular country depends upon the supply of labour, "in the long run, the question of wages is a question of population". All other things being equal, "the amount of wages received by each man must diminish as the claimants increase. . . ." But if wages depend upon population, population is itself dependent upon the supply of food. "If two countries, equal in all other respects, differ solely in this—that in one the national food is cheap and abundant, and in the other scarce and dear, the population of the former country will inevitably increase more rapidly than the population of the latter. And, by a parity of reasoning, the average rate of wages will be lower in the former than in the latter, simply because the labour-market will be more amply stocked."[17]

Buckle's theory, in short, is that food depends upon Climate; wealth and population depends on food; the distribution of wealth depends on population; and Civilization springs from Wealth. The ancient civilizations of Asia, Africa and America "were seated in hot climates; and in all of them the rate of wages was very low, and therefore the condition of the labouring classes very depressed. In Europe, for the first time, civilization arose in a colder climate: hence the reward of labour was increased, and the distribution of wealth rendered more equal than was possible in countries where an excessive abundance of food stimulated the growth of population." Buckle gives Ireland as an instance of a nation possessing a cheap national food and therefore suffering from pitiful poverty. "In Ireland the labouring classes have for more than two hundred years been principally fed by potatoes, which were introduced into their country late in the sixteenth, or early in the seventeenth century. Now, the peculiarity of the potato is, that until the appearance of the late disease, it was and perhaps still is, cheaper than any other food equally wholesome. If we compare its reproductive power with the amount of nutriment contained in it, we find that one acre of average land sown with potatoes will support twice as many persons as the same quantity of land sown with wheat. The consequence is, that in a country where men live on potatoes, the population will, if other things are tolerably equal, increase twice as fast as in a country where they live on wheat. And so it has actually occurred. Until a very few years ago, when the face of affairs was entirely altered by pestilence and emigration, the population of Ireland was, in round numbers, increasing annually three per cent; the population of England during the same period increasing one and a half per cent. The result was, that in these two countries the distribution of wealth was altogether different. Even in England the growth of population is somewhat too rapid; and the labour-market being overstocked, the working classes are not sufficiently paid for their labour. But their condition is one of sumptuous splendour, compared to that in which only a few years ago the Irish were forced to live. The misery in which they were plunged has no doubt always been aggravated by the ignorance of their rulers, and by that scandalous misgovernment which, until very recently, formed one of the darkest blots on the glory of England. The most active cause, however, was, that their wages were so low as to debar them, not only from the comforts, but from the common decencies of civilized life; and this evil condition was the natural result of that cheap and abundant food, which encouraged the people to so rapid an increase, that the labour-market was constantly gorged."[18]

Buckle's book is full of detailed examples of the way in which climate, soil and food, have influenced the development of particular Civilizations. He cites Egypt, Peru and Mexico, and traces important similarities between these countries. In all, he finds similar physical circumstances have led to a similar distribution of wealth and power. In all, plentiful food has involved over-population. In all, slavery and luxury have existed side by side.

India, with its plentiful supply of rice and hence its vast population, admirably illustrates the irresistible power of Nature in shaping man's destiny. "We find the upper classes there," says Buckle, "enormously rich, and the lower classes miserably poor. We find those by whose labour the wealth is created, receiving the smallest possible share of it; the remainder being absorbed by the higher ranks in the form either of rent or of profit. And as wealth is, after intellect, the most permanent source of power, it has naturally happened that a great inequality of wealth has been accompanied by a corresponding inequality of social and political power. It is not, therefore, surprising that from the earliest period to which our knowledge of India extends, an immense majority of the people, pinched by the most galling poverty, and just living from hand to mouth, should always have remained in a state of stupid debasement, broken by incessant misfortune, crouching before their superiors in abject submission, and only fit either to be slaves themselves or to be led to battle to make slaves of others. . . . In India, slavery, abject, eternal slavery, was the natural state of the great body of the people; it was the state to which they were doomed by physical laws utterly impossible to resist. The energy of those laws is, in truth, so invincible, that wherever they have come into play, they have kept the productive classes in perpetual subjection. There is no instance on record of any tropical country, in which wealth having been extensively accumulated, the people have escaped their fate; no instance in which the heat of the climate has not caused an abundance of food, and the abundance of food caused an unequal distribution, first of wealth, and then of political and social power. Among nations subjected to these conditions, the people have counted for nothing; they have had no voice in the management of the state, no control over the wealth their own industry created. Their only business has been to labour; their only duty to obey. . . . Nor was it until civilization arose in Europe, that other physical laws came into operation, and therefore other results were produced. In Europe, for the first time, there was some approach to equality, some tendency to correct that enormous disproportion of wealth and power, which formed the essential weakness of the greatest of the more ancient countries. As a natural consequence, it is in Europe that everything worthy of the name of civilization has originated. . . ."[19]

Even intellectual development, according to Buckle, is influenced by physical agents. Earthquakes, tempests, hurricanes and pestilences, which he collectively describes as "Aspects of Nature", affect man's outlook. Where Nature is most violent, Man is awed by its power, a sense of his own inferiority and insignificance steals over him, and the vast grandeur of the forces which confront him, inflames his imagination and extinguishes his reason. Conversely where Nature is temperate, man being less appalled by its majesty, grows inquisitive, and begins to appreciate that what at first seemed arbitrary is in fact orderly. In countries where earthquakes frequently occur, where men are constantly threatened by dangers they can neither anticipate nor avert, their feeling of helplessness leads them to accept supernatural explanations of the disasters which overwhelm them. Even in Europe where such phenomena are rare, it is precisely in those countries in which earthquakes and volcanic eruptions are most frequent: Spain, Portugal and Italy, that superstition is most rife, and supernatural rather than natural explanations most common. When the "Aspects of Nature" are formidable, the imaginative rather than intellectual faculties predominate. It is not therefore surprising that the Italian and Spanish peninsulas have produced many of Europe's greatest painters and sculptors, and that their literature abounds with writers of poetic genius. On the other hand Italy's contribution to scientific knowledge has been small when compared with the contributions made by her artists to European culture, and Spain and Portugal between them have added little to physics or chemistry.

The effects of the "Aspects of Nature" were more conspicuous in the old tropical Civilizations than in Europe. "The devastations of animals hostile to man, the ravages of hurricanes, tempests, earthquakes, and similar perils, constantly pressed upon them, and affected the tone of their national character. For the mere loss of life was the smallest part of the inconvenience. The real mischief was, that there were engendered in the mind, associations which made the imagination predominate over the understanding; which infused into the people a spirit of reverence instead of a spirit of inquiry; and which encouraged a disposition to neglect the investigation of natural causes, and ascribe events to the operation of supernatural ones. . . . With extremely few exceptions, health is more precarious, and disease more common, in tropical climates than in temperate ones. Now, it has been often observed, and indeed is very obvious, that the fear of death makes men more prone to seek supernatural aid than they would otherwise be. So complete is our ignorance respecting another life, that it is no wonder if even the stoutest heart should quail at the sudden approach of that dark and untried future. On this subject the reason is perfectly silent; the imagination, therefore, is uncontrolled. The operation of natural causes being brought to an end, supernatural causes are supposed to begin. Hence it is, that whatever increases in any country the amount of dangerous disease, has an immediate tendency to strengthen superstition, and aggrandize the imagination at the expense of the understanding. This principle is so universal, that, in every part of the world, the vulgar ascribe to the intervention of the Deity those diseases which are peculiarly fatal, and especially those which have a sudden and mysterious appearance. In Europe it used to be believed that every pestilence was a manifestation of the divine anger; and this opinion, though it has long been dying away, is by no means extinct, even in the most civilized countries. Superstition of this kind will of course be strongest, either where medical knowledge is most backward, or where disease is most abundant. In countries where both these conditions are fulfilled, the superstition is supreme; and even where only one of the conditions exists, the tendency is so irresistible, that, I believe, there are no barbarous people who do not ascribe to good or evil deities, not only extraordinary diseases, but even many of the ordinary ones to which they are liable. Here, then, we have another specimen of the unfavourable influence, which, in the old civilizations, external phenomena exercised over the human mind."[20]

The different effects of Nature on thought may be seen by contrasting the Art, Literature and Religion of India and Greece. In India the works of Nature are of startling magnitude: in Greece they are in every way smaller, feebler and less threatening. "In the great centre of Asiatic civilization, the energies of the human race are confined, and as it were intimidated, by the surrounding phenomena. Besides the dangers incidental to tropical climates, there are those noble mountains which seem to touch the sky, and from whose sides are discharged mighty rivers, which no art can divert from their course, and which no bridge has ever been able to span. There, too, are impassable forests, whole countries lined with interminable jungle, and beyond them, again, dreary and boundless deserts; all teaching Man his own feebleness, and his inability to cope with natural forces. . . . But in Greece, the aspects of nature are so entirely different, that the very conditions of existence are changed. Greece, like India, forms a peninsula; but while in the Asiatic country every thing is great and terrible, in the European country every thing is small and feeble."[21]

Differences in the "Aspect of Nature" account for corresponding intellectual differences. The ancient literature of India consists mostly of Poetry, and all it contains "is calculated to set the reason of man at open defiance. An imagination, luxuriant even to disease, runs riot on every occasion. . . . Not only in literature, but also in religion and in art, this tendency is supreme. To subjugate the understanding, and exalt the imagination, is the universal principle. In the dogmas of their theology, in the character of their gods, and even in the forms of their temples, we see how the sublime and threatening aspects of the external world have filled the mind of the people with those images of the grand and the terrible, which they strive to reproduce in a visible form, and to which they owe the leading peculiarities of their national culture."[22]

In Greece, where the "Aspects of Nature" are comparatively

mild, a different outlook developed. "The human mind was less appalled, and less superstitious; natural causes began to be studied; physical science first became possible; and Man, gradually waking to a sense of his own power, sought to investigate events with a boldness not to be expected in those other countries, where the pressure of Nature troubled his independence, and suggested ideas with which knowledge is incompatible.

"The effect of these habits of thought on the national religion must be very obvious to whoever has compared the popular creed of India with that of Greece. The mythology of India, like that of every tropical country, is based upon terror." Thus, for example, the worship of the God Siva is general. "Siva is represented to the Indian mind as a hideous being, encircled by a girdle of snakes, with a human skull in his hand, and wearing a necklace composed of human bones. He has three eyes; the ferocity of his temper is marked by his being clothed in a tiger's skin; he is represented as wandering about like a madman, and over his left shoulder the deadly cobra di capella rears its head. This monstrous creation of an awe-struck fancy has a wife Doorga, called sometimes Kali, and sometimes by other names. She has a body of dark blue; while the palms of her hands are red, to indicate her insatiate appetite for blood. She has four arms, with one of which she carries the skull of a giant; her tongue protrudes, and hangs lollingly from her mouth; round her waist are the hands of her victims; and her neck is adorned with human heads strung together in a ghastly row.

"If we now turn to Greece, we find, even in the infancy of its religion, not the faintest trace of anything approaching to this. For, in Greece, the causes of fear being less abundant, the expression of terror was less common. The Greeks, therefore, were by no means disposed to incorporate into their religion those feelings of dread natural to the Hindus. The tendency of Asiatic civilization was to widen the distance between men and their deities; the tendency of Greek civilization was to diminish it. Thus it is, that in Hindostan all the gods had something monstrous about them; as Vishnu with four hands, Brahma with five heads, and the like. But the gods of Greece were always represented in forms entirely human. In that country, no artist would have gained attention if he had presumed to portray them in any other shape. He might make them stronger than men, he might make them more beautiful; but still they must be men. The analogy between God and Man, which excited the religious feelings of the Greeks, would have been fatal to those of the Hindus. . . . The Greek gods had not only human forms, but also human attributes, human pursuits, and human tastes. . . . In Greece, Man being less humbled, and, as it were, less eclipsed, by the external world, thought more of his own powers, and human nature did not fall into that discredit in which it elsewhere sank."[23]

Civilizations outside Europe have all been subordinated to the external influence of Nature, but if we would understand the history of France or England, for instance, we must make Man our principal study. In such countries, Nature being comparatively weak, people have discovered how to tame it and bend its energies to their will. No longer are the most productive countries necessarily those in which man is most active, for he has learned to overcome the deficiencies of Nature. "If a river is difficult to navigate or a country difficult to traverse, our engineers can correct the error, and remedy the evil. If we have no rivers, we make canals; if we have no natural harbours, we make artificial ones." This tendency "to impair the authority of natural phenomena" is partly the result of the growth of towns. ". . . The more men congregate in great Cities, the more they will become accustomed to draw their materials of thought from the business of human life, and the less attention they will pay to those peculiarities of nature, which are the fertile source of superstition, and by which, in every civilization out of Europe, the progress of man was arrested."

Since European Civilization is characterized by the diminishing influence of Nature, and the increasing influence of intellectual factors, "a discovery of the laws of European history is resolved, in the first instance, into a discovery of the Laws of the human mind. These mental laws, when ascertained, will be the ultimate basis of the history of Europe. . . ."[24] The question therefore arises: "How are such laws to be discovered?" Buckle examines the metaphysical method of investigating Mind, and finds it unsatisfactory, partly because "the metaphysical method is one by which no discovery has ever yet been made in any branch of knowledge", and partly because the philosopher bases his system "on the supposition that, by studying a single mind, he can get the laws of all minds. . . ." Individual introspection, in which the observer and the observed are inseparable, has proved fruitless: only a comprehensive survey of many minds can elucidate intellectual laws. Moreover, "In metaphysics, it will invariably be found, that if two men of equal ability, and equal honesty, employ different methods in the study of mind, the conclusions which they obtain will also be different;" whereas in physics, "There are several methods of proceeding, all of which lead to the same results." Metaphysicians, divided between antagonistic schools of thought, and condemned by their own methods to an inescapable subjectivity, have achieved very little. "There is no other study which has been so zealously prosecuted, so long continued, and yet remains so barren of results. . . . It is impossible to avoid a suspicion that there is some fundamental error in the manner in which these inquiries have been prosecuted." "I believe," says Buckle, "that, by mere observation of our own minds . . . it will be impossible to raise psychology to a science. . . ." He concludes by reminding metaphysicians of Berkeley's admission: "Upon the whole, I am inclined to think that the far greater part, if not all, of those difficulties which have hitherto amused philosophers, and blocked up the way to knowledge, are entirely owing to ourselves. That we have first raised a dust, and then complain we cannot see."[25]

As the metaphysical method is unequal to the task of discovering the laws determining intellectual growth, "we are, therefore, driven to the only remaining method, according to which mental phenomena are to be studied, not simply as they appear in the mind of the individual observer, but as they appear in the actions of Mankind at large."[26] The historical, not the philosophical method, is best suited to discovering what those factors are which influence the intellect and hence determine the course of Europe's development.

Civilization progresses as a result of moral and intellectual improvements. "There can be no doubt that a people are not really advancing, if, on the one hand, their increasing ability is accompanied by increasing vice, or, if, on the other hand, while they are becoming more virtuous, they likewise become more ignorant." The problem therefore is to determine: "Which of these two parts or elements of mental progress is the most important?"[27] Once this is decided the inferior element may be subordinated to the law of the superior, and the force determining Europe's destiny will stand revealed.

It is, of course, possible that advances in civilization are partly ascribable to gradual increases in the growth of man's brain as a physical organ. Buckle, however, maintains that there is no evidence available to confirm this theory, whereas there is every reason to suppose that alteration in the intellectual environment effects extensive change. "Whatever, therefore, the moral and intellectual progress of men may be, it resolves itself not into a progress of natural capacity, but into a progress, if I may so say, of opportunity. . . . The child born in a civilized land is not likely, as such, to be superior to one born among barbarians; and the difference which ensues between the acts of the two children will be caused, so far as we know, solely by the pressure of external circumstances; by which I mean the surrounding opinions, knowledge, associations; in a word, the entire mental atmosphere in which the two children are respectively nurtured. . . .

"On this account it is evident, that if we look at mankind in the aggregate, their moral and intellectual conduct is regulated by the moral and intellectual notions prevalent in their own time. There are, of course, many persons who will rise above those notions, and many others who will sink below them. But such cases are exceptional, and form a very small proportion of the total amount of those who are nowise remarkable either for good or for evil. An immense majority of men must always remain in a middle state, neither very foolish nor very able, neither very virtuous nor very vicious, but slumbering on in a peaceful and decent mediocrity, adopting without much difficulty the current opinions of the day, making no inquiry, exciting no scandal, causing no wonder, just holding themselves on a level with their generation, and noiselessly conforming to the standard of morals and of knowledge common to the age and country in which they live."

The majority of people unthinkingly follow prevailing intellectual fashions, but these fashions constantly change, and are "never precisely the same even in the most similar countries, or in two successive generations in the same country. . . . This extreme mutability in the ordinary standard of human actions shows that the conditions on which the standard depends must themselves be very mutable. . . ."[28] Yet the outstanding feature of moral truths is that they remain almost completely stationary. Thus, as fixed moral principles cannot explain the continual movement of European history, progress must inevitably be attributed to intellectual laws.

Buckle spends much energy defending the paradox that moral ideas remain stationary while other branches of knowledge advance. "To do good to others," he says, "to love your neighbour as yourself; to forgive your enemies; to restrain your passions; to honour your parents; to respect those who are set over you: these, and a few others, are the sole essentials of morals; but they have been known for thousands of years, and not one jot or tittle has been added to them by all the sermons, homilies, and text-books which moralists and theologians have been able to produce. But, if we contrast this stationary aspect of moral truths with the progressive aspect of intellectual truths, the difference is indeed startling. All the great moral systems which have exercised much influence have been fundamentally the same; all the great intellectual systems have been fundamentally different. In reference to our moral conduct, there is not a single principle now known to the most cultivated Europeans, which was not likewise known to the ancients. In reference to the conduct of our intellect, the moderns have not only made the most important additions to every department of knowledge that the ancients ever attempted to study, but besides this, they have upset and revolutionized the old methods of inquiry; they have consolidated into one great scheme all those resources of induction which Aristotle alone dimly perceived; and they have created sciences, the faintest idea of which never entered the mind of the boldest thinker antiquity produced."[29]

Buckle illustrates the theory that intellectual rather than moral laws are the mainspring of progress by examining the way in which two of the greatest evils disfiguring history have diminished. These, in order of importance, he regards as persecution and war. "It is to the diffusion of knowledge, and to that alone, that we owe the comparative cessation of what is unquestionably the greatest evil men have ever inflicted on their own species. For that religious persecution is a greater evil than any other, is apparent, not so much from the enormous and almost incredible number of its known victims, as from the fact that the unknown must be far more numerous, and that history gives no account of those who have been spared in the body, in order that they might suffer in the mind. We hear much of martyrs and confessors—of those who were slain by the sword, or consumed in the fire; but we know little of that still larger number who, by the mere threat of persecution, have been driven into an outward abandonment of their real opinions; and who, thus forced into an apostasy the heart abhors, have passed the remainder of their life in the practice of a constant and humiliating hypocrisy. It is this which is the real curse of religious persecution. For in this way, men being constrained to mask their thoughts, there arises a habit of securing safety by falsehood, and of purchasing impunity with deceit. In this way fraud becomes a necessity of life; insincerity is made a daily custom; the whole tone of public feeling is vitiated, and the gross amount of vice and of error fearfully increased."[30]

Buckle regarded war as the second greatest evil known to Mankind although he believed it to be a curse that was diminishing. For nearly forty years after Waterloo England had remained at peace. But that this was so, was in no way the result of moral progress. For a thousand years moralists and theologians had failed to point out a single evil caused by war which was not already fully appreciated. "Since, then, the actions of men respecting War have been gradually changing, while their moral knowledge respecting it has not been changing, it is palpably evident that the changeable effect has not been produced by the unchangeable cause." Buckle traces the decline of war to the growth of knowledge among the intellectual classes, which has led to an increase in their power, and to a corresponding decline in the ability and authority of the army. In the savage state, where the intellect is still unawakened, a man is of no account "unless he has killed an enemy; and the more he has killed, the greater the reputation he enjoys". In such a society, "military glory is most esteemed, and military men most respected".[31] But, as civilization advances, an intellectual class emerges, interested in the preservation of peace, preferring argument to force, and hostile to the pretensions of the soldiers. In countries like our own, the love of fighting is extinct, not because of any new moral teaching, but because the progress of civilization has formed certain classes of society which desire peace, and have the power to overrule the warmongers.

Three other factors Buckle discusses, which, in his view, have diminished the warlike spirit: the invention of gunpowder, discoveries in political economy, and improvements in communications. Gunpowder necessitated the formation of professional armies, and instead of every man being at sometime a soldier, fighting became confined to regular troops and Mercenaries. The military spirit was thus restricted to a small class, and a check imposed on the lust for conquest, "the most fatal of those diseased appetites by which even civilized countries are too often afflicted".[32] Political Economy, by teaching governments to appreciate the true nature of trade, and by exposing the fallacy that it is in the commercial interest of one country to injure the trade of another, diverted commerce into peaceful channels, and substituted free and friendly trade for policies of force and fraud. Finally the invention of the Railway, by bringing countries into closer contact with each other, helped to dissipate foolish prejudices which sustained misunderstandings between nations and proved only too frequently a cause of war. "Thus, for instance, the miserable and impudent falsehoods which a large class of English writers formerly directed against the morals and private character of the French, and, to their shame be it said, even against the chastity of French women, tended not a little to embitter the angry feelings then existing between the two first countries of Europe; irritating the English against French vices, irritating the French against English calumnies. In the same way, there was a time when every honest Englishman firmly believed that he could beat ten Frenchmen; a class of beings whom he held in sovereign contempt, as a lean and stunted race, who drank claret instead of brandy, who lived entirely off frogs; miserable infidels, who heard mass every Sunday, who bowed down before idols, and who even worshipped the Pope. On the other hand, the French were taught to despise us, as rude unlettered barbarians, without either taste or humanity; surly, ill-conditioned men, living in an unhappy climate, where a perpetual fog, only varied by rain, prevented the sun from ever being seen; suffering from so deep and inveterate a melancholy, that physicians had called it the English spleen; and under the influence of this cruel malady constantly committing suicide, particularly in November, when we were well known to hang and shoot ourselves by thousands. . . . It may be said without the slightest exaggeration, that every new railroad which is laid down, and every fresh steamer which crosses the Channel, are additional guarantees for the preservation of that long and unbroken peace which, during forty years, has knit together the fortunes and the interests of the two most civilized nations of the earth."[33]

In estimating the relative efficacy of moral and intellectual factors in determining human progress, Buckle concludes that the latter exerts a far more powerful influence than the former. Great crimes, however appalling they may appear to contemporaries, are soon forgotten. "The desolation of countries and the slaughter of men are losses which never fail to be repaired, and at the distance of a few centuries every vestige of them is effaced. The gigantic crimes of Alexander or Napoleon become after a time void of effect, and the affairs of the world return to their former level." But amid endless change one thing endures for ever. "The discoveries of great men never leave us; they are immortal, they contain those eternal truths which survive the shock of empires, outlive the struggles of rival creeds, and witness the decay of successive religions."[34]

As the history of European Civilization is principally the history of the development and diffusion of knowledge, it ought not to be difficult to ascertain the laws which govern progress. But unfortunately, historians have carefully preserved trifling details, and overlooked what is really significant. We have innumerable "anecdotes of Kings and Courts; interminable relations of what was said by one Minister, and what was thought by another; and what is worse than all, long accounts of campaigns, battles, and sieges", but no attempt is made to understand the great tidal movements of history that lie beneath the surface. The ignorance and want of judgement displayed by most historians in the selection of their material led Buckle to complain that "whoever now attempts to generalize historical phenomena must collect the facts, as well as conduct the generalization. He finds nothing ready to his hand. He must be the mason as well as the architect; he must not only scheme the edifice, but likewise excavate the quarry. . . . History, instead of being ripe, as it ought to be, for complete and exhaustive generalizations, is still in so crude and informal a state, that not the most determined and protracted industry will enable any one to comprehend the really important actions of mankind, during even so short a period as two successive centuries."[35]

When it became clear to Buckle that he was attempting the impossible, he abandoned his original scheme of writing a general history of Civilization and decided to restrict his inquiry to the history of England alone. He selected his own country because the laws of its development could be studied without undue reference to outside influences. The task Buckle set himself was to study the intellectual progress of England, as "until that is done, the annals of any people can only present an empirical succession of events, connected by such stray and casual links as are devised by different writers, according to their different principles". Whenever the history of England failed to illustrate the laws governing the growth and distribution of knowledge, Buckle proposed to investigate the history of other countries to supply the deficiency. "Thus, for instance, in Germany, the accumulation of knowledge has been far more rapid than in England; the laws of the accumulation of knowledge may, on that account, be most conveniently studied in German history, and then applied deductively to the history of England. In the same way, the Americans have diffused their knowledge much more completely than we have done; I, therefore, purpose to explain some of the phenomena of English civilization by those laws of diffusion, of which, in American civilization, the workings may be most clearly seen, and hence the discovery most easily made. Again, inasmuch as France is the most civilized country in which the protective spirit is very powerful, we may trace the occult tendencies of that spirit among ourselves, by studying its obvious tendencies among our neighbours. With this view, I shall give an account of French history, in order to illustrate the protective principle, by showing the injury it has inflicted on a very able and enlightened people. . . . The French, as a people, have, since the beginning or middle of the seventeenth century, been remarkably free from superstition; and, notwithstanding the efforts of their government, they are very averse to ecclesiastical power. . . . Hence, my intention is to give a view of Spanish history; because in it we may trace the full results of that protection against error which the spiritual classes are always eager to afford."[36]

Religion, Literature and Government, which are ordinarily supposed to be causes of progress, Buckle regarded as conditioned by the societies in which they develop. Thus, for example, to regard Religion as initiating progress is to confuse cause with effect. "The truth is, that the religious opinions which prevail in any period are among the symptoms by which that period is marked. When the opinions are deeply rooted, they do, no doubt, influence the conduct of men; but before they can be deeply rooted, some intellectual change must first have taken place. We may as well expect that the seed should quicken in the barren rock, as that a mild and philosophic religion should be established among ignorant and ferocious savages. . . . If either a religion or a philosophy is too much in advance of a nation, it can do no present service, but must bide its time, until the minds of men are ripe for its reception. Of this innumerable instances will occur to most readers. Every science and every creed has had its martyrs; men exposed to obloquy, or even to death, because they knew more than their contemporaries, and because society was not sufficiently advanced to receive the truths which they communicated. . . . History is full of evidence of the utter inefficiency even of the noblest principles, when they are promulgated among a very ignorant nation."[37] In the same way that a religion unsuited to the needs and understanding of a people, will be misunderstood, neglected or condemned; so the ablest books and the most novel ideas will fall into oblivion unless they harmonize to some extent with ideas current at the time.

The view that European civilization owes its advance to the actions of governments, Buckle thought so extravagant a notion that it was "difficult to refute with becoming gravity". It appeared to him, however, to be so dangerous and widespread a fallacy that he contrived to combat it earnestly enough. The rulers of a country, he argues, are subject like everybody else to the traditions and prejudices which prevail at the time. "Such men are, at best, only the creatures of the age, never its creators. Their measures are the result of social progress, not the cause of it." It is not rulers who have originated political improvements, but "bold and able thinkers, who discern the abuse, denounce it, and point out how it is to be remedied". After every possible delay the government at last succumbs to popular pressure, "and the reform being accomplished, the people are expected to admire the wisdom of their rulers, by whom all this has been done". Moreover, "every great reform which has been effected, has consisted, not in doing something new, but in undoing something old". It is therefore evident "that the progress of civilization cannot be due to those who on the most important subjects have done so much harm, that their successors are considered benefactors, simply because they reverse their policy. . . ."[38] Seeing that it is the tendency of every government to overstep its proper function and to meddle with matters which are not its concern, and seeing that "the love of exercising power has been found to be so universal that no class of men who have possessed authority have been able to avoid abusing it", it follows that the efforts of government are, even where successful, merely negative; and where they are more than negative are positively injurious. It is therefore erroneous to "ascribe the progress of Europe to the wisdom of its rulers".[39]

Buckle believed that in a country which had been educated to freedom "every system must fall if it opposes the march of opinions, and gives shelter to maxims and institutions repugnant to the spirit of the age".[40] Because government action is at best a necessary evil, it follows that "the only safe course for the legislator is to look upon his craft as consisting in the adaptation of temporary contrivances to temporary emergencies. His business is to follow the age, and not at all to attempt to lead it. . . . For he may rely upon it, that the movements of society have now become so rapid, that the wants of one generation are no measure of the wants of another; and that men, urged by a sense of their own progress, are growing weary of idle talk about the wisdom of their ancestors, and are fast discarding those trite and sleepy maxims which have hitherto imposed upon them, but by which they will not consent to be much longer troubled."[41] Since in politics no certain principles have yet been discovered, success is to be achieved only by "compromise, barter, expediency, and concession". "To meet new emergencies by old maxims," is to court disaster. "Innovation is the sole ground of security."[42]

Since neither religion, literature nor legislation, suffice to account for the progress of mankind, Buckle concludes that the growth of European civilization "is solely due to the progress of knowledge". . . .[43] On the one hand he discovers in "scepticism" the antecedent of all progress; on the other hand, he attributes resistance to new ideas to a credulous theological spirit. "To scepticism we owe that spirit of inquiry, which, during the last two centuries, has gradually encroached on every possible subject; has reformed every department of practical and speculative knowledge; has weakened the authority of the privileged classes, and thus placed liberty on a surer foundation; has chastised the despotism of princes; has restrained the arrogance of the nobles; and has even diminished the prejudices of the clergy. In a word, it is this which has remedied the three fundamental errors of the olden time: errors which made the people, in politics too confiding; in science too credulous; in religion too intolerant." To doubt established ideas is the necessary preliminary of acquiring new knowledge, but scepticism is nevertheless "an abomination to the ignorant; because it disturbs their lazy and complacent minds; because it troubles their cherished superstitions; because it imposes on them the fatigue of inquiry; and because it rouses even sluggish understandings to ask if things are as they are commonly supposed". . . .[44] Again and again enlightened scepticism has been confronted by an obdurate clergy, by the forces of tradition, and by restrictive governments. Thus the history of Modern Europe is the history of the conflict between the spirit of protection and the spirit of scepticism.

The history of England in particular clearly reveals the nature of this widespread struggle. For long ages the theological spirit in this country triumphantly smothered independent thought, and the fate of a heretic awaited any who dared to challenge the omniscience of the Church. In such a stifling atmosphere superstition flourished, absurdities were accepted with unquestioning credulity, and the epoch is only too well described as "the age of faith". Since the sixteenth century, however, a great change has taken place. "The

Reformation, by destroying the dogma of an infallible Church, weakened the reverence which was paid to ecclesiastical antiquity," and a new zest for scientific inquiry arose. Although the early Stuarts did all in their power to resist the tendencies of their age, "the spirit which they wished to quench had reached a height that mocked their control".[45] There were checks and recessions in the progress of enlightenment, but if an occasional breaker receded, the tide was none the less coming in.

The successes of science in the seventeenth century, and the researches of Boyle in particular, show how old ways of thought were yielding to new. "In the whole of his physical inquiries, Boyle constantly insists upon two fundamental principles: namely, the importance of individual experiments, and the comparative unimportance of the facts which, on these subjects, antiquity has handed down. These are the two great keys to his method: they are the views which he inherited from Bacon, and they are also the views which have been held by every man who, during the last two centuries, has added anything of moment to the stock of human knowledge. First to doubt, then to inquire, and then to discover, has been the process universally followed by our great teachers. So strongly did Boyle feel this, that though he was an eminently religious man, he gave to the most popular of his scientific works the title of *The Sceptical Chemist*; meaning to intimate, that until men were sceptical concerning the chemistry of their own time, it would be impossible that they should advance far in the career which lay before them." In the seventeenth century the reactionary party, consisting of the majority of the clergy, entirely failed to discredit that inquisitive and experimental spirit which they found offensive to their prejudices and detrimental to their power. They failed because the physical sciences "taught men to require a severity of proof which it was soon found that the clergy were, in their own department, unable to supply".[46] As knowledge advanced, events which had previously been regarded as supernatural, such as plagues and eclipses, were found to be explicable, and thus the scope and reputation of theology diminished as that of science increased. In short, ignorance breeds superstition while knowledge dispels it.

Buckle regarded the history of the reign of Charles II as particularly instructive; for the great improvements effected during it owed practically nothing to the government. Indeed, these improvements were made despite "the miserable incompetence of the king, the idle profligacy of his court, the unblushing venality of his ministers". The problem of explaining how such men could effect such improvements, and how, in face of unparalleled disasters like the Great Fire, the Great Plague and the appearance of a Dutch fleet in the Medway, such wonderful progress could be made in the extension of toleration, the freeing of the Press and the reduction of tyrannical power, "our political compilers are unable to answer; because they look too much at the peculiarities of individuals, and too little at the temper of the age in which those individuals live. Such writers do not perceive that the history of every civilized country is the history of its intellectual development, which kings, statesmen, and legislators are more likely to retard than to hasten; because, however great their power may be, they are at best the accidental and insufficient representatives of the spirit of their time; and because, so far from being able to regulate the movements of the national mind, they themselves form the smallest part of it, and, in a general view of the progress of Man, are only to be regarded as the puppets who strut and fret their hour upon a little stage; while, beyond them, and on every side of them, are forming opinions and principles which they can scarcely perceive, but by which alone the whole course of human affairs is ultimately governed."[47]

After considering the development of the sceptical spirit in England, Buckle turns to French history, and discovers the same processes at work there; although, as the theological spirit in France was more powerfully entrenched, enlightened ideas were more vigorously resisted, and advances in knowledge and toleration were more effectively delayed. "In France, a long train of events, had, from an early period, given to the clergy a share of power larger than that which they possessed in England. The results of this were for a time decidedly beneficial, inasmuch as the church restrained the lawlessness of a barbarous age, and secured a refuge for the weak and oppressed. But as the French advanced in knowledge, the spiritual authority, which had done so much to curb their passions, began to press heavily upon their genius, and impede its movements. That same ecclesiastical power, which to an ignorant age is an unmixed benefit, is to a more enlightened age a serious evil."[48] The greater power of the French clergy involved a greater preoccupation with things ecclesiastical, at the expense of profane literature, secular politics, and natural science. In an atmosphere of religious strife, "it would have been idle to expect any of those maxims of charity to which theological faction is always a stranger." Toleration, the necessary preliminary of scepticism, and hence of intellectual advance, withered under the ferocious heat engendered by religious bigotry. Such were the results "of that accursed spirit, which, whenever it has had the power, has punished even to the death those who dared to differ from it; and which, now that the power has passed away, still continues to dogmatize on the most mysterious subjects, tamper with the most sacred principles of the human heart, and darken with its miserable superstitions those sublime questions that no one should rudely touch, because they are for each according to the measure of his own soul, because they lie in that unknown tract which separates the Finite from the Infinite, and because they are as a secret and individual convenant between Man and his God".[49]

The growth of scepticism in France began in the reign of Henry IV, a king whose career displayed his personal indifference to creeds. The toleration granted to heresy by the Edict of Nantes as well as the writings of Rabelais, Montaigne and Charron, reveal a spirit hostile to theological pretensions and conducive to the spread of knowledge. The process thus begun was assisted throughout the reign of Louis XIII by Richelieu, who, despite the fact that he was a Cardinal, subordinated the interests of the Church to those of the State, thus weakening ecclesiastical power while strengthening the secular arm. But Richelieu's work was only "the political expression of that bold and sceptical spirit which cried havoc to the prejudices and superstitions of men. For, the government of Richelieu was successful, as well as progressive; and no government can unite these two qualities, unless its measures harmonize with the feelings and temper of the age." It is not sufficient, therefore, only to examine the surface of political events, it is necessary to investigate those undercurrents of opinion of which a country's political history is only one manifestation; and it is because so many historians have studied the past without ever attempting to trace the growth of knowledge, that history appears to be "a barren field, which, bearing no fruit, is unworthy of the labour that is wasted on the cultivation of so ungrateful a soil".[50]

While Richelieu was secularizing French politics and setting ancient traditions at naught, Descartes in the sphere of science and philosophy was doing exactly the same thing: fighting prejudice, and destroying old errors. The similarity of the services rendered to Europe by these two men affords yet another instance of the way in which a country's political history is related to its intellectual progress. The analogy between Descartes and Richelieu is very striking. "The same disregard of ancient notions, the same contempt for theological interests, the indifference to tradition, the same determination to prefer the present to the past: in a word, the same essentially modern spirit, is seen alike in the writings of Descartes, and in the actions of Richelieu. What the first was to philosophy, that was the other to politics. But, while acknowledging the merits of these eminent men, it behoves us to remember that their success was the result, not only of their own abilities, but likewise of the general temper of their time. The nature of their labours depended on themselves; the way in which their labours were received, depended on their contemporaries. Had they lived in a more superstitious age, their views would have been disregarded, or, if noticed, would have been execrated as impious novelties."[51]

During the seventy years following the accession of Henry IV, "the mind, according to the natural conditions of its growth, first doubted what it had long believed, and then tolerated what it had long hated". This process occurred a generation later in France than in England because of the prevalence there of those feelings "which are fatal to all knowledge, because, looking on antiquity as the sole receptacle of wisdom, they degrade the present in order that they may exaggerate the past: feelings which destroy the prospects of man, stifle his hopes, damp his curiosity, chill his energies, impair his judgment, and under pretence of humbling the pride of his reason, seek to throw him back into that more than midnight darkness from which his reason alone has enabled him to emerge". But delayed as the movement was, "both countries followed the same order of development in their scepticism, in their knowledge, in their literature, and in their toleration. In both countries, there broke out a civil war at the same time, for the same object, and, in many respects, under the same circumstances. In both, the insurgents, at first triumphant, were afterwards defeated; and the rebellion being put down, the governments of the two nations were fully restored almost at the same moment: in 1660 by Charles II; in 1661, by Louis XIV. But there the similarity stopped. At this point there began a marked divergence between the two countries; which continued to increase for more than a century, until it ended in England by the consolidation of the national prosperity, in France by a revolution more sanguinary, more complete, and more destructive, than any the world has ever seen. This difference between the fortunes of such great and civilized nations is so remarkable, that a knowledge of its causes becomes essential to a right understanding of European history. . . . The cause of this difference is to be sought in the existence of that spirit of protection which is so dangerous and yet so plausible, that it forms the most serious obstacle with which advancing civilization has to contend."[52]

Buckle devotes considerable space to contrasting the protective spirit in France and England. Since nearly all governments before the seventeenth century were aristocratic, the more powers the nobles exerted, the more formidable was the spirit of protection. In England the circumstances of the Norman conquest favoured a reduction of the influence of the barons. Whereas in France land was held by prescription, in England the nobles owed their estates to royal grants, and even the most powerful peers were too feeble to contend with the crown, except with the assistance of the people. "The English aristocracy being thus forced, by their own weakness, to rely on the people, it naturally followed, that the people imbibed that tone of independence, and that lofty bearing, of which our civil and political institutions are the consequence, rather than the cause. It is to this, and not to any fanciful peculiarity of race, that we owe the sturdy and enterprising spirit for which the inhabitants of this island have long been remarkable. It is this which has enabled us to baffle all the arts of oppression, and to maintain for centuries liberties which no other nation has ever possessed. . . .

"But the habits of self-government which, under these circumstances, were cultivated in England, were, under opposite circumstances, neglected in France. The great French lords being too powerful to need the people, were unwilling to seek their alliance. The result was, that, amid a great variety of forms and names, society was, in reality, only divided into two classes—the upper and the lower, the protectors and the protected. And, looking at the ferocity of the prevailing manners, it is not too much to say, that in France, under the feudal system, every man was either a tyrant or a slave."[53]

The people of England, not being subjected to the same "protection" as Frenchmen, became accustomed to self-government, and it was the habit of independence that Englishmen gradually acquired, rather than any legislation, which proved the real guarantee of their liberty. "For it is not by the wax and parchment of lawyers that the independence of men can be preserved. Such things are the mere externals; they set off liberty to advantage; they are as its dress and paraphernalia, its holiday-suit in times of peace and quiet. But, when the evil days set in, when the invasions of despotism have begun, liberty will be retained, not by those who can show the oldest deeds and the largest charters, but by those who have been most inured to habits of independence, most accustomed to think and act for themselves, and most regardless of that insidious protection which the upper classes have always been so ready to bestow."[54]

Under Louis XIV and Napoleon the protective spirit in France assumed a new form, and the power of the aristocracy was largely replaced by that of the Crown. This not only involved a transfer of authority, but a tendency to centralization. The ill effects of this change Buckle was quick to condemn; for he was always alert to the evil of government interference. "In France," he says, "all improvements of any importance, all schemes for bettering even the material condition of the people must receive the sanction of government; the local authorities not being considered equal to such arduous tasks. In order that inferior magistrates may not abuse their power no power is conferred upon them. The exercise of independent jurisdiction is almost unknown. Every thing that is done must be done at head quarters. The government is believed to see every thing, know every thing, and provide for every thing. To enforce this monstrous monopoly there has been contrived a machinery well worthy of the design. The entire country is covered by an immense array of officials. . . . In fact, the whole business of the state is conducted on the supposition that no man either knows his own interest, or is fit to take care of himself." In order that the French may not make imprudent wills, the Government "has limited the right of bequest; and, for fear that they should bequeath their property wrongly, it prevents them from bequeathing the greater part of it at all. In order that society may be protected by its police, it has directed that no one shall travel without a passport. And when men are actually travelling, they are met at every turn by the same interfering spirit, which, under pretence of protecting their persons, shackles their liberty. . . . The people, even in their ordinary amusements, are watched and carefully superintended. Lest they should harm each other by some sudden indiscretion, precautions are taken similar to those with which a father might surround his children. In their fairs, at their theatres, their concerts, and their other places of public resort, there are always present soldiers, who are sent to see that no mischief is done, that there is no unnecessary crowding, that no one uses harsh language, that no one quarrels with his neighbour. Nor does the vigilance of the government stop there. . . . Its prying eye follows the butcher to the shambles, and the baker to the oven. By its paternal hand, meat is examined lest it should be bad, and bread is weighed lest it should be light. . . . It is enough to say that in France, as in every country where the protective principle is active, the government has established a monopoly of the worst kind; a monopoly which comes home to the business and bosoms of men, follows them in their daily avocations, troubles them with its petty, meddling spirit, and, what is worse than all, diminishes their responsibility to themselves; thus depriving them of what is the only real education that most minds receive—the constant necessity of providing for future contingencies, and the habit of grappling with the difficulties of life. . . . Men can never be free, unless they are educated to freedom. And this is not the education which is to be found in schools, or gained from books; but it is that which consists in self-discipline, in self-reliance, and in self-government. These in England are matters of hereditary descent. . . . What with us is competition, with them is monopoly. That which we effect by private companies, they effect by public boards. They cannot cut a canal, or lay down a railroad, without appealing to the government for aid. With them, the people look to the rulers; with us, the rulers look to the people. . . . The French, always treated as children, are, in political matters, children still. And as they have handled the most weighty concerns in that gay and volatile spirit which adorns their lighter literature, it is no wonder that they have failed in matters where the first condition of success is, that men should have been long accustomed to rely upon their own energies. . . ."[55]

The difference between the English Civil War and the Fronde in France shows how different has been the political development of the two countries. The Great Rebellion was effected by the people, while the leaders of the Fronde were exclusively aristocratic—as was inevitable in a nation in which the protective spirit was so strong and the enjoyment of liberty so restricted. The English Civil War was "a movement from below, an uprising from the foundations, or as some will have it, the dregs of society". But in France the rank and file "had been so long accustomed to look with timid reverence to the upper classes, that even when they rose in arms, they could not throw off the ideas of submission which were quickly discarded by our ancestors".[56]

The protective spirit was as detrimental to the intellectual life of France as it was to its political development. Buckle devotes an entire chapter to examining the effect of royal patronage and censorship upon literature and thought. He does so on the principle that "to write the history of a country without regard to its intellectual progress, is as if an astronomer should compose a planetary system without regard to the sun, by whose light alone the planets can be seen, and by whose attraction they are held in their course, and compelled to run in the path of their appointed orbits". . . .[57]

"In every country," says Buckle, "where royal patronage has been long and generally bestowed, the spirit of literature, instead of being progressive, has become reactionary. An alliance has been struck up between those who give and those who receive. By a system of bounties, there has been artificially engendered a greedy and necessitous class; who, eager for pensions, and offices, and titles, have made the pursuit of truth subordinate to the desire of gain, and have infused into their writings the prejudices of the court to which they cling. Hence it is, that the marks of favour have become the badge of servitude. . . . In no age have literary men been rewarded with such profuseness as in the reign of Louis XIV: and in no age have they been so mean-spirited, so servile, so utterly unfit to fulfil their great vocation as the apostles of knowledge and the missionaries of truth. . . . To gain the favour of the king, they sacrificed that independent spirit which should have been dearer to them than life. They gave away the inheritance of genius; they sold their birthright for a mess of pottage. . . . If the government can corrupt the intellect, and if the intellect will yield to the government, the inevitable result must be, despotism in politics, and servility in literature. This was the history of France under Louis XIV: and this, we may rest assured, will be the history of every country that shall be tempted to follow so attractive but so fatal an example."[58]

If France suffered greatly from a protective spirit which crushed knowledge, restricted commerce and destroyed that political independence which is the necessary condition of permanent improvement, she did at least have a revolution; and except for a few brief intervals, there were usually writers found to protest against the whole system and to keep a love of liberty alive. In order to understand fully how disastrous the protective spirit can be in thwarting progress, and thus to appreciate the true nature of a force which has always been at work in England, but which, because resisted, is often hard to discern, we must consider the history of Spain, where the conditions of national improvement have been most flagrantly violated, and where ignorance and superstition have always prevailed.

Spain, like the tropics, is designated by Nature as the seat and refuge of superstition. Famines, epidemics and earthquakes have been more prominent there than anywhere else in Europe. The soil is arid, rain is infrequent, and life is therefore always insecure. Under these circumstances superstition is easily excited, and ambitious priests have had little difficulty in imposing themselves on the people. The Islamic attack on Spain early in the eighth century involved that country in a crusade which lasted for more than twenty generations, and greatly added to the power of the clergy, who were regarded as the natural leaders of the Holy War. In yet another way their influence was increased by the Mohammedan invasion. Continual warfare made the Spaniards poor; "poverty caused ignorance; ignorance caused credulity; and credulity, depriving men both of the power and of the desire to investigate for themselves, encouraged a reverential spirit, and confirmed those submissive habits, and that blind obedience to the Church, which forms the leading and most unfortunate peculiarity of Spanish history". So powerful was the influence of the clergy that "the theological element became not so much a component of the national character, but rather the character itself".[59] Unquestioning loyalty to the king was combined by Spaniards with reverence for the clergy. The readiness with which sovereigns were obeyed, was inspired by the same submissive spirit which characterized the people's relation to the Church; and the habit of looking to one or other for protection was strengthened by centuries of resistance to Islam. There could be little hope of driving the Mohammedans back into Africa unless every resource was used to the full and every command accepted without hesitation. Thus abject loyalty and slavish superstition went hand in hand, and the history of Spain shows the fruits of such a partnership. Her policy for a considerable period was to avoid contact with other powers, and her isolation from the rest of Europe was emphasized by the Pyrenees. The peculiar character of her institutions is entirely the result of internal events. Just as the scientist attempts to arrive at truth by excluding, as far as possible, every disturbing circumstance which might upset his experiments or falsify his results, so the philosophic historian in his search for the laws determining human behaviour, tries to isolate phenomena so as to observe them more accurately. It is for this reason that Spain's development is of particular significance.

In the century after the Mohammedans were driven from the country, Spain's "power advanced with a speed of which the world had seen no example since the days of the Roman Empire. So late as 1478 Spain was still broken up into independent and often hostile states; Granada was possessed by the Mohammedans; the throne of Castile was occupied by one prince, the throne of Aragon by another. Before the year 1590, not only were these fragments firmly consolidated into one kingdom, but acquisitions were made abroad so rapidly as to endanger the independence of Europe. The history of Spain, during this period, is the history of one long and uninterrupted success. That country, recently torn by civil wars, and distracted by hostile creeds, was able in three generations to annex to her territory the whole of Portugal, Navarre, and Roussillon. By diplomacy or by force of arms, she acquired Artois and Franche Comte, and the Netherlands; also the Milanese, Naples, Sicily, Sardinia, the Balearic Islands, and the Canaries. One of her kings was emperor of Germany; while his son influenced the councils of England, whose queen he married. The Turkish power, then one of the most formidable in the world, was broken and beaten back on every side. The French monarchy was humbled. French armies were constantly worsted; Paris was once in imminent jeopardy; and a king of France, after being defeated on the field, was taken captive, and led prisoner to Madrid. Out of Europe, the deeds of Spain were equally wonderful. In America, the Spaniards became possessed of territories which covered sixty degrees of latitude, and included both the tropics. Besides Mexico, Central America, Venezuela, New Granada, Peru, and Chili, they conquered Cuba, San Domingo, Jamaica, and other islands. In Africa, they obtained Ceuta, Melilla, Oran, Bougiah, and Tunis, and overawed the whole coast of Barbary. In Asia, they had settlements on each side of the Deccan; they held part of Malacca; and they established themselves in the Spice Islands. Finally, by the conquest of the noble archipelago of the Philippines, they connected their most distant acquisitions, and secured a communication between every part of that enormous empire which girdled the world."[60]

These great achievements, however, depended too much on the talents of individuals, and not sufficiently on the enterprise of the people. For all her apparent grandeur the foundation of Spain was unsound, as the decay of her vast empire in the seventeenth century showed. But then any country which obeys its rulers with indiscriminate loyalty, "is sure to decay; inasmuch as, in the ordinary course of affairs, incapable rulers must sometimes arise. Directly this happens, the deterioration begins; for the people will follow wherever they are led, and will yield to foolish counsels the same obedience that they had before paid to wise ones. This leads us to perceive the essential difference between the civilization of Spain and the civilization of England. We, in England, are a critical, dissatisfied, and captious people, constantly complaining of our rulers, suspecting their schemes, discussing their measures in a hostile spirit, allowing very little power either to the Church or to the Crown, managing our own affairs in our own way, and ready, on the slightest provocation, to renounce that conventional, lip-deep loyalty, which, having never really touched our hearts, is a habit lying on the surface, but not a passion rooted in the mind. . . . The consequence is, that our progress is uninterrupted, whether our kings are good or whether they are bad. Under either condition, the great movement goes on. Our sovereigns have had their full share of imbecility and of crime. Still, even men like Henry III and Charles II were unable to do us harm. In the same way, during the eighteenth and many years of the nineteenth century, when our improvement was very conspicuous, our rulers were very incompetent. Anne and the first two Georges were grossly ignorant; they were wretchedly educated, and nature had made them at once weak and obstinate. Their united reigns lasted nearly sixty years; and after they had passed away, we, for another period of sixty years, were governed by a prince who was long incapacitated by disease, but of whom we must honestly say that, looking at his general policy, he was least mischievous when he was most incapable. This is not the place to expose the monstrous principles advocated by George III." It is, however, certain that "neither his contracted understanding, nor his despotic temper, nor his miserable superstition, nor the incredible baseness of that ignoble voluptuary who succeeded him on the throne, could do aught to stop the march of English civilization, or to stem the tide of English prosperity. We went on our way rejoicing, caring for none of these things. We were not to be turned aside from our path by the folly of our rulers, because we know full well that we hold our own fate in our own hands, and that the English people possess within themselves those resources and that fertility of contrivance by which alone men can be made great, and happy, and wise."[61]

The greatness of Spain had been achieved by a long line of able and intelligent princes, under whom the country appeared to flourish. "But, what followed when they were withdrawn from the scene, showed how artificial all this was, and how rotten, even to the core, is that system of government which must be fostered before it can thrive, and which, being based on the loyalty and reverence of the people, depends for success not on the ability of the nation, but on the skill of those to whom the interests of the nation are entrusted."[62]

To understand the decline of Spain in the seventeenth century it is necessary to know something of its sovereigns, and of these Charles II was characteristic. "He possessed," says Buckle, "nearly every defect which can make a man ridiculous and contemptible. His mind and his person were such as, in any nation less loyal than Spain, would have exposed him to universal derision. Although his death took place while he was still in the prime of life, he looked like an old and worn-out debauchee. At the age of thirty-five, he was completely bald; he had lost his eyebrows; he was paralysed; he was epileptic; and he was notoriously impotent. His general appearance was absolutely revolting, and was that of a drivelling idiot. To an enormous mouth, he added a nether jaw protruding so hideously that his teeth could never meet, and he was unable to masticate his food. His ignorance would be incredible, if it were not substantiated by unimpeachable evidence. He did not know the names of the large towns, or even of the provinces, in his dominions; and during the war with France he was heard to pity England for losing cities which in fact formed part of his own territory. Finally, he was immersed in the most grovelling superstition; he believed himself to be constantly tempted by the devil; he allowed himself to be exorcized as one possessed by evil spirits; and he would not retire to rest, except with his confessor and two friars, who had to lie by his side during the night.

"Now it was that men might clearly see on how sandy a foundation the grandeur of Spain was built. When there were able sovereigns, the country prospered; when there were weak ones, it declined. Nearly everything that had been done by the great princes of the sixteenth century, was undone by the little princes of the seventeenth. So rapid was the fall of Spain, that in only three reigns after the death of Philip II, the most powerful monarchy existing in the world was depressed to the lowest point of debasement, was insulted with impunity by foreign nations, was reduced more than once to bankruptcy, was stripped of her fairest possessions, was held up to public opprobrium, was made a theme on which school-boys and moralists loved to declaim respecting the uncertainty of human affairs, and, at length, was exposed to the bitter humiliation of seeing her territories mapped out and divided by a treaty in which she took no share, but the provisions of which she was unable to resent. Then, truly, did she drink to the dregs the cup of her own shame. Her glory had departed from her, she was smitten down and humbled. Well might a Spaniard of that time who compared the present with the past, mourn over his country, the chosen abode of chivalry and romance, of valour and of loyalty. The mistress of the world, the queen of the ocean, the terror of nations, was gone; her power was gone, no more to return."[63]

The degradation into which the Spaniards sank was only partly the consequence of their blind loyalty to the throne; a loyalty which induced them to follow the perversest of courses, provided they were led by a king. The theological spirit in Spain being stronger than elsewhere, ignorance was consequently more pronounced, and this very ignorance helped to perpetuate unquestioning submission to Church and State. The clergy, "by discouraging all inquiry, and fettering all freedom of thought, had at length reduced the country to such a plight, that the faculties of men, rusted by disuse, were no longer equal to fulfil the functions required from them; so that in every department, whether of political life, or of speculative philosophy, or even of mechanical industry, it was necessary that foreigners should be called in, to do that work, which the natives had become unable to perform."[64]

As late as 1770 ecclesiastical resistance to learning was so bigoted that at Salamanca, "the seat of the most ancient and most famous University in Spain", the discoveries of Newton were not taught because his system "was not so consonant with revealed religion as the system of Aristotle". All over the country the same attitude to truth prevailed. "The Duke de Saint Simon, who, in 1721 and 1722, was the French ambassador at Madrid, sums up his observations by the remark that, in Spain, science is a crime, and ignorance a virtue. Fifty years later, another shrewd observer, struck with amazement at the condition of the national mind, expresses his opinion in a sentence equally pithy and almost equally severe. Searching for an illustration to convey his sense of the general darkness, he emphatically says, that the common education of an English gentleman would, in Spain, constitute a man of learning. Those who know what the common education of an English gentleman was eighty years ago, will appreciate the force of this comparison, and will understand how benighted a country must have been, to which such a taunt was applicable."[65]

Spain's rapid deterioration was halted in the eighteenth century. Under Philip V, new and enlightened policies were inaugurated, although exclusively with foreign assistance. From his accession, to the death of Charles III, a period of nearly ninety years, reforms continued uninterruptedly. "For three generations, there was no pause on the part of the government; not one reaction, not one sign of halting. Improvement upon improvement, and reform upon reform, followed each other in swift succession."[66] But just as the gains of the sixteenth century were thrown away in the seventeenth century, so the improvements made by the enlightened rulers of the eighteenth century were dissipated by their successors. The impermanence of the progress made during the "Age of Reason" shows how little legislators can effect when their policies are opposed to national prejudices. "No reform can produce real good, unless it is the work of public opinion, and unless the people themselves take the initiative. In Spain, during the eighteenth century, foreign influence, and the complications of foreign politics, bestowed enlightened rulers upon an unenlightened country. The consequence was, that, for a time, great things were done. Evils were removed, grievances were redressed, many important improvements were introduced; and a spirit of toleration was exhibited, such as had never before been seen in that priest-ridden and superstitious land. But the mind of Spain was untouched. While the surface, and as it were the symptoms, of affairs were ameliorated, affairs themselves remained unchanged. Below that surface, and far out of reach of any political remedy, large general causes were at work, which had been operating for many centuries, and which were sure, sooner or later, to force politicians to retrace their steps, and compel them to inaugurate a policy which would suit the traditions of the country, and harmonize with the circumstances under which those traditions had been formed."[67]

On the death of Charles III the reaction came. Charles IV, who succeeded him, was "a king of the true Spanish breed, devout, orthodox, and ignorant. It was now seen how insecure everything was, and how little reliance can be placed on reforms, which, instead of being suggested by the people, are bestowed on them by the political classes. . . . In less than five years everything was changed. The power of the Church was restored; the slightest approach towards free discussion was forbidden; old and arbitrary principles, which had not been heard of since the seventeenth century, were revived; the priests re-assumed their former importance; literary men were intimidated, and literature was discouraged; while the Inquisition, suddenly starting up afresh, displayed an energy, which caused its enemies to tremble, and proved that all the attempts which had been made to weaken it, had been unable to impair its vigour, or to daunt its ancient spirit. . . . Once more was Spain covered with darkness; once more did the shadows of night overtake that wretched land."[68]

More than once in the nineteenth century, leaders of the Spanish liberal movement momentarily succeeded in establishing constitutions. But their success proved short lived. "The forms of constitutional government they could bestow; but they could not find the traditions and the habits, by which the forms are worked. They mimicked the voice of liberty; they copied her institutions; they aped her very gestures. And what then? At the first stroke of adverse fortune, their idol fell to pieces. Their constitutions were broken up, their assemblies dissolved, their enactments rescinded. The inevitable reaction quickly followed. After each disturbance, the hands of the government were strengthened, the principles of despotism were confirmed, and the Spanish liberals were taught to rue the day, in which they vainly endeavoured to impart freedom to their unhappy and ill-starred country. . . . The Spaniards have had everything except knowledge. They have had immense wealth, and fertile and well-peopled territories, in all parts of the globe. . . . They have had their full share of great statesmen, great kings, great magistrates, and great legislators. They have had many able and vigorous rulers; and their history is ennobled by the frequent appearance of courageous and disinterested patriots, who have sacrificed their all, that they might help their country. The bravery of the people has never been disputed; while, as to the upper classes, the punctilious honour of a Spanish gentleman has passed into a bye-word, and circulated through the world. . . . Yet all these great qualities have availed them nothing, and will avail them nothing, so long as they remain ignorant. What the end of all this will be, and whether in their unhappy country the right path will ever be taken, is impossible for anyone to say. But if it is not taken, no amelioration which can possibly be effected will penetrate below the surface. The sole course is, to weaken the superstition of the people; and this can only be done by that march of physical science, which, familiarizing men with conceptions of order and of regularity, gradually encroaches on the old notions of perturbation, of prodigy, and of miracle, and by this means accustoms the mind to explain the vicissitudes of affairs by natural considerations, instead of, as heretofore, by those which are purely supernatural. . . . While the human intellect has been making the most prodigious and unheard-of strides, while discoveries in every quarter are simultaneously pressing upon us, and coming in such rapid and bewildering succession, that the strongest sight, dazzled by the glare of their splendour, is unable to contemplate them as a whole . . . while the veil is being rudely torn, and nature, violated at all points, is forced to disclose her secrets, and reveal her structure, her economy, and her laws, to the indomitable energy of man; while Europe is ringing with the noise of intellectual achievements . . . Spain sleeps on, untroubled, unheeding, impassive. . . . There she lies, at the further extremity of the continent, a huge and torpid mass, the sole representative now remaining of the feelings and knowledge of the Middle Ages. And, what is the worst symptom of all, she is satisfied with her own condition. Though she is the most backward country in Europe, she believes herself to be the foremost. She is proud of every thing of which she should be ashamed. She is proud of the antiquity of her opinions; proud of her orthodoxy; proud of the strength of her faith; proud of her immeasurable and childish credulity; proud of her unwillingness to amend either her creed or her customs; proud of her hatred of heretics, and proud of the undying vigilance with which she has baffled their efforts to obtain a full and legal establishment on her soil."[69]

Buckle's book concludes with an examination of the history of Scotland, which, in his opinion, despite apparent contradictions, shows as does the history of Spain, that "nothing is casual or accidental; and the whole march of affairs is governed by general causes, which, owing to their largeness and remoteness, often escape attention, but which, when once recognized, are found to be marked by a simplicity and uniformity, which are the invariable characteristics of the highest truths that the mind of man has reached".[70] At first sight, Scotland seems to present a paradox: it has remained grossly superstitious despite a bold and inquisitive literature, and the people have succumbed to the clergy, despite constant opposition to their kings. Herein lies the peculiarity of the history of Scotland. "The same people have long been liberal in politics, and illiberal in religion." They have produced a brilliant and sceptical literature without letting it in any way weaken their superstition, or instil into them "wiser and larger maxims on religious matters".[71] The dilemma, however, is resolvable; and what looks like an exception to the rule that scepticism and enlightenment go hand in hand, turns out not to be so.

In Scotland every circumstance has been favourable to ecclesiastical power. Ignorance and danger, the parents of superstition, bred their infant, theology; and there, by the fifteenth century, the clergy had obtained more influence than in any other country in Europe, Spain alone excepted. Even the Reformation did nothing to reduce the Church's power. To overthrow Catholicism was not to destroy superstition. Against "that dark and ill-omened principle . . . there is only one weapon, and that weapon is knowledge. . . . When the Protestant Reformation was effected, the Scotch were excessively ignorant, and, therefore, in spite of the Reformation, they remained excessively superstitious." All that had happened was that the spirit had transmigrated, and, as so often happens, the reformers had contrived to "slay the carcass, and spare the life".[72] Because in Scotland Protestantism had been established by the nobles, who sought thereby to destroy the power of a hostile Church, it did not, as in England, involve a real change of heart among the people. The new Presbyter was but the old Priest writ large.

In the sixteenth and seventeenth centuries, the Scottish clergy, despite the fact that they were "a restless and unscrupulous body, greedy after power, and grossly intolerant of whatever opposed their own views", performed one important service for the nation. "At a most hazardous moment they kept alive the spirit of national liberty. . . . It was they who taught their countrymen to scrutinize, with a fearless eye, the policy of their rulers. It was they who pointed the finger of scorn at kings and nobles, and laid bare the hollowness of their pretensions. They ridiculed their claims, and jeered at their mysteries. . . . By discountenancing that pernicious and degrading respect which men are too apt to pay to those whom accident, and not merit, has raised above them, they facilitated the growth of a proud and sturdy independence, which was sure to do good service at a time of need."[73] The only reason why the clergy adopted this unfamiliar role was that the rulers of Scotland either neglected or persecuted Protestantism. The comforts of the Establishment were unknown north of the Tweed, so that Church and State, instead of slumbering together in peaceful oblivion, found themselves in constant and angry collision. In this struggle the clergy looked to the people for support, converted them to democratic beliefs and with their aid won the victory.

The liberal spirit with which the clergy opposed political tyranny, was not applied to Church government. The Kirk established an ecclesiastical despotism which must in comparison have made the rule of the Stuarts seem perfect freedom; and the people, accustomed even in temporal matters to follow their spiritual leaders, willingly accepted the yoke. In a short time the clergy were supreme. "The theories of a single profession outweighed those of all other professions; and not only war, but also trade, literature, science, and art, were held of no account unless they ministered to the general feeling. A state of society so narrow and so one-sided, has never been seen in any other country equally civilized."[74]

Clerical power in Scotland was wielded largely from the pulpit, where the only limit to the length of a sermon was the preacher's loquacity and physical stamina. Buckle regarded the craving of congregations for endless exhortation as evidence of their depraved dependence on the Church. "It is not surprising that the clergy, who, at no period, and in no nation, have been remarkable for their meekness, or for a want of confidence in themselves, should, under circumstances so eminently favourable to their pretensions, have been somewhat elated, and should have claimed an authority even greater than that which was conceded to them." So obsessed with power did they become that "they did not scruple to affirm that by their censures they could open and shut the kingdom of heaven".[75]

Part of the secret of clerical power in Scotland was the way in which people were intimidated by the Church's teaching on evil spirits, Hell, and the terrible nature of divine justice. Satan, so it was taught, was for ever at work in the world, personally appearing to further his stratagems, more often than not cunningly disguised. Such was his impudence that he "frequently appeared to the clergy, and tried to coax them over to his side. In that, of course, he failed; but, out of the ministry, few, indeed, could withstand him. . . . The clergy were constantly preaching about him, and preparing their audience for an interview with their great enemy. The consequence was, that the people became almost crazed with fear. Whenever the preacher mentioned Satan, the consternation was so great, that the church resounded with sighs and groans. The aspect of a Scottish congregation in those days, is, indeed, hard for us to conceive. Not unfrequently the people, benumbed and stupefied with awe, were rooted to their seats by the horrible fascination exercised over them, which compelled them to listen, though they are described as gasping for breath, and with their hair standing on end."[76]

To terror of the devil in this world, was added an infinitely greater terror of everlasting torments to come. "The clergy boasted, that it was their special mission to thunder out the wrath and curses of the Lord. In their eyes, the Deity was not a beneficent being, but a cruel and remorseless tyrant. They declared that all mankind, a very small portion only excepted, were doomed to eternal misery. And when they came to describe what that misery was, their dark imaginations revelled and gloated at the prospect. In the pictures which they drew, they reproduced and heightened the barbarous imagery of a barbarous age. They delighted in telling their hearers, that they would be roasted in great fires, and hung up by their tongues. They were to be lashed with scorpions, and see their companions writhing and howling around them. They were to be thrown into boiling oil and scalding lead. A river of fire and brimstone, broader than the earth, was prepared for them; in that, they were to be immersed; their bones, their lungs, and their liver, were to boil, but never be consumed. At the same time, worms were to prey upon them; and while these were gnawing at their bodies, they were to be surrounded by devils, mocking and making pastime of their pains."[77]

This terrible suffering "was the work of the God of the Scottish clergy. It was not only his work, it was his joy and his pride. For, according to them, hell was created before man came into the world; the Almighty, they did not scruple to say, having spent his previous leisure in preparing and completing this place of torture, so that, when the human race appeared, it might be ready for their reception. Ample, however, as the arrangements were, they were insufficient; and hell, not being big enough to contain the countless victims incessantly poured into it, had, in these latter days, been enlarged. There was now sufficient room. But in that vast expanse there was no void, for the whole of it reverberated with the shrieks and yells of undying agony. They rent the air with horrid sound, and, amid their pauses, other scenes occurred, if possible, still more excruciating. Loud reproaches filled the ear: children reproaching their parents, and servants reproaching their masters. Then indeed, terror was rife, and abounded on every side. For, while the child cursed his father, the father, consumed by remorse, felt his own guilt; and both children and fathers made hell echo with their piercing screams, writhing in convulsive agony at the torments which they suffered, and knowing that other torments more grievous still were reserved for them."[78]

Buckle obtained this picture of Scottish divinity from reading hundreds of sermons. In the passages quoted above he gives ten references to the works of the seventeenth- and eighteenth-century divines in which every detail he mentions may be found.* Reading these sermons he describes as "the most painful literary task I ever undertook, since, in addition to the narrowness and the dogmatism which even the best of such compositions contain, there is, in these productions, a hardness of heart, an austerity of temper, a want of sympathy with human happiness, and a hatred of human nature, such as have rarely been exhibited in any age."[79]

Not satisfied with terrifying their flock into abject submission, the Scottish clergy condemned every form of pleasure which might, even momentarily ease their anxiety. "It was improper to care for beauty of any kind," for to do so was to become entrapped in the snare of the evil one. Indeed "the world afforded nothing worth looking at save and except the Scottish Kirk, which was incomparably the most beautiful thing under heaven". It was even forbidden by the dour elders of the Church to make merry at marriages, a custom which Buckle suggests first arose from the notion "that a contract, so often productive of misery, might, at all events, begin with mirth".[80] The moroseness of the Scots is "the natural product of the gloomy and ascetic opinions inculcated by their religious teachers". So thoroughly did they do their work that "the people still bear the marks of the lash".[81]

The teaching of the clergy involved a calumny on the Almighty, for they represented "the Great Author of our being" as using "His omnipotence in so cruel a manner as to endow His creatures with tastes, instincts, and desires, which He not only forbids them to gratify, but which, if they do gratify, shall bring on themselves

* Buckle's History contains extensive footnotes throughout, and nearly every statement made in it is supported by reference to authority. These footnotes provide evidence of an immensely varied reading.

eternal punishment. . . . Many of the clergy persist in attacking the pleasures of the world, forgetting that, not only the world, but all which the world contains, is the work of the Almighty, and that the instincts and desires, which they stigmatize as unholy, are part of his gifts to man."[82] The history of the Kirk provides a corrective for Protestants who suppose, as they are only too inclined to do, "that there is something in their creed which protects them against those hurtful extravagances which have been, and, to a certain extent, still are, practised in the Catholic Church. Never was a greater mistake."[83]

When, in the eighteenth century, the ideas of the enlightenment reached Scotland, they affected the intellectual classes as powerfully as elsewhere, but not unfortunately with the same happy results: the dispersion of superstition and ignorance. The deductive habits of thought natural to theology, had become so deeply engrained that no one was able to escape them. Even Hutcheson* believed "that, by arguing from a certain number of original principles, he could construct the theory and explain the march of human affairs, with little or no aid from the experience of the past, or, indeed of the present".[84] Because "for one person who can think, there are at least a hundred persons who can observe", truths arrived at by the deductive method have never been well understood or widely diffused. Whereas, "we find historically that the establishment of the modern inductive philosophy, with its varied and attractive experiments, its material appliances, and its constant appeal to the senses, has been intimately connected with the awakening of the public mind, and coincides with that spirit of inquiry, and with that love of liberty, which have been constantly advancing since the sixteenth century". The spread of inductive science is nearly always easy and rapid because it "gives the first place to facts, is essentially popular, and has on its side those innumerable persons, who will not listen to the more refined and subtle teachings of deductive science".[85] Thus it was that the enlightened ideas of a number of great thinkers, because they were reached by the deductive method, appealed only to a small portion of society, and left the vast masses as ignorant as before; and thus it is that the country of "such fearless thinkers as George Buchanan, David Hume, and Adam Smith, is awed by a few noisy and ignorant preachers, to whom it allows a licence, and yields a submission, dis-

* Hutcheson, Francis (1694–1746), was a prominent Scottish philosopher, who first coined the phrase "the greatest happiness for the greatest number". His principal work was *Inquiry into the Origin of Our Ideas of Beauty and Virtue.*

graceful to the age, and incompatible with the commonest notions of liberty. A people, in many respects very advanced, and holding upon political subjects enlightened views, do, upon all religious subjects, display a littleness of mind, an illiberality of sentiment, a heat of temper, and a love of persecuting others, which shows that the Protestantism of which they boast has done them no good; that, in the most important matters, it has left them as narrow as it found them; and that it has been unable to free them from prejudices which make them the laughing-stock of Europe, and which have turned the very name of the Scottish Kirk into a bye-word and a reproach among educated men."[86]

Such is Buckle's solution of the dilemma posed by Scottish history, and such are the arguments he adduces to explain how despite, "a noble and enlightened literature", the people remained in darkness, "refusing to listen to those great masters of wisdom which their country possessed".[87] That the "marks of the lash" were visible at the time he wrote, Buckle firmly believed. "I speak," he says, "not on vague rumour, but from what I know as existing at the present time, and for the accuracy of which I vouch and hold myself responsible. I challenge anyone to contradict my assertion, when I say that, at this moment, nearly all over Scotland, the finger of scorn is pointed at every man, who, in the exercise of his sacred and inalienable right of free judgment, refuses to acquiesce in those religious notions, and to practise those religious customs, which time, indeed, has consecrated, but many of which are repulsive to the eye of reason, though to all of them, however irrational they may be, the people adhere with sullen and inflexible obstinacy. Knowing that these words will be widely read and circulated in Scotland, and averse as I naturally am to bring on myself the hostility of a nation, for whose many sterling and valuable qualities I entertain sincere respect, I do, nevertheless, deliberately affirm, that in no civilized country is toleration so little understood, and that in none is the spirit of bigotry and of persecution so extensively diffused."[88]

This outline of Buckle's philosophy of history has tried to set out his principal ideas, but has done no more than hint at the scope of his thought. To read so long and serious a work is, nowadays, a formidable undertaking, but the student of *The History of Civilization in England* is rewarded, not only by deeper insight into the nature of Victorian historical speculation, but by acquaintance with a dialectical skill and a sustained eloquence of which quotation can give but scant impression.

CHAPTER VI

BUCKLE AND HIS CRITICS

THE facts of history are sometimes alleged to speak for themselves; but Clio is a reticent muse however garrulous her votaries. Historians, who attempt to interpret as well as to narrate, often introduce more into the past than they deduce from it. Straus and Renan, Seeley and Gore, studied the same documents, but different presuppositions led them to opposite conclusions. "There is no single history . . . which does not derive its individual character from the particular standpoint of the author."[1] Macaulay and Buckle, living in the prosperous 'fifties, saw signs of progress wherever they looked; in the years of disillusionment following the Treaty of Versailles, historians found nothing but evidence of the decline of the West. Mitford saw in the Peloponnesian War, "as in a mirror, the progress and the struggles of his own age".[2] Grote's history of Greece was coloured by its author's views on the great Reform Bill, and Froude's account of the Reformation was inspired by the controversy which Tractarianism provoked. "What you call the spirit of past ages," says Goethe's Faust, "is but the spirit of this or that worthy gentleman in whose mind those ages are reflected."

Nobody appreciated more clearly than Buckle the way in which people's ideas and beliefs are influenced by prevailing climates of opinion. "A man," he maintains in his essay on Mill, "is nowise responsible for his creed. . . . Whether, for instance, he is a Mohammedan or a Christian, will usually resolve itself into a simple question of his geographical antecedents. He who is born in Constantinople will hold one set of opinions; he who is born in London will hold another set. . . ."[3] "The general condition of society in former days," he remarks elsewhere, "compelled even the ablest writers to believe the most childish absurdities."[4] He does not, however, appear to have recognized that his own *History of Civilization*, despite its originality, inevitably expressed many characteristic ideas of his time; and similarities between his opinions and those of such writers as Bagehot, Herbert Spencer, Lecky and Taine, must partly be attributed to the influence of a common ethos.

As many early Victorian radical traditions had their roots in pre-revolutionary France, Buckle resembles to some extent an eighteenth-century thinker. He had, for instance, little to add to the idea of progress propounded by the Enlightenment, believing like Condorcet in the perfectibility of Man and in the supremacy of Reason. In the eighteen-fifties this optimism was so widespread that Carlyle's scepticism about progress was generally attributed to dyspepsia. "Progress," wrote Herbert Spencer, "is not an accident but a necessity. . . . It is certain that man must become perfect." Tennyson might question the existence of God and of immortality, but never progress:

"Yet I doubt not through the ages one increasing purpose runs,
And the thoughts of men are widened with the process of the suns."

Writing in 1880, Leslie Stephen refers to Buckle as representative of "that curious tone of popular complacency which was prevalent some thirty years ago, when people held that the devil had finally committed suicide upon seeing the Great Exhibition, having had things pretty much his own way till Luther threw the inkstand in his face". . . .[5] In a skit, reminiscent of Newman's criticism of liberalism,* John Phillimore parodies Buckle's idea of Progress.

"This is the creed, let no man chuckle,
Of the great thinker, Henry Buckle:
I believe in fire and water
And in fate, dame Nature's daughter;
I believe in steam and rice,
Not in virtue or in vice,
I believe that all the gases
Have the power to raise the masses. . . ."[6]

Buckle's political views were formed by reading Adam Smith, and as his early manhood coincided with the rise and triumph of the Anti-Corn-Law League, he also learned much from the events of his own time. While still a student he became familiar with the theory that protection is the great obstacle to the accumulation and diffusion

* "Virtue is the child of knowledge, and vice of ignorance. Therefore, e.g. education, periodical literature, railroad travelling, ventilation, drainage, and the arts of life, when fully carried out, serve to make a population moral and happy." Newman. *Apologia Pro Vita Sua.* Appendix on Liberalism.

of wealth, and that government is at best a necessary evil. Thereafter he came to regard history "as a sort of vast Anti-Corn-Law agitation, with the substitution of knowledge for cheap bread, of ecclesiastical corporations for the Landlord-ring by which protection was maintained, and of theological dogmas for the inferior article forced by them on the public. Or again we may say that he looked on theology as the pestilent system of governmental interference with industry and trade, raised to a transcendental value and personified in a false representation of the Deity".[7]

Just as Buckle's attitude to progress and politics owed much to the eighteenth century, so his confidence in Man's rationality, power, and essential goodness, derived from Locke, Helvétius, Bentham and Mill. "The powers of man," he writes, "so far as experience and analogy can guide us, are unlimited; nor are we possessed of any evidence which authorizes us to assign even an imaginary boundary at which the human intellect will, of necessity, be brought to a stand."[8] Human reason he describes in another passage, as "that divine spark which even the most corrupt society is unable to extinguish".[9] This confidence in Man's rationality gave Buckle an exalted opinion of human virtue. "An enlarged experience," he says, "proves that Mankind is not so radically bad as we from our infancy are taught to believe. . . . It is the solitary misanthrope, brooding over his fancied wrongs, who is most prone to depreciate the good qualities of our nature, and exaggerate its bad ones. Or else it is some foolish and ignorant monk, who, dreaming away his existence in an idle solitude, flatters his own vanity by denouncing the vices of others; and thus declaiming against the enjoyments of life, revenges himself on that society from which by his own superstition he is excluded. These are the sort of men who insist most strongly on the corruption of our nature, and on the degeneracy into which we have fallen."[10]

Such faith in man's fundamental rationality is difficult to sustain when confronted with the stubborn facts of history. Mark Pattison, who reviewed Buckle's first volume, suggests that its author made insufficient allowance for "the sleeping volcano of passion", which at any moment might erupt "with irresistible violence".[11] More recently, Pareto, reinforced by a greater knowledge of psychology, has criticized Buckle on the ground that his reasoning "is sound provided one accepts that all human conduct is logical. . . . But that proposition is false. . . . Many very important actions are non-logical."[12]

Macaulay has been called "the last of the Augustans", who always remained the man of 1832. In the same way Buckle might be described as the last of the eighteenth-century radicals, who remained the man of 1846. They have much in common. Both pursued truth in the same spirit of boisterous triumph, both had an amazing power of assimilating knowledge, both were happiest in the seclusion of their own libraries. Moreover, there is a close analogy in the quality of their work. "Both," says Leslie Stephen, "have a superlative self-confidence, combined with an animated glow of enthusiasm in proclaiming the future destinies of their party; both have a luminous style which never gives the reader the trouble of a second glance, a power of marshalling facts and arguments so as to give a satisfactory fulness and symmetry to their work.... Both, again, represent that sort of one-sided common sense which is alternately irritating and satisfactory.... Both of them looked forwards to the same millennium when cultivation (as Macaulay puts it) is to reach the summit of Helvellyn, and though Buckle called himself a Radical rather than a Whig, their political philosophy is really an idealization of the true Whig principles, with the current traditional estimate of the glorious Revolution, the freedom of the press, trial by jury, and the other palladia of our liberties. He is at bottom a thorough John Bull, though draped in philosophic garments. If, in both cases, we occasionally resent the narrowness, the excessive exaltation of the more vulgar side of progress, we are tempted in both cases to condone the offence in consideration of the vast amount of solid common sense, and, what is perhaps better, of really generous zeal for great causes, contempt for the petty foppery of effeminate prejudices, and hearty appreciation of their predecessors in the same cause."[13]

Although Buckle was indebted to previous thinkers for most of his ideas, his synthesis of history as a whole was nevertheless original. Many of his critics failed to appreciate this, although Sidgwick regarded the charge of plagiarism as unjust. "Abuse him as you like," he writes to a friend, "he is the first Englishman who has attempted to write scientific history, and I for one paid a tribute to that attempt in the intense interest with which I read it."[14] A few examples will suffice to show how even Buckle's most controversial theories were derived consciously or unconsciously from previous thinkers. Dean Stanley attributes the very idea of a philosophy of history to the book of Daniel. Mill saw that statistics might usefully be applied to a study of Civilization, Coleridge regarded history as the education of the mind of Mankind, and Hazlitt explained the difference between northern and southern manners in terms of climate.

The thinkers to whom Buckle owed the greatest debt were Voltaire, Montesquieu, Adam Smith, Kant, Quételet* and Comte; although of course, much that he borrowed from them he could have found elsewhere. From Voltaire, he learned that history is not confined merely to politics and biography. From Montesquieu he learned how the forces of nature affect the life of man.[15] Adam Smith helped him to appreciate the importance of Laisser-Faire, while Kant showed him that in studying human behaviour free will can be left out of account if a sufficiently extensive view is taken, for although the conduct of men individually may be unpredictable, their behaviour in the mass conforms to certain intelligible laws.

Buckle's debt to Comte is not so easy to estimate and its extent has been the subject of dispute. Some writers have asserted that he owed everything to him. Littré says: "*il n'aurait jamais écrit un tel livre, s'il n'y avait pas eu avant lui le livre de M. Comte*".[16] Bernheim deplores the fact that Comte's work became known in Germany through repeated translations of the *History of Civilization*.[17] Hutchison Stirling refers to Buckle as a disciple of Comte who disowned his master;[18] but since he accuses him elsewhere of borrowing his ideas from Hume's Essays, and since he proclaims that "what Mr. Buckle wanted to teach in 1857 was just 105 years old", it becomes evident that Stirling's savage hostility to Positivism deprived him of consistency.[19] More friendly critics have denied, both directly and by implication, that Buckle was deeply indebted to Comte. Lecky, for example, maintained that he was primarily indebted to Montesquieu, and M. Bouillier says that he applied the philosophy of Mill to history.[20] Indeed it is from Mill himself that we have the most authoritative denial that Buckle was a disciple of Comte. ". . . It may be affirmed without presumption," he writes, "that they neither saw the same truths, nor fell into the same errors, nor defended their opinions, either true or erroneous, by the same arguments. Indeed, it is one of the surprising things in the case of Mr. Buckle . . . that being a man of kindred genius, of the same wide range of knowledge, and devoting himself to speculations of the same kind, he profited so little by M. Comte."[21]

* Many of Buckle's critics and some of the writers to whom he was indebted are not well known today. In Appendix III the reader will find short notes on some of the less familiar authors mentioned in this Chapter.

It is hardly surprising that similarities should be noticed in the works of the two writers. They wrote on the same subject and were both indebted to the same predecessors. But apart from their belief that Mankind is subject to Law, an idea which was a commonplace of eighteenth-century thought, their method and conclusions are often entirely different. Buckle regarded Comte's theory of Government as "so monstrously and obviously impracticable, that if it were translated into English the plain men of our Island would lift their eyes in astonishment, and would most likely suggest that the author should for his own sake be immediately confined".[22] There is some resemblance between Comte's law of the Three States and Buckle's account of Man's progress from superstition to science, but the idea of development through such a series of stages may equally be seen in Saint-Simon, Turgot and Vico. To refute the shallow judgement that Buckle was "the English Comte" only becomes necessary because it has been so repeatedly affirmed.

From the day of its publication the *History of Civilization* became the subject of violent discussion and criticism. "*Son livre*," says Etienne, "*fût une espèce de conquête soudaine et violente de l'attention publique, soudaine par cette rare surprise d'un homme jeune et obscur qui, du jour au lendemain, se plaçait au nombre des esprits les plus puissants des trois royaumes, violente grâce au ton provoquant d'un grand nombre de ses pages. . . . Son succès fût surtout un succès de discussion. L'Angleterre, l'Ecosse, l'Irlande, argumentèrent contre Buckle dans tous les organes de la publicité. On eut dit que le temps des Luther et des Knox était revenu: pas un journal, pas un recueil qui ne mit en avant trois ou quatre thèses contre le nouveau docteur en positivisme.*"[23]

The hostility Buckle provoked was admittedly of his own making, for his criticism was always outspoken and many reviewers had injuries to avenge. Oxford and Cambridge, at the time when he wrote, were still predominantly clerical, and thus his contempt for their scholarship and his attacks on many of their most cherished dogmas, scarcely inclined them to charity. Both the Church and the Universities resented what they regarded as outrageous slanders poured upon them by a mere dilettante, who believed he could educate himself, and who actually dared to challenge their monopoly of wisdom and learning. But even the flood of academic censure to which Buckle was subjected, was thought by some to be inadequate. M. Gratry, a priest and philosopher, regarded it as "*vraiment honteux pour l'Angleterre d'être, en effet, le pays du monde ou l'on accueille le mieux cette espèce d'écrivains*".[24] The *History of Civilization* contains repeated attacks on the methods usually employed by historians, and such criticism, although well merited, was not invariably well received. If Buckle's challenging generalizations were a step in the right direction, then those who believed that a few random reflections constituted philosophic history were sadly deluded. If he was right, they were wrong. Moreover, as Mill has pointed out, "The English invariably mistrust the most evident truths if he who propounds them is suspected of having general ideas". Buckle was often angrily opposed by writers whose self-esteem he had injured and whose "endowed opinions" he had called in question.

Criticism of him is as remarkable for its irrelevance and inaccuracy as for its extent. Even Oettingen, normally a sensible thinker, used a preposterous argument to demolish Buckle's statistical thesis. "In round numbers," says the History, "for every twenty girls, there are twenty-one boys born." This statement claims only to be approximate. It is introduced to illustrate the way that statistics can ascertain information about the masses which observation of individuals cannot supply. Even if these rough figures could be shown to be wrong, the general contention would still stand. Yet Oettingen believes he has made a telling point when he says that if still-born children are included in the estimate, the proportion should be expressed as twenty-two and twenty two-hundredths of a boy.[25] Similarly Maine wins an easy victory by misrepresenting what Buckle said and then proving him wrong. He accuses Buckle of having "derived all the distinctive institutions of India and the peculiarities of its people from their consumption of rice". This, he says, "ought to be a caution against overbold generalization", particularly as rice was no longer the staple food of the people of India.[26] In fact Buckle was almost certainly right about the consumption of rice, and Maine wrong. Moreover Buckle asserts in his book that in southern India rice was being replaced by ragi. But even if he were entirely mistaken, it would not follow, as Maine suggests, that bold generalization is in itself undesirable, nor would it make any difference to the proposition that the food of India was cheap and that cheap food encourages large populations. Nor did Buckle ever suggest for a moment that the character of Indians was exclusively formed by their eating rice.

If some of Buckle's critics have been satisfied merely to misrepresent him, others have been so ignorant of his writing that they have had to content themselves with repeating what they have read elsewhere. Only too often it is impossible to reconcile what detractors have found objectionable in the *History of Civilization* with what its author wrote. J. M. Robertson, the author of *Buckle and his Critics*, says: "Nothing indeed has struck me so much in the investigation of the criticism passed on Buckle as the sheer ignorance of his book on the part of most of his assailants."[27] "*Entre autre résultats,*" declares Etienne, "*ce n'était pas le moins remarquable, a nôtre avis, que l'on put savoir à quoi s'en tenir sur les opinions de l'auteur sans connaître l'auteur lui-même.*"[28]

Some of the most confident judgements on the value of Buckle's book have been passed by people who never read it from cover to cover. Macaulay notes in his diary that it was the work of "a man of talent and of a good deal of reading, but paradoxical and incoherent". From the same source we learn that he finished the book in a day, "skipping, of course".[29] Carlyle, who accused Buckle of shallow dogmatism, inordinate conceit, and of forcing the facts to fit his theory, when asked if he had read the book, replied that he had not, but that he had read extracts from it in the papers.[30] Unfortunately few critics are so candid, although their writings frequently betray that they have favoured similar methods and that their contempt is not altogether bred of familiarity with the work they condemn.

It is only fair to Macaulay and Carlyle to point out that their opinions were privately expressed, and that had they reviewed the History, they would presumably have taken more trouble to discover what it contained. There have been writers, however, who have publicly condemned Buckle, after the most casual perusal of his History, not merely in ephemeral journals but in reputedly learned books. So anxious have such critics been to combat his dangerous doctrines that they have instantly joined battle, generally on treacherous ground, without waiting to discover where their adversary was vulnerable; and so frequent have been their despatches announcing successes, that they have contrived to be proclaimed the victors. Peschel, a ponderous German scholar, provides a good example of this strategy. "Let us be warned," he says, "by the errors of Buckle, who . . . deceived himself and a willingly deluded multitude into a belief that it is possible to explain the course of the history of the most highly civilized nations by the chemical constituents of their food."[31] As the major portion of the *History of Civilization* is devoted to establishing the thesis that in Europe intellectual advances have been the dominant factor in progress, this ignorant misrepresentation is unlikely to carry weight; except with those, who like Peschel, have found time only to dip into Buckle's book. Although Peschel nowhere admits as candidly as Macaulay that he read Buckle "skipping, of course", he nevertheless makes a mistake which betrays how slight was his acquaintance with the work he criticized. According to Buckle, says Peschel, sailors, who are constantly exposed to the caprice of nature, should be peculiarly superstitious. "Yet no one has ever stated that this is the case."[32] "The credulity of sailors," says Buckle in the work under review, "is notorious, and every literature contains evidence of the multiplicity of their superstitions, and of the tenacity with which they cling to them."[33]

Peschel's method was not exceptional. Max Nordau summarizes Buckle's views by saying that he assumed "that the one determining factor in the fate of nations is climate and the condition of the soil".[34] As eighteen out of the twenty Chapters of the History are concerned primarily with intellectual development, it seems possible that Herr Nordau's study of Buckle's book was confined to its first two Chapters. Almost as common among critics as ignorance and misrepresentation is the resort to insult. "I think," says Ruskin, "the impudence of the modern cockney mind is more shown in its attempt to write history than in anything else: Mr. Buckle's *History of Civilization*! Why a cock sparrow bred in Tower Ditch might as well think it could write the History of the Tower. . . . History of Civilization! The toil and martyrdom of all the great souls that God has made since the beginning of His creation; and this winter-cricket with only a chirp between his creaking legs at the fireside—he will write the history of the heaven and all its eagles!"[35] Gladstone's remarks on Buckle show the same tendency to substitute rhetoric for argument. "Quote if you choose," he says, referring to an appeal to Buckle on the condition of the clergy in the seventeenth century, "publicans on liquor laws, or slave-drivers on the capacities of blacks; cite Martial as a witness to purity, or Bacchus to sobriety; put Danton to conduct a bloodless revolution, or swear in the Gracchi as special constables; but do not set up Mr. Buckle as an arbiter of judicial measure or precision, nor let the fame of anything that is called a religion or a clergy depend upon his nod."[36] The vehemence of such language indicates the extent to which Buckle's doctrines provoked orthodox opinion.

A criticism often made of the *History of Civilization*, not without justice, is that it contains a number of unreconciled contradictions, and that its author is a confused thinker.[37] Buckle failed to appreciate, says Mr. Noel Annan, "that the historical method which he applied in his History should have led him to question his assumption that a personal God existed and the soul was immortal".[38] Dühring, who otherwise praised the work highly, objected to the rags of theology which he alleged it retained, and which he regarded as incompatible with the main thesis of the book.[39] But perhaps the most serious inconsistency of which Buckle has been accused relates to his view of the part played by individuals in history. "What Buckle himself says of the achievements of Richelieu, Adam Smith, Voltaire, and others, and of the effects of the protective spirit in France and England, and of religious intolerance in Spain and Scotland, is irreconcilable with his doctrines that great men, government, and religion have had almost no influence on Civilization."[40] The great discoveries, which Buckle regarded as the mainspring of progress, were necessarily the work of individuals, and had Newton died at the age of twenty the contribution he in fact made to science might have been long delayed. To escape this conclusion, Buckle refers to the "spirit of the age"; yet although prevailing beliefs may succeed in crushing new ideas, it is difficult to see how they can initiate them. Thought advances because individuals of genius transcend the opinions of their time: indeed if they did not, progress would be inconceivable. There is, in fact, a vicious circularity about Buckle's argument which he never recognized, and for which he has rightly been censured.

Mark Pattison was the first to accuse Buckle of failing to practise what he preached. "Will it be believed," he says, "that after laying down, at the outset, that individual experiments can effect nothing, and that certain consequences can only be traced by comprehensive observation of society in the aggregate; that after pouring unmeasured contempt on previous historians for neglecting this principle, and on the metaphysicians for their narrow method of studying the human mind in single specimens, and that after insisting that we must apply to the history of man those methods of investigation which have been found successful in other branches of knowledge, Mr. Buckle employs the remainder of his volume in exemplifying the very method of writing history which he had condemned? We have in several chapters a summary of the progress of society in France; a masterly sketch, of which it is not too much to say, that in breadth and comprehensiveness of view, no English writer on French History has yet equalled it. . . . If the details are not new—and they could not be—the whole effect is new. . . . But all this is effected without the slightest reference to the principles of historical science avowed in the opening.

"Instead of general averages, we have the opinions of eminent individuals. Instead of the fatality of social law, we have the force exerted on national life by the single will of a Louis XIV. . . . We find his history practical, entertaining, instructive, in a degree beyond that of most writers who have gone over the same ground; but by his own definition of history, it is excluded from any claim to that title. It bears the same relation to the science of history, which a narrative of the commercial fortunes of the great house of Hope, or the successes and reverses of the family of Rothschild, would bear to the science of Political Economy."[41]

In a letter to Capel, Buckle deals with this criticism. "I only ascribe," he writes of Mark Pattison's objection, "a transient influence to Louis XIV, since his work was undone by the reaction of the eighteenth century. So that my general proposition still holds good—viz., that in the *long run* (or on the general average of affairs) individuals count for nothing. Besides this, I distinctly state, in Chapter XI, that the way was *prepared* by the Protective Spirit for Louis XIV; so that even his transient influence was partly due to the action of those general causes which governed the march of the French mind."[42] Although these considerations to some extent vindicate his position, the fact that such explanation was necessary suggests that he was guilty of confusion of thought and language. It is not easy to reconcile Buckle's reference to "the way in which great thinkers control the affairs of men, and by their discoveries regulate the march of Nations",[43] with his assertion that "to a philosophic mind the actions of an individual count for little; to a practical mind they are everything. Whoever is accustomed to generalize, smiles within himself when he hears that Luther brought about the Reformation; that Bacon overthrew the ancient philosophy; that William III saved our liberties; that Romilly humanized our penal code; that Clarkson and Wilberforce destroyed slavery; and that Grey and Brougham gave us Reform. He smiles at such assertions, because he knows full well that such men, useful as they were, are only to be regarded as tools by which that work was done which the force and accumulation of preceding circumstances had determined should be done. . . . Not only are individuals, in the great average of affairs, inoperative for good; they are also, happily for mankind, inoperative for evil. Nero and Domitian caused enormous mischief, but every trace of it has now disappeared. The occurrences which contemporaries think to be of the greatest importance, and which in point of fact for a short time are so, invariably turn out in the long run to be the least important of all. They are like meteors which dazzle the vulgar by their brilliancy, and then pass away, leaving no mark behind."[44]

Ignorant as was Carlyle's comment on Buckle, it contained a germ of truth. A similar criticism has been made more learnedly by Laurent in his book on the philosophy of history. ". . . *L'historien anglais a la prétention d'étudier les faits, et sa science est, en éffet, très étendue. Mais n'aurait-il pas étudié les faits avec l'idée préconçue d'y trouver ce qu'il cherche?*"[45] In the nature of things no historian can avoid imposing *a priori* upon the past certain ideas which his study of history may verify but which it has not in the first place suggested. His choice and arrangement of facts must be made in the light of a preconceived plan and the conclusions he arrives at will depend upon the presuppositions with which he starts. But although historical thought can never be completely objective, those historians who are aware of their assumptions, and therefore better able to discount them, are the most likely to escape the ill effects of the subjectivity inherent in their method. Sydney Parkinson, who accompanied Cook on his first voyage of discovery, provides an excellent illustration of the way in which evidence, far from dictating conclusions, is often made to support preconceptions. Parkinson subscribed to the eighteenth-century belief that Man was naturally good, and that savages, who had not been corrupted by so-called civilized institutions, were supremely happy and virtuous. When he discovered that Tahitian houses had no locks on their doors it appeared to him to provide convincing proof that "locks, bolts and bars are peculiar to civilized countries, where their moral theory is the best and their moral practices too generally of the worst". The facts seemed to square with the theory, but unfortunately the explorers soon found that the natives were "prodigious expert thieves", Cook's quadrant was stolen, and nothing was safe unless constantly guarded. The absence of fastenings was due to defective carpentry.

It is inevitable that history should be written with preconceptions. "The real distinction," says Bradley, "is between the writer who has his prejudications without knowing what they are, and . . . the writer who consciously orders and creates from the known foundation of that which for him is the truth."[46] Those who are unaware of the assumptions they make, believe they are deriving valuable information from history; whereas, in fact, they are only abstracting from the past, events, which by the very principle of their selection, beg the question."

Froude in his lecture on Buckle points out how History may be made to prove anything by judicious selection of evidence. "It often seems to me," he says, "as if History was like a child's box of letters, with which we can spell any word we please. We have only to pick out such letters as we want, arrange them as we like, and say nothing about those which do not suit our purpose. . . . You may prove from History that the world is governed in detail by a special providence; you may prove that there is no sign of any moral agent in the Universe, except man; you may believe, if you like it, in the old theory of the wisdom of antiquity. . . . In all, or any of these views, History will stand your friend, History, in its passive irony, will make no objection!"[47] *The Edinburgh Review*, in its strictures on Buckle's second volume, accuses him, as does Froude, of selecting his facts to conform to his theory. "There is nothing so absurd or so untrue that some evidence may not be collected in support of it from the dusty shelves of huge libraries. . . . He (Buckle) repeats his own paradoxes till he believes them to be truths; and although he is always lauding the blessings of scepticism, there is one kind of scepticism which he is seldom disposed to practise—that, namely, which consists in a prudent distrust of his own infallibility."[48]

The *History of Civilization* is greatly affected by its author's preconceptions. Like Macaulay, Buckle tended to make up his mind too early and too decisively. He was, as Dean Milman observed, "a bit of a bigot", who "hated intolerance so much as to be blind, or nearly blind to religion".[49] Lecky, who greatly admired him, none the less thought him deficient in sympathy and understanding. "Buckle," he says, "was almost colour blind to the devotional and reverential aspect of things and he had little more power than Whately of projecting himself into the beliefs, ideals, and modes of thought of other men and ages."[50] His insistence on contrasting past and present to the detriment of the former, involved him in anachronism; and his conception of the Middle Ages, incidentally the exact opposite to Comte's, was unhistorical, because it involved judging the past in the light of nineteenth-century progress. Such comparisons enabled him to emphasize the uniformity of history but unfortunately only by ignoring its diversity. He never saw, for example, that the policy of protection which he so vigorously resented, had once served a useful purpose. If frequently it led to arbitrary tyranny, at other times it protected the weak.[51]

In addition to general attacks on Buckle's method, nearly every individual idea he put forward has been separately criticized and none more frequently than his doctrine of statistics; particularly as its fatalism seemed to imply that people could no longer be held morally responsible for their actions. So dangerous did the theory appear that it was even condemned from the pulpit.[52] Of all Buckle's ideas, this was the most characteristically Victorian,* although the particular way in which he applied it was suggested to him by the writings of Quételet, a Belgian. The thesis that statistics reveal a uniformity in human affairs looked at in the mass which cannot be observed in particular instances; and its corollary: that the historian should pay more attention to society as a whole than to the lives of great individuals, provided a valuable, if exaggerated corrective to the idea that history should be mainly biographical. Buckle's faith in statistics was so great that he was not content to rest his case there; he went on to make such extravagant claims that he discredited what was sound in his argument. In his anxiety to establish that history was a science in the same sense as was physics, he seized upon statistics, claiming that its laws were similar to those which governed the movement of the planets and that they should be studied by the same method. Here, at last, was an empirical foundation for a Science of Human Nature.

The essence of explanation is the interpretation of ideas and events in terms of the dominant beliefs of the time. In the Middle Ages thought was conditioned by theology, and in the eighteenth century by mechanics. The very language employed by historians often reveals the prevailing intellectual fashion. It is not difficult to trace the source of such phrases as: "the balance of power", or "the evolution of the State". The triumph of Natural Science in the seventeenth century led to a complete reorientation of thought. Philosophy became mechanistic rather than metaphysical. It became increasingly obsessed with the relations between cause and effect, mind and body, appearance and reality, rationalism and empiricism. Locke, Hume and Spinoza were among the first thinkers to try to apply the principles of Science to the understanding of human nature. It was inevitable

* G. M. Young, in his *Portrait of an Age*, says that the Victorian passion for statistics was encouraged by the development of Insurance. The statistical department of the Board of Trade was founded in 1832, and that of the Registrar-General in 1838. The foundation of the Royal Statistical Society in 1833, and the Royal Commissions appointed in the 'forties, all helped to foster confidence in the method.

that methods which had proved triumphantly successful in explaining the physical world should appeal to philosophers and historians, and that they should attempt, like Buckle, to discover laws determining the behaviour of society.

Positivists are right in regarding scientific method as one of the most powerful weapons in man's intellectual armoury, but what they frequently fail to realize is that physics is not the only pattern of scientific thinking, and that scientific thinking is not the only way to truth. History, if it is to be scientific as physics is scientific, ought to be disciplined, objective, and critical. But there the similarity ends. Every sphere of knowledge has to develop its own method, and, however much it may borrow from other branches of learning, retain its individuality and autonomy. Since biology provides a closer analogy to historical processes than does physics, it was Buckle's misfortune to be brought up on Newton and to write before Darwin. Mechanical laws cannot be made to fit human behaviour because man as an evolving organism is always altering the conditions to which such laws are alleged to apply. Moreover the implied assumption that man is only an elaborate machine, involves a denial of the existence of Free Will.

Buckle's confusion of thought arises partly from confusion of language. He speaks of the Laws of Statistics as if they had to be obeyed, and he is, in Acton's words, "led into the mistake of concluding that fixed Law means a necessity inherent in the essence of the thing, and that therefore whatever has an average is necessary, and could not be otherwise. . . . Alas, then, if one person in our village is to commit suicide, if nobody else will, I must! And why? Simply because one person has committed suicide there yearly for several years past. Nothing can withstand the simple rules of Arithmetic."[53] Much the same point was made by the Edinburgh Reviewer when he wrote: "To speak of the movement of the planets as *governed* by the law of gravitation is, in strictness, to put the effect for the cause. By moving in a certain manner the heavenly bodies produce uniform results; but it is a strange inversion of things to say that the uniform results regulate the motions. It is like saying that the pattern weaves the cloth, or that the nautical almanack regulates the tides. Laws, in this sense, exist only in and for the minds which conceive them. . . . So long as the word 'Law' is not supposed to imply compulsion, or the exercise of any definite influence upon human conduct, there may be no other objection to its use than that it is an inappropriate metaphor. But it is, in fact, impossible to abuse language with impunity."[54]

In attempting to use statistics to prove that man's actions are determined and that Free Will is illusory, Buckle went further than he needed to substantiate his historical theory and thereby unnecessarily provoked hostility. It would have been sufficient for his purpose merely to admit a causal connexion between men's actions and their antecedents; the question of Free Will and of moral responsibility need never have been raised. Although he overstrained statistics in his attempt to prove the regularity of human affairs, he did so in an age when many regarded man's behaviour as purely fortuitous. Thus his faith in a more exalted form of history, whose function should be to explain rather than to narrate, was of particular value at the time of his book's publication. By insisting on the importance of studying mass behaviour, he no doubt underestimated the significance of individuals and of accidents. This appeared to Grote, Lecky and Froude to be his "master error";* but if it was a fault, it was not without compensation, for few writers have so boldly extended the territories to which history lays claim.

Buckle's historical ideas have not only been attacked because they involve an invalid analogy with science, but on the more general ground that philosophies of history are illusory. "I don't believe in the philosophy of history," Bishop Stubbs proclaimed, "so I don't believe in Buckle." Apparently, for much the same reason, Darwin, greatly as he admired the literary style of the *History of Civilization*, doubted whether its generalizations were worth anything. The empirical English rightly suspect the "high *a priori* method", particularly when applied to historical interpretation; but, nevertheless, to deny the possibility of a philosophy of history is to beg the question at issue: it is to assume a form of historical nihilism in order to establish that history is meaningless. Fisher's famous introduction to his *History of Europe*, in which he proudly disclaims his ability to make any sense of the past, is characteristic of such confused thinking. He begins by saying that the pattern of the past has eluded him and in the next

* "Individuals," says Lecky, "and even accidents have had a great modifying and deflecting influence in history, and sometimes the part they have played can scarcely be overestimated. If a stray dart had struck down Mohammed in one of the early skirmishes of his career, there is no reason to believe that the world would have seen a great military and monotheistic religion arise in Arabia, powerful enough to sweep over a large part of three continents, and to mould during many centuries the lives and characters of about a fifth part of the human race." Lecky, *Historical and Political Essays*, 1908, p. 101.

breath proclaims that "the fact of progress is written plain and large on the page of history. . . ." It would be absurd to say that, as Napoleon conquered only half Europe, he was a less successful general than Paoli, who temporarily made himself master of Corsica. Yet many specialist historians seem to believe that the incontrovertible results that their limited studies permit are more fruitful than the glimpses of great truths which more extended surveys yield.

After Buckle's theory of statistics, his belief that climatic conditions affect national character has been most frequently challenged. The relation he traces between earthquakes and superstition, particularly with reference to Spain, aroused formidable controversy. The Edinburgh Reviewer even denied that any earthquake had occurred in the Spanish peninsula, apart from the famous Lisbon disaster. This ridiculous statement Buckle refuted in a footnote to his second volume. "I have certainly no right," he says, "to expect that a reviewer, composing a popular article for an immediate purpose, and knowing that when his article is read, it will be thrown aside and forgotten, should, under such unfavourable circumstances, be at the pains of mastering all the details of his subject. To look for this would be the height of injustice. He has no interest in being accurate; his name being concealed, his reputation, if he has any, is not at stake; and the errors into which he falls ought to be regarded with leniency, inasmuch as their vehicle being an ephemeral publication, they are not likely to be remembered, and they are therefore not likely to work much mischief.

"These considerations have always prevented me from offering any reply to anonymous criticisms. But the passage in *The Edinburgh Review* . . . displays such marvellous ignorance, that I wish to rescue it from oblivion, and to put it on record as a literary curiosity. . . . No reasonable person can possibly suppose that, after years of arduous and uninterrupted study, I should have committed those childish blunders with which my opponents unscrupulously taunt me. . . .

"The simple fact is, that in Spain there have been more earthquakes than in all other parts of Europe put together, Italy excepted. If the destruction of property and of life produced by this one cause were summed up, the results would be appalling. When we moreover add those alarming shocks, which, though less destructive, are far more frequent, and of which not scores, nor hundreds, but thousands have occurred, and which by increasing the total amount of fear, have to an incalculable extent promoted the growth of superstition, it is evident that such phenomena must have played an important part in forming the national character of the Spaniards. Whoever will take the trouble of consulting the following passages will find decisive proofs of the frightful ravages committed by earthquakes in Spain alone; Portugal being excluded. They all refer to a period of less than two hundred years; the first being in 1639, and the last in 1829. *Lettres de Madame de Villars, Ambassadrice en Espagne*, Amsterdam, 1759, p. 205. *Laborde's Spain*, London, 1809, vol. i. p. 169. *Dunlop's Memoirs of Spain*, Edinburgh, 1834, vol. ii. pp. 226, 227. *Boisel, Journal du Voyage d'Espagne*, Paris, 1669, 4 to, p. 243. *Mallet's Earthquake Catalogue of the British Association*, London, 1858; Report for 1853, p. 146; for 1854, pp. 26, 27, 54, 55, 57, 58, 65, 110, 140, 173, 196, 202. *Swinburne's Travels through Spain*, London, 1787, vol. i. p. 166. *Ford's Spain*, London, 1847, p. 178. *Bacon's Six Years in Biscay*, London, 1838, p. 32, compared with *Inglis' Spain*, London, 1831, vol. i. p. 393, vol. ii. p. 289–291.

"These authorities narrate the ravages committed during a hundred and ninety years. From their account it is manifest, that in Spain hardly a generation passed by without castles, villages, and towns being destroyed, and men, women, or children killed by earthquakes. But according to our anonymous instructor, it is doubtful if there ever was an earthquake in Spain; for he says of the whole Peninsula, including Portugal, 'the only earthquake known to have occurred there was that of Lisbon'."[55]

Not all Buckle's critics were so ill-informed. Leslie Stephen pertinently points out that, "Free thinking flourishes where there was once abject superstition, and therefore the country cannot by itself explain the superstition."[56] Froude, in his lecture on Buckle, raises an equally reasonable objection. "When we are told," he says, "that the Spaniards are superstitious, because Spain is a country of earthquakes, we remember Japan, the spot in all the world where earthquakes are most frequent,* and where at the same time there is the most serene disbelief in any supernatural agency whatsoever."[57] Another difficulty is that Peru, where earthquakes occur as often as anywhere else in the world, has produced no imaginative literature or painting. On the other hand, the Netherlands, where there is no recorded instance of the slightest damage being caused by tremors, have produced

* J. M. Robertson says that Froude errs in describing the Japanese as unsuperstitious, and he argues, moreover, that in so far as they are not as superstitious as Spaniards, it is because they build houses which survive moderate tremors, and which, if they collapse, fall almost as harmlessly as a tent. Robertson, p. 140.

flourishing schools of Art.[58] It might, of course, be argued that the placid climate of the Low Countries engendered an equally placid tradition of painting, whereas the wildly imaginative pictures of El Greco, produced as if by flashes of lightning, reflect the violent moods of nature. But clearly Buckle's theory has not, as he believed, the finality of Law. It provides, at best, a suggestive and illuminating half-truth.

Buckle's theory that there is no progress in moral perception, and that improvements in morality derive from the growth and diffusion of knowledge, was widely criticized. It has been pointed out that, if certain fundamental moral principles have remained essentially unchanged for a thousand years, so have the basic principles of logic, and this being so, it is inconsistent to regard the intellect as progressive and the moral faculty as stationary.[59] Another objection raised is that as moral development occurs in individual instances, it is unreasonable to suppose that Mankind collectively is incapable of improvement. Morals, like organisms, develop. "The first principles may indeed always remain the same, but the application, the propagation, the deepening and specializing of them, may be a matter of far-reaching evolution."[60]

The weightiest criticism of Buckle's theory of the static nature of the moral disposition is made by Frauenstädt in his review of Ruge's translation into German of the *History of Civilization*. On the whole, Frauenstädt regarded the book favourably. He described it as a gigantic work testifying "to immense learning and comprehensive thought". Buckle, he says, "may even boast of having begun a new era in the writing of History". But his belief that morals remain stationary appeared to Frauenstädt to contradict the most evident historical facts. In all periods certain principles have been accepted and have always been the same: to sacrifice our selfish interest for the common good, to curb our passions, to see justice done. But although these general propositions have been agreed upon in all ages, the way in which these universal principles have been interpreted has changed. "Although we still hold fast to the principle, preached millenniums ago, of the love of our neighbour, we understand the love of our neighbour quite differently from the way in which it was understood in antiquity and the middle ages. Our present-day ethics no longer approve of slavery or of a hostile attitude to foreign nations as such. Our present-day ethics no longer approve of the burning of heretics out of love of our neighbour and to the glory of God. The concept of 'neighbour' has considerably widened in the ethics of the Modern Age, compared with the ancient and Mediaeval moral ideas as to what the true love of our neighbour consists in."[61]

Even if we concede that the reinterpretation of ancient moral axioms may imply progress, the possibility still remains that such reassessments are made not because there is some inner compulsion in moral principles which ensures their constant revision, but because such ethical ideas no longer harmonize with increasing knowledge and enlightenment. On the other hand, assuming Buckle to be right when he says that moral ideas are stationary, it does not necessarily mean that they cannot exert a constant effect on mankind; nor does it follow that such pressure is a negligible factor in accounting for progress. This doctrine of the stationary nature of morality, which Buckle probably owed to Condorcet, is introduced merely to establish the supreme significance of intellectual history for a proper understanding of the past, at any rate in so far as European civilization is concerned; and just as a thorough-going determinism is more than is needed to show the causal connexions of history, so it is unnecessary to prove the immutability of morals in order to emphasize the achievements of the intellect. The exaggerated vehemence with which Buckle attacks established creeds must be attributed partly to his belief that deep-rooted fallacies and errors can only be eradicated violently. In his attempts, however, to counter orthodoxy, he was sometimes betrayed into extravagant heterodoxy. His favourite form of argument is to say either *this*, or *that*, must be accepted; and as to credit *this* is inconceivable, then *that* must be believed. Such an insistence that everything is black or white and such a complete disregard of subtle gradations of shade, may be appropriate to polemics, but is unlikely to lead to truth.

The majority of Buckle's critics have been prepared to concede, if grudgingly, that his History was the fruit of extensive learning. "I was carried away," admits Mark Pattison, "by Buckle's vast reading and the appearance of wide induction which his pages bore."[62] Leslie Stephen thought that "the extent of his knowledge and his command of all his resources was remarkable".[63] Sayce, although he was very critical of the History, and attempted to be as disparaging as possible about Buckle's learning, was unable to deny the extraordinary range of his reading. "The first impression it made upon its readers," he says, "was the vastness of the 'book learning' displayed in it. Not only was a sort of Encyclopaedic Bibliography attached to the volumes, the pages were also crowded with quotations from books and pamphlets of all kinds, many of them of the obscurest character. The author seemed determined to crush all opposition to his theories by the mere weight and number of his references without any consideration of their cogency or value. . . ."[64] Such is the testimony of Buckle's declared opponents, to which might be added the evidence of his History, of his Common Place Books, and of his friends. But Acton and Hutchison Stirling, two of Buckle's bitterest critics, refused to admit even this much, and their attempt to discredit his scholarship, since it is to be presumed that they acted in as good faith as their rancour would allow, only displays their own ignorance of the extent of his knowledge.

"The theoretical portion," says Acton in his review of the History "is completely overgrown and hidden by the mass of matter which is collected to support it, and on which Mr. Buckle has brought to bear all the reading of a lifetime. The wonderful accumulation of details and extravagance of quotation have the manifest purpose of dazzling and blinding his readers by the mere mass of apparent erudition. 'So learned a man cannot be mistaken in his conclusions', is no doubt what they are expected to say." Elsewhere in the review, Acton refers to "the dishonest affectation of knowledge by which Mr. Buckle deludes his readers", accuses Buckle of being unacquainted "with scarcely four or five of the most common writers of antiquity", affirms that "the practice of reading the books one is to write about was beneath so great a philosopher", and decides that "the ostentation of his slovenly erudition is but an artifice of ignorance". In so far as one can find in this obloquy any statement of fact, it is that Buckle had not read the books he discusses and that he was unacquainted with classical authors. Suffice it to say that Acton had no possible means at the time of telling what Buckle had not read, and that we, who have,* know how absurd such accusations are. But then possibly Acton regarded it as a duty to belabour the infidel, and in that pious task any stick does. "In his laborious endeavour," concludes Acton's review, "to degrade the history of mankind, and of the dealings of God with Man, to the level of one of the natural sciences, he has stripped it of its philosophical, of its divine, and even of its human

* Apart from Buckle's printed Common Place Books, which make repeated references to different Authors of Antiquity, the Huth Collection of Buckle Manuscripts contains rough notes on a considerable number of the books he was supposed not to have read.

character and interest. . . . We could not allow a book to pass without notice into general circulation and popularity which is written in an impious and degrading spirit, redeemed by no superiority or modesty of learning, by no earnest love of truth, and by no open dealing with opponents."[65] No earnest love of truth! Of all Buckle's qualities this is the one for which he has been most often praised and which his life and his work displays again and again. It is unfortunate that Acton, for all his card-indexes, never managed, like Buckle, to write a great book; and it is curious to think that if he were to be judged by what he has actually printed, his reputation for impartiality and learning would depend on essays like that on the *History of Civilization*.

Stirling's attempt to discredit Buckle's scholarship is of much the same order as Acton's, and his criticism contains the same share of emotive language and falsehood. He describes the list of books quoted in the History as "a vainglorious catalogue of most ordinary volumes"; he says that Buckle's reading consisted of a superficial acquaintance with Hume, Voltaire, and Gibbon, and that he was "a flushed and conceited boy".[66] As Buckle was only forty when he died, as his book was a mere fragment of what he hoped to write, and as, while there was so much to do, he very sensibly refused to waste time answering his critics, they were left with the field to themselves. One cannot help suspecting that the decline in Buckle's reputation must partly be attributed to utterly irresponsible criticism made by authors who should have known better than to lend their names to groundless slanders. Stirling, unlike Acton, had he desired to find out anything about Buckle's reading, could have read Huth's life or looked at the Common Place Books. But the author of *The Secret of Hegel*, the best-kept secret in philosophical literature, was far too eager to refute an opponent whose views undermined his own murky transcendentalism to be bothered with the accuracy of his accusations.

Buckle fully realized that he would provoke angry hostility, but he knew that the historian must not look to the world for reward. "Not for him, are those rewards which, in other pursuits, the same energy would have earned; not for him, the sweets of popular applause; not for him, the luxury of power; not for him, a share in the councils of his country; not for him, a conspicuous and honoured place before the public eye. . . . So far from looking for these things, he should rather be prepared for that obloquy which always awaits those, who, by opening up new veins of thought, disturb the prejudices of their contemporaries. While ignorance, and worse than ignorance, is imputed to him, while his motives are misrepresented, and his integrity impeached, while he is accused of denying the value of moral principles, and of attacking the foundation of all religion, as if he were some public enemy, who made it his business to corrupt society, and whose delight it was to see what evil he could do; while these charges are brought forward, and repeated from mouth to mouth, he must be capable of pursuing in silence the even tenor of his way, without swerving, without pausing, and without stepping from his path to notice the angry outcries which he cannot but hear, and which he is more than human if he does not long to rebuke. These are the qualities, and these the high resolves, indispensable to him, who, on the most important of all subjects, believing that the old road is worn-out and useless, seeks to strike out a new one for himself, and, in the effort, not only perhaps exhausts his strength, but is sure to incur the enmity of those who are bent on maintaining the ancient scheme unimpaired. To solve the great problem of affairs; to detect those hidden circumstances which determine the march and destiny of nations; and to find, in the events of the past, a key to the proceedings of the future, is nothing less than to unite into a single science all the laws of the moral and physical world. Whoever does this, will build up afresh the fabric of our knowledge, rearrange its various parts, and harmonize its apparent discrepancies. Perchance, the human mind is hardly ready for so vast an enterprise. At all events, he who undertakes it will meet with little sympathy, and will find few to help him. And let him toil as he may, the sun and noontide of his life shall pass by, the evening of his days shall overtake him, and he himself have to quit the scene, leaving that unfinished which he had vainly hoped to complete. He may lay the foundation; it will be for his successors to raise the edifice. Their hands will give the last touch; they will reap the glory; their names will be remembered when he is forgotten. It is, indeed, too true, that such work requires, not only several minds, but also the successive experience of several generations. Once, I own, I thought otherwise. Once, when I first caught sight of the whole field of knowledge, and seemed, however dimly, to discern its various parts and the relation they bore to each other, I was so entranced with its surpassing beauty, that the judgment was beguiled, and I deemed myself able, not only to cover the surface, but also to master the details. Little did I know how the horizon enlarges as well as recedes, and how vainly we grasp at the fleeting forms, which melt away and elude us in the distance. Of all that I had hoped to do, I now find but too surely how small a part I shall accomplish. In those early aspirations, there was much that was fanciful; perhaps there was much that was foolish. Perhaps, too, they contained a moral defect, and savoured of an arrogance which belongs to a strength that refuses to recognize its own weakness. Still, even now that they are defeated and brought to nought, I cannot repent having indulged in them, but, on the contrary, I would willingly recall them, if I could. For such hopes belong to that joyous and sanguine period of life, when alone we are really happy; when the emotions are more active than the judgment; when experience has not yet hardened our nature; when the affections are not yet blighted and nipped to the core; and when the bitterness of disappointment not having yet been felt, difficulties are unheeded, obstacles are unseen, ambition is a pleasure instead of a pang, and the blood coursing swiftly through the veins, the pulse beats high, while the heart throbs at the prospect of the future. Those are glorious days; but they go from us, and nothing can compensate their absence. To me, they now seem more like the visions of a disordered fancy, than the sober realities of things that were, and are not."[67]

Much of Buckle's originality derives from his solitary education. Had he followed his father and gone to Cambridge, he might have succumbed to orthodoxy. Nevertheless, not having been at a University had disadvantages. He suffered from many of the distinctive faults, says Lecky, "of a writer who had mixed little with men, and had formed his mind almost exclusively by solitary, unguided study".[68] Leslie Stephen came to the same conclusion. "Buckle," he wrote, "had always a touch of the spoilt child. . . . He congratulated himself, it seems, upon not having been exposed to the atmosphere of antiquated prejudice at a University. Yet some men of less intellectual vigour have passed through Oxford and Cambridge without becoming hopeless slaves of obsolete dogmas. It might have done Buckle no harm to learn that parsons are not invariably provided with horns and hoofs; and in College he might have met that admirable instructor who receives so little gratitude—the youth who maintains that he is as good a man as you, and has an unpleasant habit of proving his words. As it was, Buckle's mental fibre was always rather soft. He was more of the youthful genius lecturing an admiring audience of feminine relatives than of the controversial athlete throwing down the gauntlet to rival champions."[69] Despite the substantial truth of these remarks, Buckle would almost certainly have lost more than he would have gained had he gone to a University. "Every Man who rises above the common level," says Gibbon in his Autobiography, "has received two educations: the first from his teachers; the second, more personal and important, from himself." Gibbon's indictment of Oxford shows how little his own scholarship owed to its instruction, and indeed the number of celebrated thinkers of the Victorian Age, who, like Mill, Huxley and Herbert Spencer were self-educated, suggests that neither Oxford nor Cambridge were indispensable.

The fact that Buckle's History came out two years before *The Origin of Species* was published, was far more serious than his lack of a university education. He "was singularly unfortunate", says Lecky, "in the time in which he appeared. From the days of Bacon and Locke to the days of Condillac and Bentham, it had been the tendency of advanced liberal thinkers to aggrandize as much as possible the power of circumstances and experience over the individual, and to reduce to the narrowest limits every influence that is innate, transmitted, or hereditary. They represented man as essentially the creature of circumstances, and his mind as a sheet of blank paper on which education might write what it pleased." Then came Darwin's book, "and from that time the supreme importance of inborn and hereditary tendencies has become the very central fact in English philosophy".[70] The idea that human capabilities have remained stationary was no longer tenable. In nature everything develops. "The human intellect today possesses capacities, which man at the prehistoric stage of culture never possessed, and which remain denied to the present-day Hottentot. . . . The cerebral system of a Fijian islander, even if he was educated from infancy in Charles Darwin's home, would not exhibit the centuries long development of the central nervous system of Europeans."[71]

Buckle published his History at the very moment when the ideas of Hume, Hartley and Mill were just about to be superseded by the teaching of Darwin and Spencer. The *History of Civilization*, according to Leslie Stephen, "has thus been left, as it were, stranded on a shore from which the tide of speculation has ebbed. . . ."[72] Its Author, says the same critic elsewhere, "was, I think, a man of extraordinary powers. . . . He went wrong just from not having the Darwinian clue. The stronger a man is, the further he goes in the wrong direction, once started."[73] Grant Allen even goes so far as to assert that Darwin's discovery completely outmoded not only Buckle, but Hegel and Comte as well. "There is no department," he says, "of human thought or human action which evolutionism leaves exactly where it stood before the advent of the Darwinian conception. In nothing is this fact more conspicuously seen than in the immediate obsolescence (if one may so speak) of all the statistical pre-Darwinian philosophies which ignored development, as soon as ever the new progressive evolutionary theories had fairly burst upon an astonished world. Dogmatic Comte was left forthwith to his little band of devoted adherents; shadowy Hegel was relegated with a bow to the cool shades of the common-rooms of Oxford; Buckle was exploded like an inflated wind-bag. . . ."[74]

The idea of evolution was, of course, older than *The Origin of Species*. Darwin's importance was that he securely established what had long been suspected. The simultaneous publication of Wallace's work, the evolutionary theories of the geologists, the popular concept of development as reflected in Tennyson's poetry, and the organic view of the State found in the writings of Herder and Hegel, show how widely diffused was the idea long before 1859. Immediately Buckle read Darwin he accepted his theory, but he did not live to appreciate its full implications, and his History suffers from the essentially unhistorical assumption that human nature is everywhere uniform.

Buckle's failure to consider human development in terms other than those of mechanical causality diminished the value of his work. The idea of evolution does not displace that of causality, it presupposes it, and is a much richer concept. "The fundamental principle of history is not *causality*, as Buckle assumed, but *evolution* according to the principle of *immanent teleology*."[75] If the *History of Civilization* had been written at the time of the Franco-Prussian War, instead of during the Crimean War, it could not possibly have been described either as "an Utilitarian cul-de-sac", or as a "positivist fabrication".[76]

Maine once told Lecky that "he knew no modern reputation which had declined so much in so short a time as Buckle's".[77] There are several reasons for his fall from favour: the unjust treatment he received from some of his critics; the unfinished nature of his work; academic suspicion of philosophies of history; the collectivist reaction to the political views he advocated; the inaccuracy of his predictions about the new era of peace; and his failure to reckon with evolution. If Buckle had lived even as long as Macaulay, his views would have probably changed sufficiently to meet many of these objections. Had he survived to be as old as Carlyle he might have been ranked with him as an historian. As it is, his book is but the fragment of a fragment, consisting of an unfinished introduction to a work he never even began.

Buckle, realizing that he could not possibly finish his book, determined to restrict his survey to a history of England alone. The Edinburgh reviewer foretold when the first volume was published that the scheme would never be completed. "The construction of so gigantic a plan shows a misconception of the capacity of the human intellect and the length of human life. A very simple rule of three sum might convince Mr. Buckle (if he were open to conviction) that the chance that his work will be a mere Cyclopean ruin is incalculably great."[78] As even the introduction was never finished, the title of the book is unfortunate. "*Ce titre indique le livre que l'auteur voulait écrire, non celui qu'il a écrit. Comme plus d'un historien philosophe, il n'a bâti que le vestibule de son temple.*"[79] Had Buckle lived to be sixty it is probable he would at any rate have completed his revised scheme. "They do not know," he used to say in answer to critics like the Edinburgh reviewer, "the amount of material I have collected."[80]

The astonishing thing about this unfinished History is not so much that it left its author vulnerable to criticism, but that it should have caused such controversy and exerted such influence. "It must," says Acton, "have powerfully appealed to something or other in the public mind . . . in order to have won so rapid a popularity."[81] The ferment the book created among professional philosophers and historians has been compared with that provoked by Schopenhauer. Both writers "furnished endless material for thought".[82] Miss Martineau, who was disgusted by the History, saw at least that it might be esteemed, "by those who value a piece of writing in proportion to the amount of thought which it compels",[83] and Bernard Shaw described it as "a work of the mind-changing sort".[84] Buckle himself was fully aware that inertia rather than error is the enemy of knowledge, and that since truth evolves from conflicing opinions, a book, whatever blunders it may contain, which sets people talking and thinking, performs an important service. "Authors of new ideas, the proposers of new contrivances, and the originators of new heresies are benefactors of their species. Whether they are right or wrong, is the least part of the question. They tend to excite the mind; they open up the faculties; they stimulate us to fresh inquiry; they place old subjects under new aspects; they disturb the public sloth; and they interrupt, rudely, but with most salutary effect, that love of routine, which, by inducing men to go grovelling on in the ways of their ancestors, stands in the path of every improvement, as a constant, an outlying, and, too often, a fatal obstacle."[85]

Macaulay desired to write a history which young ladies would prefer to the latest novel, and there is no doubt that he achieved this modest ambition. Buckle's work was too serious and philosophical to appeal to the ordinary Victorian girl despite Henry Fawcett's story about "a female disciple of the new prophet who went about proclaiming that she was 'panting for a wider generalization'."[86] From the time of its publication it became one of the classics most read by radical working men, and as late as 1895, J. M. Robertson was able to write: "At this moment, with all the affectation of having buried Buckle that prevails in the literary world, there are hundreds of non-literary men who can testify how he has taught them to regard history in an enlightened and reflective fashion. . . ."[87] In Stevenson's story, *The Wrecker*, one of the crew takes the *History of Civilization* as his reading for the voyage, although it must be admitted that it generally sent its student to sleep and that when he awoke, "he was almost invariably in the humour for brown sherry. The connection was so well established that 'a glass of Buckle' or a bottle of 'Civilization' became current pleasantries on board the *Currency Lass*." Other students, however, have been more fortunate, and, as Dr. Gooch says, the book "has marked an epoch in the life of readers all over the world".[88] It "fluttered the dovecotes of the Imperial Acadamy at St. Petersburg".[89] In Rumania, Professor Xenepol studied and admired it. In Czechoslovakia, Masaryk discussed it with his fiancée. Even Cavour read it on the way back from Plombières. But it was in England and Germany that it exerted its profoundest effect.[90] Reading Buckle decided Lecky on a career of historical research.[91] Winwood Reade, the author of *The Martyrdom of Man*, acknowledges his influence,[92] and Westermarck's debt to the *History of Civilization* was considerable. Moreover Buckle's effect was not confined to the nineteenth century. In the Preface to his book on *Climate and the Energy of Nations*, published during the Second World War, Mr. Markham describes how he came across the History and there read a passage which started him on his work.[93] In Germany Buckle's book "won a mighty influence", since, according to Bernheim, "it just hit the middle of the materialistic, scientific and socialistic intellectual currents of the time", and because "rough, exaggerated views are more easily accepted than accurately balanced opinions".[94]

One of Buckle's greatest achievements was to broaden the scope of historical thought, and this largely accounts for the interest he aroused and the influence he exerted. His writing, "for all its occasional shallowness, signifies a great broadening of the horizons of history. The vivid geographical sense, the eager Victorian exploration of exotic scenes and esoteric learning",[95] the emphasis on studying whole societies rather than individuals, and the belief that it is possible to make sense out of the apparent chaos of the past, made his book very different from the numerous political narratives which confined history within the narrowest bounds. "Buckle," says Lecky, "opened out wider horizons than any previous writer in the field of history. No other English historian has sketched his plan with so bold a hand, or has shown so clearly the transcendent importance of studying not merely the actions of soldiers, politicians, and diplomatists, but also those great connected evolutions of intellectual, social, and industrial life on which the type of each succeeding age mainly depends. To not a few of his contemporaries he imparted an altogether new interest in history, and his admirable literary talent, the vast range of topics which he illuminated with a fresh significance, and the noble enthusiasm for knowledge and for freedom that pervades his work, made its appearance an epoch in the lives of many who have passed far from its definite conclusions."[96] Although J. R. Green hated most of Buckle's ideas, he could not but sympathize with his protest against "drum and trumpet" history. Buckle, however, appreciated more fully than Green the importance of what Whitehead has called the "Climate of opinion," what Comte, borrowing from Lamarlk, called "Milieu", and what in the *History of Civilization* is referred to as "the spirit of the age". When one recalls the praise lavished on Macaulay's third chapter and the revolution in historical writing it is alleged to have begun, and when one remembers its neglect of science and philosophy it seems curious that Buckle, writing only a few years later, and devoting nearly every page of his book to social and intellectual matters, should not receive at least a share of the credit.

If the faults of Buckle's History have been avidly seized upon, its merits have not escaped notice; and many of the writers whose criticisms have been examined, praised as well as condemned it. Mark Pattison, for example, opened his Review with these words: "This volume is certainly the most important work of the season; and it is perhaps the most comprehensive contribution to philosophical history that has ever been attempted in the English language. It is full of thought and original observation; but it is no speculative creation of a brilliant theorist. It is learned in the only true sense of the word."[97] Pattison was not alone in thinking that the History was a work of the very greatest importance. "This," says Theodore Parker of the first volume, "is the most important work, in its line, from a British hand, which the world has seen for many a year. The theme is one of the greatest in the world. The author has treated it better, with more learning and profound comprehension, than any of his English predecessors. . . . The author's style is clear and distinct, not ambitious or ornamented. We often pause to admire a great thought, a wide and felicitous generalization, or a nice account of some special detail, nay, to question the truth of a statement of fact, or of a philosophic induction; we never stop to puzzle over a difficult sentence. . . Mr. Buckle has given us one of the most important contributions which any Englishman has yet made to the philosophy of human history. . . . We congratulate the author on his success. We are sure the thoughtful world will give him a thoughtful welcome, and if his future volumes, which we anxiously look for, shall equal this, he is sure of a high place in the estimation of mankind."[98] Although Lecky's early enthusiasm waned as he grew older, his immediate impression of Buckle's work was one of unstinted admiration. "I wish you would read Buckle's *History of Civilization*," he writes to a friend; "it is, I think, one of the most interesting books and the very best history I have ever read. I have gone over nearly all of it several times, and each time with increasing admiration and amazement. I am convinced he will one day be regarded as one of the greatest men England has ever produced."[99]

Such lavish praise might be attributed to an ephemeral enthusiasm; certainly Lecky revised his opinion although he always held Buckle in high esteem. But not every eulogy was written in the first flush of excitement at the time when the History came out. J. M. Robertson's book, in itself as sincere a tribute as any author could desire, was published in 1895. Alfred Benn, writing early in the present century, affirms that "for sheer intellectual power Buckle probably surpassed all his contemporaries. . . . His ideation, copious, brilliant, and suggestive, seems not to have been more unsound than that of some other writers who passed at the time for far safer guides. His critical attitude towards men and things was independent, robust, and sincere. His style, while lacking refinement, was strong, lucid, interesting, and sometimes rose to heights of moving eloquence not easily matched in modern philosophic literature. These qualities at once secured him a large popular audience both in England and abroad; nor, to judge by the constant reprints of his unfinished work, has the lapse of nearly half a century exhausted their fascination for the young. . . . Most imaginative works, if they have any merit at all, not only stimulate but instruct; they tell us something new about nature or human life. A history or a philosophical treatise has no permanent value unless it is to some extent a work of art, giving us, together with new facts and ideas, an exalted sense of intellectual energy and curiosity, of capacity to cope with the materials of thought for ourselves. Buckle's work performed both services in a very eminent degree. Quite apart from his own particular theories, it opened out an enormous range of facts gathered from every department of learning; it introduced to the notice of the English reading public an array of great figures, especially in the intellectual history of France, whom they hardly knew even by name before; it associated with precise achievements the names of others who before had been merely the objects of a vague traditional admiration; doing in this way for the heroes of science and philosophy what Macaulay and Carlyle had done for the heroes of literature." Benn concludes his estimate of Buckle's importance by pointing out how valuable were some of his doctrines at the time when he wrote: a time when England needed to be "liberated from the religious terrorism which had been weighing on her since the Peace of 1814. It was necessary that a man should stand up and teach her people the very reverse of what Keble and Newman had taught; that religious intolerance and exclusiveness, instead of being brought back, should be much more thoroughly expelled from our political and social arrangements; that superstitious gloom, instead of being encouraged, should be dispelled by education; that priestly authority is not a blessing but a curse; that the Middle Ages, so far from offering a picture of ideal justice and romantic spirituality, were really what Voltaire had shown them to be, a period of barbarism, delusion, profligacy, and oppression."[100]

The *History of Civilization* was the work of a man dedicated to a single purpose, who spent more than half his life preparing in solitary seclusion the materials for his vast enterprise. When at length the first volume appeared, many thought that in comprehensiveness, boldness, erudition and eloquence, it had few equals in any age. With the possible exception of Herbert Spencer, Buckle stimulated sociological thought more vigorously than any other nineteenth-century writer, and played a considerable, although often unacknowledged part, in creating the intellectual movement of which Bagehot and Lecky were representatives. Whatever the faults of the book, said a reviewer in *Fraser's*, "the merits of the author are sterling. He sought knowledge for its own sake; for knowledge he gave up his youth, his talents, his fortune, and possibly his life."[101]

Buckle himself believed that his book was of value in that it helped to discredit some of the mistaken notions, which prevailed when he wrote, about the purpose and method of history. "I am deeply convinced," he says, "that the time is fast approaching when the history of Man will be placed on its proper footing; when its study will be recognized as the noblest and most arduous of all pursuits; and when it will be clearly seen, that, to cultivate it with success, there is wanted a wide and comprehensive mind, richly furnished with the highest branches of human knowledge. When this is fully admitted, history will be written only by those whose habits fit them for the task; and it will be rescued from the hands of biographers, genealogists, collectors of anecdotes, chroniclers of courts, of princes, and of nobles—those babblers of vain things, who lie in wait at every corner, and infest this the public highway of our national literature. . . . If I have done anything towards bringing these intrusions into discredit, and inspiring historians themselves with a sense of the dignity of their own calling, I shall have rendered in my time some little service, and I shall be well content to have it said, that in many cases I have failed in executing what I originally proposed."[102]

Buckle's History contains great faults. In it are to be found mistaken principles, erroneous facts and false predictions. Its optimism, its faith in reason, its suspicion of the most charitable activities of government and its contempt of clericalism, have long since been discredited. Yet works of genius have a perennial power. As knowledge increases they may need to be modified, but their insight is never outmoded. The conceptions of a Gibbon are of more value than the corrections of a Bury. Out of date as the *History of Civilization* may be, it remains suggestive, vigorous, instructive and readable. Few Victorian writers did as much as Buckle to revolutionize the idea of history. His book secured the widest hearing which philosophical ideas can hope to attain; and had he lived long enough to fulfil his majestic ambition, he must have been recognized for what he was: one of the first figures of the great age of literary historians.

APPENDIX I

HUTH'S CRITICISM OF *PILGRIM MEMORIES*

HUTH regarded *Pilgrim Memories* as a worthless book. "There is much in it," he says, "about 'Oneness' and the 'Ideal'. We are told that Christ and the chief priest and elders were in the habit of talking Greek to each other; and we are treated to such brilliant flights of eloquence and imagination as the passage: 'How Elysian were life, all gathering for each other, on the strand of our little star-island, the beautiful shells of natural law, and bathing in the gleaming sea of the Infinite!' What is even more curious to anyone who ever met Buckle, is the extraordinary fact that in most cases Mr. Glennie seems to monopolize the conversation, while Mr. Buckle only ventures to put in occasionally a 'Well?' or 'How so?' or announce the fact that it is time for lunch. But if the reader be indulgent he will pass this over; considering that the unequal length of the paragraphs may be due to the fact that Mr. Glennie has had thirteen years to work up the arguments he urged, while Mr. Buckle's interjections come very usefully to help Mr. Glennie along, and wind him up again, as it were, when he has run down. However, this indulgence cannot last long. For looking more carefully at Mr. Buckle's reported conversation, we feel irresistibly impelled to exclaim with *The Athenaeum*, 'In Mr. Buckle's lifetime he talked sense, but here he is made to talk nonsense.' Occasionally, indeed, we do come across a sentence, a fragment, an oasis in the dreary waste of words, which Buckle's friends would recognize as his; such as his quotation to Mr. Glennie: 'I can find you an argument, but not understanding.' And yet, notwithstanding this natural deficiency, Mr. Glennie has undertaken to supply Mr. Buckle with arguments—some from passages in the *History of Civilization*, some from his *Miscellaneous and Posthumous Works*, and others, to judge from internal evidence, from his own dreams. . . .

"The next long conversation which Mr. Glennie reports to us, is on the non-effect of moral truth on the progress of civilization. What Buckle is made to say, when there is anything at all in his remarks, is merely a succession of extracts from the *History of Civilization*; and what Mr. Glennie says, is chiefly remarkable for the way in which he utterly misunderstands Buckle's position, and the way in which he ventures to say things which, not only Buckle, but any educated man, could easily refute. However, Mr. Buckle was, as usual, woefully defeated, and meekly says, 'Well, I think it is time for lunch.' After lunch, however, Buckle takes heart of grace, and renews the conversation, with the new weapon of the state of morality in the Middle Ages. 'Mr. Buckle thought he had me there,' says Mr. Glennie. But how miserable was his defeat! Mr. Glennie was quite calm; his cheeks blanched not; he firmly withstood the shock; and then quietly overwhelmed his antagonist with a speech of two or three pages in length. It was Prince Giglio and Captain Hedzoff over again. Mr. Glennie's argument was, of course, quite unanswerable. Mr. Buckle had, indeed, caught a Tartar when he 'thought he had him there', and could only slink away crestfallen to the innermost recesses of his tent.

"It is a remarkable thing, and speaks volumes for Mr. Buckle's courage, that notwithstanding his repeated and almost invariable defeats, he should still continue to wage an impotent war against his invincible antagonist. The subject of the next conversation is the materialistic view of the Greatest Happiness, a subject in which Buckle was deeply interested. In this the reader will notice with astonishment, that, while Mr. Glennie delivers himself of some three hundred lines of print, Buckle is unable to manage even one hundred. Perhaps some Philistine, who has not read Mr. Glennie's volume, may urge that Buckle, being a good writer and conversationalist, might have made his sentences more pithy, straight, and to the point; while Mr. Glennie laboured on, like the horse in the mill, ever circling, but never nearer to the point around which he works. But if he reads, he will find this theory untenable, for Buckle's style in this conversation is no better than Mr. Glennie's. . . .

"It would be wearisome to the reader, and perhaps it is not possible for me, exhaustively to criticize all the conversations which Mr. Glennie has reported. We cannot read them without seeing that he is deeply indebted to Buckle; that the barren soil has brought forth something it would not otherwise have been capable of. But the crop is so intermingled with tares and weeds that it is valueless. What I have just said of the last conversation is again applicable to the next: it is all Mr. Buckle encouraging Mr. Glennie to state his opinions, and no Mr. Buckle then stating his, and examining where they differed. But that the conversation took place as Mr. Glennie writes it, I, for one, do not believe. We may allow, for instance, that Mr. Glennie quoted Aristotle in the original Greek, as he before says that he quoted Socrates. The thing is possible, though hardly probable. But, that he had to add a translation for Buckle's benefit!

". . . What is the value of conversations recorded as are these? They give us no new knowledge, for all that is of value in them had been already published before Mr. Glennie wrote. They give us not only no true idea of what Buckle was in conversation, but they do give us a most wrong and harmful and untrue idea. Buckle is used simply as a peg upon which Mr. Glennie may hang his own views; Buckle begs explanations, and Mr. Glennie explains; Buckle says 'how so?' and Mr. Glennie adds some more explanation. . . . Buckle is always wandering from the subject: logical Mr. Glennie is always bringing him back. Buckle seeks to escape by turning the conversation: victorious Mr. Glennie, with true magnanimity allows it. Buckle has the misfortune to utter the word 'toleration'; but Mr. Glennie is instantly down upon him with:—'I exceedingly dislike the word. Toleration, properly speaking, can be, and has in fact historically been, offered only by those who endeavoured to carry off their inability to suppress, by an insolent assumption of superiority in permitting. Letting the word, however, pass, my views', &c., &c. As if Mr. Glennie ever dared to talk like this! or as if Buckle, despite his marvellous patience, would have allowed so insolent an 'assumption of superiority of permitting'! Mr. Glennie here talks some four hundred lines; while Buckle does not take even one hundred and fifty. Mr. Glennie quotes a passage from the Greek Testament, and translates it for Buckle's benefit. Therefore we must draw the conclusion that Buckle did not know Greek, while Mr. Glennie knew Aristotle's works, Socrates, and the New Testament, by heart. He is indeed a wonderful man, with a wonderful memory; a memory, however, which nevertheless is strangely unable to retain Buckle's conversation. . . . If these conversations are valueless, there yet remains a good deal of description of scenery, which may be interesting, though it cannot, of course, differ very much from the descriptions in Murray's Guide, if both be true. But the reader will find that the resemblance is even greater than he would at first have been led to expect, as though 'Murray' had had a prophetic view of what Mr. Glennie was going to write, and had forestalled him." (Huth II, Appendix, *Mr. Glennie's Memories.*)

APPENDIX II

GLENNIE AND BUCKLE'S TOMBSTONE

EVEN Buckle's gravestone led to a quarrel between Glennie and Alfred Huth. In *Pilgrim Memories*, Glennie gives the following account of the marking of the tomb. "I was, I believe, myself the first to make any inquiry about Mr. Buckle's grave. In answer to a letter of mine, Dr. Barclay thus wrote, under date Beirut, November 24, 1864, 'I also wrote, at the same time to Mr. Rogers, H. B. M. Consul at Damascus, asking, as you desired, for a pencil-sketch of the grave; and in reply was informed that not even a stone or mark of any kind indicated the spot of interment! Shortly afterwards, Mr. Rogers came on to Beirut, when I spoke to him on the subject, and showed him your letter.' Towards the close of 1865, Mr. Rogers was visited by his sister. And through her zeal it was that, in the autumn of 1866, nearly four years and a half after his death, the grave of Mr. Buckle was, at length, marked by a simple monument." (Glennie, p. 468. Footnote.)

"I do not know," is Huth's comment, "what impression this passage leaves on the mind of the reader; but on my first perusal it appeared to me that Mr. Glennie claimed for himself the honour of having directed the attention of Miss Rogers to the fact that there was no memorial marking Buckle's last resting-place. No doubt Mr. Glennie did not suppose that such a construction could be put upon his words, and will be only too happy to have the matter clearly set forth. The truth is, he had not the remotest connection with it. He no doubt did write a letter to Dr. Barclay asking for the particulars of Buckle's death, and no doubt asked at the same time for a sketch or photograph of the tomb which he, as every one else, supposed was there, for the purpose of ornamenting his *Pilgrim Memories*. Dr. Barclay wrote back to say there was none; and there the matter dropped. This was in November, 1864. Towards the end of 1865, Miss Rogers went out to join her brother, who was Consul at Damascus; and on February 8th, 1866, accompanied him to the Protestant cemetery, to visit the grave of a near relative. She went with the full expectation of also seeing Buckle's tomb; and was greatly surprised, and very much shocked, to find nothing but a rounded mound over his remains. . . .

"The tomb was finished by 30th October, 1866; and up to the year 1871, or 1872, Mr. Glennie, I understand, had not even heard that there was one; but, happening to see a photograph of it in Major Bell's copy of the *History of Civilization*, he wrote on the 26th February, 1875, to Mrs.

Bell: 'I remember seeing in Major Bell's copy of Buckle's *History of Civilization* a photograph of his tombstone. I should be very much obliged if your Miss Rogers would kindly give the particulars of the time, circumstance, &c., of the erection of the tombstone.' This Miss Rogers did; and the account I have given, showing that to Miss Rogers is entirely and solely due the honour of the first initiation, as the subsequent erection of the tombstone, is no doubt what Mr. Glennie intended to convey to his readers; but he has been unfortunate in his choice of language, and this explanation therefore became necessary." (Huth II, pp. 290–3.)

APPENDIX III

SHORT BIOGRAPHIES OF BUCKLE'S CRITICS

ALLEN, Grant (1848–99). An English writer. He edited a shortened version of Buckle's Common Place Books and, amongst other works, wrote a life of Darwin.

BENN, Alfred (1843–1916). An English philosopher. He was educated chiefly at home. In 1866 he left England and thereafter lived in Switzerland and Italy. He wrote several books on Greek philosophy and a two-volume *History of English Rationalism in the Nineteenth Century* (1906).

BERNHEIM, Ernst (1859–1942). A German historian. He was a professor at the University of Greifswald. He was one of the editors of *Deutsche Reichstagsacten unter Ruprecht*. This work, consisting of three volumes, covered the first decade of the fifteenth century.

BOUILLIER, Francisque (1813–99). A French philosopher. In 1839 he became professor of philosophy at Lyons. He wrote several books including *Histoire et Critique de la Révolution Cartésienne* (1842).

DÚRHING, Eugen (1833–1901). A German economist and philosopher. He is best known for the attack made on him by Marx and Engels. He belonged to the positivistic school and was strongly anti-semitic.

ÉTIENNE, LOUIS (1799–1885). A Professor of Roman Law at Aix (1843–50). He wrote a book on Justinian's Institutes and contributed articles on positivism and history to the *Revue des Deux Mondes* in 1868.

FRAUENSTADT, Julius (1813–79). A German philosopher. He studied philosophy and theology at Berlin and became one of Schopenhauer's most ardent admirers. He edited the first complete edition of Schopenhauer's Collected Works (1874) and wrote several important books on morals, philosophy and theology.

GRATRY, Auguste (1805–72). A French Roman Catholic theologian. In 1863 he became a professor of ethics at the Sorbonne. He published, among other works, an attack on the doctrine of Papal Infallibility. His greatest work is *Cours de Philosophie*, 6 vols., 1857.

LAURENT, Franc (1810–87). A Belgian historian and jurist. He was a liberal and progressive thinker who wrote mainly about law. He introduced savings banks into Belgium.

LITTRÉ, Maximilien (1801–81). A French philosopher and physician He was a prodigious worker and published a number of books on a variety of subjects, including a five-volume *Dictionnaire*. He made a particular study of positivism.

Nordau, Max (1849–1923). A Jewish doctor and journalist. His most famous book is *Degeneration* (1893). This consists of an unbalanced and prudish attack on the abnormality of men of genius.

Oettingen, Alexander (1827–1905). A German theologian. He was professor of theology at Dorpat (1854–91). His chief work is *Die Moralstatistik und die christliche Sittenlehre* (1874).

Peschel, Oscar (1826–75). A German geographer and a pioneer in modern geomorphology.

Quételet, Lambert (1796–1874). He was a Belgian astronomer and statistician. In his greatest book, *Sur l'Homme*, he shows how the theory of probabilities may be applied to the "average man".

Robertson, John (1856–1933). A journalist, author and politician. He stood as a Radical for Tyneside (1906–18), and was Parliamentary Secretary to the Board of Trade (1911–15). He wrote a number of books on Shakespeare. His book *Buckle and his Critics* was published in 1895.

Sayce, Reverend Archibald (1845–1933). A philologist, archaeologist and Egyptologist. He was Professor of Assyriology at Oxford (1891–1919). He published a considerable number of books. His *Reminiscences* came out in 1923.

Stirling, James (1820–1909). A Scottish philosopher. He studied medicine and practised until 1851. In 1865 he completed his two-volume book *The Secret of Hegel*. The school of Idealism, especially in the Scottish universities, owed much to his influence. In 1889 he gave the Gifford lectures at Edinburgh.

NOTE ON SOURCES

HELEN TAYLOR who edited the *Miscellaneous and Posthumous Works of Henry Thomas Buckle*, and who wrote the Biographical Notice at the beginning of the work, kept copies of letters sent to her about Buckle and draft copies of her replies. These letters are now in the Mill–Taylor Collection of the British Library of Political and Economic Science. The letters of Emily Shirreff, who knew Buckle well and who contributed a memoir to Helen Taylor's Biography, are particularly interesting and important.

Another great friend of Buckle's, Mrs. Huth, collected material for a biography, which was used by her son, Alfred Huth, the author of the *Life and Letters of Henry Thomas Buckle*. This material is now in the author's possession. Huth used this collection extensively in writing his book, but his omissions suggest that he was asked not to publish parts of it. For example, no mention of the Strickland family is made in the book although Huth possessed a number of papers relating to them. The collection also contains some interesting information sent to Huth after his book came out.

Besides Huth's two-volume Life, which contains a full bibliography, and Helen Taylor's "Biographical Notice", John Stuart Glennie, who met Buckle travelling in Egypt in 1861, wrote a book entitled *Pilgrim Memories, or Travel and Discussion in the Birth-Countries of Christianity with the late Henry Thomas Buckle*. This is an unreliable work, but contains an appendix reprinting an interesting article by Charles Hale, an American traveller, who, like Glennie, met Buckle in the East. *Pilgrim Memories* was published twelve years after the journey it describes, although Glennie immediately on his return home wrote an article for *Fraser's Magazine* entitled: *"Mr. Buckle in the East"*. There is only one book dealing with Buckle as an historian: *Buckle and his Critics*, by J. M. Robertson.

The following abbreviations are used throughout: M/T for the Mill–Taylor Collection. The figures in Roman numerals denote the number of the volume in the collection, and the Arabic numerals the page (e.g. M/T, IV, p. 73 means Volume four, page seventy-three of the Mill–Taylor Collection). *The Life and Writings of Henry Thomas Buckle* by Alfred Henry Huth, in two volumes, are referred to as Huth, I or Huth, II. Wherever chapter and verse is not given for a quotation, or statement of fact, it should be assumed that the omitted reference is to Huth's biography.

Helen Taylor's *Miscellaneous and Posthumous Works of Henry Thomas Buckle*, in three volumes, 1872, is referred to as Taylor, Vol. I, II, or III. The books: *Buckle and his Critics* and *Pilgrim Memories* are denoted by the names of their Authors, respectively: Robertson and Glennie. References to the *History of Civilization in England* are given thus: Buckle, Vol. I, II or III. Longman's edition of 1872, republished several times in the nineteenth century, has been used. The dates of books mentioned in the notes which follow, refer to the editions used in this work.

NOTES

CHAPTER I

THE SOLITARY STUDENT

1. Taylor, Vol. I, 1872, p. xxi. The extract quoted was written by Miss Shirreff, a great friend of Buckle.

2. F. Edwards to A. H. Huth, 20th Jan., 1880. Author's Collection.

3. British Museum. Additional Manuscripts 28509 F. 235. H. T. Buckle to Griffin and Co. Undated.

4. S. W. Strickland to Mrs. A. Huth, 24th Feb., 1876. Author's Collection.

5. John Buckle to J. S. Mill, 31st Dec., 1868. M/T, I, p. 122.

6. F. Edwards to A. H. Huth, 20th Jan. and 7th May, 1880. The information about Annie Holloway comes from several letters between Edwards, her brother-in-law, and Alfred Huth. The story of the proposal was also known to Mary Buckle, who wrote two letters about it to Alfred Huth, one of which ends: "I feel sure you will respect my feelings in this matter. Any allusions to the escapade of youth in the history of his life, I think would be inopportune if not uncalled for."

7. S. Strickland to Mrs. A. Huth, 24th Feb., 1876. Author's Collection.

8. Charles Hale. "Personal Reminiscences of the late H. T. Buckle." *Atlantic Monthly*, XI, April 1863. Reprinted in Glennie, p. 501.

9. Buckle, Vol. I, p. 348.

10. S. M. Ellis. *A Mid-Victorian Pepys*, 1923, p. 147.

11. Taylor, Vol. I, 1872, pp. xxxvi–xxxvii. This passage was written by Miss Shirreff. Many critics have blamed Buckle's shortcomings on his lack of a university education, for example, Leslie Stephen in the *Dictionary of National Biography*. See above p. 181.

12. H. T. Buckle to T. Parker, 9th July, 1858. Weiss, *Life of Theodore Parker*, Vol. I, 1865, p. 468. Quoted in Huth, I, p. 157.

13. Huth, I, p. 19. I have been unable to trace this journal, part of which was certainly lost, and the rest of which was probably destroyed. Huth in his life of Buckle says: "His diary only begins again with the 21st March, 1850. But in such a manner that is almost impossible to believe but that some of it, at least, has been lost." Huth, I, p. 53. This remark, and the fact that Huth uses extracts from the journal not quoted by Helen Taylor, whose book came out in 1872, suggests that he had access to most of the

diary as late as 1880, when his own work was published. On the other hand, John Buckle wrote to J. S. Mill, on 31st December, 1868, as follows: "His journal I never saw, for his sisters took possession of it and I think they burnt it for reasons they deemed sufficient." M/T, I, p. 122. They could hardly have burnt it all since Helen Taylor was sent at any rate part of the journal by Miss Shirreff in August 1869. M/T XVII, p. 51. But there was good reason for destroying at least some sections of it (see above p. 109) and this may well have been done.

14. Helen Taylor quotes Buckle's journal for 7th March, 1843, on page xv of her Biographical Notice. "What he then wrote," she continues, "is possibly, probably even, what will be found under the head 'Chaıles I' in Volume II of the Common Place Books." Huth, however, gives convincing reasons for thinking she is mistaken. Huth, I, p. 28, footnote 21.

15. Taylor, Vol. I, 1872, p. xvi.

16. H. T. Buckle to Lord Kintore, Feb. 1853. Huth, I, pp. 63–4.

17. Taylor, Vol. I, 1872, p. xxxiv–xxxv. This extract was written by Miss Shirreff.

18. Buckle's Journal, 16th Jan. and 17th Dec., 1842. Huth, I, p. 27.

19. Charles Hale. "Personal Reminiscences of the late H. T. Buckle." *Atlantic Monthly*, Vol. XI, April 1863. Reprinted in Glennie, p. 498.

20. *The Chess Player's Magazine*, Vol. II, Feb. 1864, p. 33.

21. The Westminster Chess Club Papers, No. 62, June 1873. "Mr. Buckle as a Chess Player", by Captain H. A. Kennedy. Quoted in Huth, I, pp. 24–5.

22. Huth, I, p. 62. Huth gives a special Chess Bibliography. Vol. II, pp. 307–11.

23. I can find no written evidence of this story which was told by Edmund Gosse.

24. H. T. Buckle to Miss Shirreff, 28th Oct., 1856. Huth, I, p. 124.

25. The Westminster Chess Club Papers, No. 62, June 1873. "Mr. Buckle as a Chess Player", by Captain H. A. Kennedy. Quoted in Huth, I, pp. 18–19.

26. *Fraser's Magazine*, Vol. 66, p. 343. Katherine Hare told Helen Taylor that Buckle had hoped that his Common Place Books would be published if he were prevented by illness, or death, from finishing his History. K. Hare to Miss H. Taylor, 2nd July, 1868. M/T, XVII, p. 7.

27. Taylor, Vol. I, 1872, p. xix.

28. *The Life and Letters of Charles Darwin*. Edited by Francis Darwin. Vol. I, 1887, pp. 74–5.

29. Charles Hale. *Atlantic Monthly*, Vol. XI, April 1863. Reprinted in Glennie, 501. Buckle frequently talked about style. Glennie, writing

about his journey with Buckle in the East, says, "He had studied all its artifices, and chiefly in Hume, Berkeley, and Burke".

30. H. Taylor to Mrs. A. Huth. Undated. M/T, XVII, p. 11.

31. Taylor, Vol. I, 1872, p. xxxii. This extract was written by Miss Shirreff who spoke from personal experience. Buckle had given her considerable help with her book, e.g. Buckle to Miss Shirreff, 8th Dec., 1854. Huth, I, pp. 86–7.

32. *The Life and Letters of Charles Darwin*. Edited by Francis Darwin. Vol. II, 1887, p. 386.

33. H. T. Buckle to Miss Shirreff, Oct. 1858. Taylor, Vol. I, 1872, p. xliii.

34. H. T. Buckle to J. W. Parker, 22nd Feb., 1856. Huth, I, p. 116.

35. H. T. Buckle to Reverend G. Capel, 24th Oct., 1857. Huth, I, p. 141.

36. John Buckle to J. S. Mill, 31st Dec., 1868. M/T, I, p. 122.

37. Eliza Strickland. Author's Collection. This extract comes from a brief memoir of Buckle, which she probably wrote for A. H. Huth. Since Huth makes no mention of her in his biography, although he possessed this memoir and some of Buckle's letter to her, he presumably refrained from doing so at her request.

38. Taylor, Vol. I, 1872, p. xxiv.

39. *Fraser's Magazine*, Vol. 66, p. 344.

40. Alexander Gray's Memoir of Buckle. Huth II, p. 201.

41. John Timbs. *A Century of Anecdote*, Vol. II, 1860, p. 155.

42. J. A. Longmore. *The Athenaeum*, 1873. "Reminiscences of Mr. Buckle", p. 114.

43. Kate Stanley to her brother, Lyneph, 30th April, 1860. *The Amberley Papers*, Vol. I, 1937, p. 76.

44. John Buckle to J. S. Mill, 31st Dec., 1868. M/T, I, p. 122.

45. E. Shirreff to H. Taylor, Jan., 1869. M/T, XVII, p. 48.

46. Eliza Strickland's Memoir. Author's Collection.

47. H. T. Buckle to Miss Shirreff, 12th May, 1855. Huth, I, p. 89. Even Stuart-Glennie, whose admiration for Buckle was not unmingled with malice, says: "There was no finer trait, perhaps in Mr. Buckle's character than his intellectual ardour and generosity." Glennie, p. 53.

48. H. T. Buckle to E. Shirreff, 15th Jan., 1856. Huth, I, p. 105.

49. Huth, II, pp. 107–108.

50. E. Shirreff to H. Taylor, Jan. 1869. M/T, XVII, p. 48. She is replying to John Buckle's letter to Mill (M/T, I, p. 122), in which, among other things, he says, Henry Buckle "was fond of money and a very saving

man". Regardless of consistency, John later in the same letter accuses his cousin of extravagant self-indulgence.

51. *The Letters and Memoirs of Sir William Hardman*, second series. Edited by S. M. Ellis, 1923, p. 68. Mrs. Grote is not a witness whose evidence should be taken seriously.

52. H. T. Buckle to Mrs. A. Huth, 23rd March, 1861. Huth, II, p. 50. Buckle was inclined to give people with whom he proposed to stay elaborate instructions about his requirements. "I drink hardly anything but claret," he wrote to Capel. "Pure and sound, but *not* expensive—Julien, or some *vin ordinaire*. It is advisable to know something of the place one gets it from, otherwise it may be unwholesome. . . . Mr. Mayo also wishes me to drink German Seltzer Water." H. T. Buckle to Reverend G. Capel, 16th June, 1861. Author's Collection.

53. Huth, II, p. 60. This extract was written by Mrs. A. Huth.

54. Taylor, Vol. III, 1872, p. 529.

55. H. T. Buckle to H. Huth, 12th Dec., 1860. Author's Collection.

56. Taylor, Vol. I, 1872, p. xxii. The extract was written by Miss Shirreff.

57. Charles Hale. *Atlantic Monthly*, Vol. XI, April 1863. Printed in Glennie, pp. 496–7.

58. J. A. Longmore. *The Athenaeum*, Jan. 1873, p. 115.

59. H. T. Buckle to Mrs. Annie Hutchinson, 1860. Huth, II, p. 29.

60. Journal, 24th June, 1856. Huth, I, p. 127. Footnote 14. See also Huth, II, p. 18, 17th Aug., 1859. "He accidentally fell down stairs and fainted away."

61. Huth, II, pp. 69, 72. See also Buckle's letter to Mrs. Grote, 17th May, 1861, in which he says: "This is the first day I have been well enough to write, and the trembling of my hand will, I fear, make this difficult to decipher." Huth, II, p. 67.

62. H. T. Buckle to Miss Shirreff, 22nd Dec., 1856. Huth, I, p. 126.

63. H. T. Buckle to Mrs. Grey, 30th June, 1856. Taylor, Vol. I, 1872, p. xix.

64. Journal, 11th Dec., 1852. Huth, I, pp. 65–6.

65. H. T. Buckle to Eliza Strickland, 26th Dec., 1852. Author's Collection.

66. H. T. Buckle to Sir F. Madden, 10th May, 1854. British Museum. Additional Manuscripts Eg. 2845 F345.

67. H. T. Buckle to Miss Shirreff, July, 1855. Huth, I, p. 96.

68. H. T. Buckle to Miss Shirreff, 29th June, 1855. Huth, I, pp. 94–5.

69. Taylor, Vol. I, 1872, p. xxi–xxv.

70. Kate Stanley to her brother, Lyneph, 30th April, 1860. *The Amberley Papers*, Vol. I, 1937, p. 76.

71. H. T. Buckle to Mrs. Maria Grey, 18th Sept., 1854. Huth, I, p. 83.

72. Huth II, pp. 73–4. The extract was written by Mrs. A. Huth.

73. H. T. Buckle to Miss Shirreff, 8th Oct., 1854. Huth, I, pp. 84–5.

74. Huth, II, p. 105. It has been hinted that Buckle was morbidly interested in flagellation. In 1872 the publisher, J. C. Hotten, issued a prospectus of books which he asserted came from Buckle's secret library of erotic literature. Hotten was almost certainly maligning Buckle in order to divert attention from his own dubious method of obtaining these books which were concerned with flagellation. (See Ivan Bloch, *Sexual Life in England Past and Present*. pp. 579–80.) There is a curious reference to the subject, which it would probably be a mistake to take seriously, in a letter written by Mrs. Huth to her sons. "I would have petitioned Mr. Buckle," she writes, "to give the boy (Alfred) a good whipping such as Mr. B. delights in giving. . . ." Mrs. A. Huth to her sons, 2nd March, 1862. Author's Collection.

75. Huth, I, p. 111. 22nd July, 1855.

76. H. T. Buckle to J. Parker, 11th July, 1856. Huth, I, p. 118.

77. H. T. Buckle to J. Parker, 17th Feb., 1857. Huth, I. pp. 129–30. The terms on which the second edition were published are enumerated in the following letter from Buckle to J. Parker. "I have just received your letter in which you state the engagements of your House with me in that of the forthcoming second edition of volume I of my *History of Civilization*. You shall print and publish at your own cost and risk two thousand copies—that when the edition is ready for publication you are to pay me Five hundred pounds for it;—that you give me twelve copies; and that you supply what are required for Reviews.—It is of course also understood that this engagement is confined to the second edition—beyond which neither of us is bound. This engagement I willingly ratify and I think it not only fair but liberal on your part." H. T. Buckle to J. Parker, 17th April, 1858. Henry E. Huntington Library, San Marino, California.

78. Taylor, Vol. I, 1872, p. xxxix.

79. H. T. Buckle to Miss Shirreff, 28th Aug., 1858. Huth, I, p. 120.

80. H. T. Buckle to Reverend G. Capel, 19th Nov., 1860. Author's Collection.

81. Taylor, Vol. I, 1872, p. xl–xli. This extract was written by Miss Shirreff.

82. Janet Ross, *The Fourth Generation*. 1912, p. 118.

83. *Letters to William Allingham*. Edited H. Allingham, 1911, p. 163.

84. Taylor, Vol. I, 1872, p. xlvii.

85. Herbert Spencer. *An Autobiography*. Vol. II, 1904, p. 19.

86. H. T. Buckle to Mrs. Grey, 30th April, 1857. Huth, I, p. 140.

87. *The Greville Memoirs*, 1852–60, edited by Lytton Strachey and Roger Fulford. Vol. VII, p. 350. Macmillan, 1938.

88. Eve and Creasey, *Life and Work of John Tyndall*. 1945, p. 76.

89. *Life and Letters of Charles Darwin*. Vol. II, 1887, p. 315. See also more letters of Charles Darwin, Vol. II, p. 156. The History particularly appealed to scientists. Charles Lyell described it as "full of talent and having the merit of setting people thinking". *Life, Letters and Journals of Sir Charles Lyell, Bart*. Vol. II, 1881, p. 279.

90. J. S. Mill to H. S. Chapman, 24th Feb., 1863, from a copy of the original made by the late Sir Frederick B. Chapman for Professor James M. McCrimmon, University of Illinois.

91. *Letters of James Russell Lowell*. Edited by Charles Norton. Vol. I, 1894, pp. 317–18.

92. Anton Chekov. *The Cherry Orchard*. Penguin Classics. *Three Plays*, p. 48.

93. Olga Metchinkoff, *Life of Elsie Metchinkoff*. 1921. "Buckle's *History of Civilization* had at that time a very great influence on the young Russian mind." P. 29.

94. D. Mackenzie Wallace, *Russia*. Vol. I, 1877, pp. 167–8. Buckle was influential even in Czechoslovakia. Masaryk, in 1884, wrote a thesis on him, and it was while reading Buckle with Miss Garrigue that they became engaged. Paul Selver, *Masaryk*. 1940, p. 83.

95. Samuel G. Arnold to H. T. Buckle, 10th Feb., 1862. Author's Collection.

96. Theodore Parker to Miss Cobbe, 4th Dec., 1857. Weiss, *Life and Correspondence of Theodore Parker*. Vol. I, 1865, p. 463.

97. Theodore Parker to Professor Henry Rogers, 29th Dec., 1857. Weiss, *Life and Correspondence of Theodore Parker*. Vol. I, 1865, pp. 333–4.

CHAPTER II

FAME AND MISFORTUNE

1. This phrase of Channing's was used by Sir Charles Lyell to describe the opposition to Buckle's election. *Life, Letters and Journals of Sir Charles Lyell*. Vol. II, 1881, p. 280.

2. Sir Frederick Pollock. *Personal Remembrances of Sir Frederick Pollock*. Vol. II, 1887, p. 69.

3. H. T. Buckle to J. Parker, 10th March, 1858. Huth I, pp. 254–5.

4. H. T. Buckle to Miss Shirreff, 26th Oct., 1857. Huth, I, pp. 264–5.

5. H. T. Buckle to Miss Shirreff, 4th Feb., 1858. Huth, I, pp. 265–6.

6. H. T. Buckle to Mrs. Grey, 11th Aug., 1857. Huth, I, p. 262.

7. H. T. Buckle to Mrs. Bowyear, Oct. 1858. Huth, I, pp. 275–6.

8. H. T. Buckle to Mrs. Woodhead, 8th March, 1859. Huth I, p. 288.

9. Journal, 1st April, 1859. Quoted Taylor, Vol. I, 1872, p. xlvii.

10. H. T. Buckle to Mrs. Bowyear, April 1859. Huth, I, p. 295.

11. H. T. Buckle. "Mill on Liberty". *Fraser's Magazine*, May 1859. Reprinted in Taylor, Vol. I. The extracts quoted are on pp. 67–9.

12. H. T. Buckle to J. Parker, 9th March, 1859. Huth, I, p. 284.

13. H. T. Buckle to J. Parker, 30th July, 1859. M/T, VII, p. 54.

14. John Stuart Mill. *Utilitarianism*. Everyman Edition, p. 90. This edition includes Mill's Essay on Liberty from which this quotation comes.

15. H. T. Buckle. "Mill on Liberty." *Fraser's Magazine*, May 1859. Reprinted Taylor, Vol. I, p. 56.

16. See, for example, Buckle's letter to Parker, written 24th June, 1859, about the exact number of months of Pooley's imprisonment. Huth, II, pp. 2–3.

17. H. T. Buckle. "Mill on Liberty." *Fraser's Magazine*, May 1859. Reprinted, Taylor, Vol. I, p. 57–8.

18. This information about Pooley's madness is based on *The Case of Thomas Pooley* and *Bygones Worth Remembering*, 2 Vols., 1905, by G. J. Holyoake.

19. John T. Coleridge to the Home Secretary, 2nd Dec., 1857. *The Law Magazine and Law Review*. Vol. VII, 1859, p. 277.

20. H. T. Buckle. "Letter to a Gentleman respecting Pooley's case." Printed in Taylor, Vol. I, 1872, p. 78.

21. *The Law Magazine and Law Review*. Vol. VII, No. XIV, 1859, p. 278.

22. H. T. Buckle to J. Parker, 11th May, 1859. Huth, I, pp. 306–8.

23. H. T. Buckle to Miss Shirreff, 10th May, 1859. Taylor, Vol. I, 1872, pp. xlvii–xlviii.

24. H. T. Buckle to Miss Shirreff, 13th May, 1859. Huth, I, pp. 313–17.

25. *The Law Magazine and the Law Review*, Vol. VII, No. XIV, 1859, pp. 270–82.

26. H. T. Buckle to J. Parker, 31st May, 1859. Huth, I, p. 318.

27. A letter to the Editor from Mr. J. D. Coleridge. *Fraser's Magazine*, No. 59, June 1859, pp. 635–6. A few extracts from this letter are printed in Taylor, Vol. I, pp. 80–1.

28. A letter to the Editor from Mr. J. D. Coleridge. *Fraser's Magazine*, No. 59, June 1859. Printed, Taylor, Vol. I, 1872, pp. 80–1. *The Law Magazine*, which was horrified by Buckle's attack on Judge Coleridge, nevertheless felt that his son's defence was unfortunate. "One consequence of the controversy," it says, "has been, that Mr. Coleridge, in his reply, has been provoked to use language to the man who has improperly aspersed the character of Sir J. Coleridge, which of course it would, in some instances, have been better to have avoided." *The Law Magazine and the Law Review*, Vol. VII, August 1859, p. 281.

29. H. T. Buckle to Reverend G. Capel, 30th May, 1859. Huth, I, p. 318.

30. H. T. Buckle to J. D. Parker, 9th June, 1859. Huth, I, p. 319.

31. "Letter to a Gentleman respecting Pooley's case." Printed in Taylor, Vol. I, 1872, pp. 71–9.

32. H. T. Buckle to Reverend G. Capel, 24th Oct., 1859. Huth, II, p. 8.

33. George Holyoake. *Sixty Years of an Agitator's Life*, Vol. II, 1892, p. 96. When Holyoake said: "Mr. Mill would give money," he spoke from personal experience. Mill once lent him £70. M/T, I, pp. 35–41.

34. Huth, II, pp. 11–12.

35. H. T. Buckle to T. Parker, 5th July, 1859. Weiss, *Life and Correspondence of Theodore Parker*, Vol. I, 1865, pp. 469–70. Reprinted in Huth, II, pp. 13–14.

36. Reverend G. Capel to Mrs. A. Huth, 25th July, 1859. Author's Collection. Part of this letter is printed in Huth, II, p. 16.

37. H. T. Buckle to Miss E. Strickland, 2nd Sept., 1859. Author's Collection.

38. Taylor, Vol. I, 1872, p. l.

39. *The Letters and Private Papers of W. M. Thackeray*. Edited by Gordon Ray. Vol. IV, 1946, pp. 181 and 238. Priauex "was fond of giving sumptuous dinners to somewhat select parties". These dinners always ended up with Chateau Yquem. Herbert Spencer. *An Autobiography*, Vol. II, 1904, p. 229.

40. W. M. Thackeray to H. T. Buckle, 15th March, 1860. *The Letters and Private Papers of W. M. Thackeray*. Edited by Gordon Ray. Vol. IV, 1946, p. 181.

41. Mrs. Grote. *The Personal Life of George Grote*, 1873, p. 267.

42. Caroline Fox. *Memoirs of Old Friends*. Vol. I, 1882, p. 189. Caroline Fox was told this by Mill.

43. S. M. Ellis. *The Letters and Memoirs of Sir William Hardman*. Second Series, 1923, 1863–65, p. 68.

44. *The Amberley Papers*. Kate's Journal, 27th April, 1860. Vol. I, 1937, p. 75.

45. Edward Huth to his mother, Mrs. A. Huth, 18th Sept., 1860. Author's Collection.

46. H. T. Buckle to the Huth boys, 18th Sept., 1860. Huth, II, pp. 32–3.

47. Huth, II, p. 76. Written by Mrs. Huth.

48. Herbert Spencer. *An Autobiography*. Vol. II, 1904, p. 91. Spencer thought the Huths "very nice intelligent people".

49. Huth, II, pp. 38–59. This account of Buckle was written by Mrs. A. Huth.

50. H. T. Buckle to Mrs. Woodhead, 17th Jan., 1860. Huth, II, pp. 27–8.

51. H. T. Buckle to Mrs. Bowyear, Nov. 1860. Huth, II, p. 36.

52. H. T. Buckle to J. Parker, 20th Dec., 1860. Henry E. Huntington Library, San Marino, California.

53. H. T. Buckle to Mrs. Grote, 17th May, 1861. Huth, II, p. 67.

54. Huth, II, pp. 68–9.

55. H. T. Buckle to Mrs. Grote, 6th June, 1861. Huth, II, p. 71.

56. H. T. Buckle to S. W. Strickland, 2nd July, 1861. Author's Collection.

57. H. T. Buckle to Mrs. Mitchell, 31st July, 1861. Huth, II, pp. 81–2. Fanny Mitchell was married to Alexander Mitchell, M.P., of Carolside. Earleton, Berwickshire. Some years after his death she married Lord Reay,

58. H. T. Buckle to Mrs. Grey, 25th Aug., 1861. Huth, II, pp. 84–5.

59. H. T. Buckle to his aunt, Mrs. Ward, 15th Sept., 1861. Huth, II, pp. 86–7.

60. Huth, II, pp. 89–106. Written by Mrs. A. Huth.

61. Taylor, Vol. I, 1872, p. 524.

62. H. T Buckle to Mrs. A. Huth, 12th Oct., 1861. Author's Collection. Partly printed in Huth, II, p. 110.

63. H. T. Buckle to Mrs. Grote, 18th Oct., 1861. Huth, II, p. 111–12.

CHAPTER III

THE NILE VOYAGE

1. Mrs. Huth to her sons, 20th Oct., 1861. With one or two exceptions, the letters quoted in this chapter are in the Author's Collection. Wherever a letter is printed in Huth's biography the page reference is given.

2. H. T. Buckle to Mrs. A. Huth, 29th Oct., 1861.

3. H. T. Buckle to Mrs. A. Huth, 5th Nov., 1861. Huth, II, pp. 122–3.

4. E. Huth to Mrs. A. Huth, 24th Oct., 1861.

5. E. Huth to Mrs. A. Huth, 28th Oct., 1861.

6. A. H. Huth to Mrs. A. Huth, 2nd Nov., 1861.

7. E. Huth to Mrs. A. Huth, 11th Nov., 1861.

8. H. T. Buckle to Mrs. A. Huth, 15th Nov., 1861.

9. Janet Ross. *The Fourth Generation*, 1912, p. 119. These precautions were not as absurd as may appear. Eddy had very weak eyes.

10. H. T. Buckle to Mrs. A. Huth, 5th Nov., 1861. Huth, II, p. 122.

11. H. T. Buckle to Mrs. A. Huth, 15th Nov., 1861. Huth, II, p. 125. Where Huth's printed version of a letter is inaccurate, or contains omissions, I have followed the original. In the above passage, for example, Huth leaves out the sentence beginning: "They are most excellent boys . . ." I have made no attempt to indicate such alterations.

12. Huth, II, p. 138.

13. A. H. Huth to Mrs. A. Huth, 13th Dec., 1861. Huth, II, p. 137.

14. H. T. Buckle to Mrs. A. Huth, 14th Dec., 1861. Huth, II, pp. 131–3.

15. E. Huth to Mrs. A. Huth, 12th Dec., 1861. Huth, II, pp. 135–6.

16. H. T. Buckle to Miss Shirreff (?), 7th Feb., 1862. Huth, II, pp. 139–41. I have been unable to trace the original of this letter.

17. J. A. Longmore. *The Athenaeum*, 25th Jan., 1873, p. 115. Extracts from Longmore's "Reminiscences of Mr. Buckle" are reprinted by Huth. Huth, II, pp. 142–5.

18. H. T. Buckle to Mrs. A. Huth, 15th Jan., 1862. Huth, II, pp. 147–8.

19. Huth, II, p. 255. This extract comes from an appendix to Huth's biography devoted to a criticism of Glennie's *Pilgrim Memories*, 1880.

20. W. R. Holmes to the Editor of the *Daily News*. *Daily News*, 20th Oct., 1876. Holmes was the British Consul at Bosna Serai. This letter was a copy of one originally written to Sir H. Elliot denying Turkish atrocities, and quoting Glennie as an authority.

21. J. S. Stuart-Glennie. *Travellers and Correspondents*, 1877. Glennie wrote a full account of the episode which he sent to the editor of the *Daily News*. The *Daily News* refused to print it, so Glennie published his letter as a separate pamphlet.

22. Glennie, pp. 5–7.

23. "There is this difference between the conversations recorded by Mr. Longmore and Mr. Glennie—that while at Esneh Buckle said that he was unable to explain the phenomena (of Spiritualism) on any known

physical laws . . . at Aswan he is declared to have believed they *were* supernatural." Huth, II, pp. 148–9. Huth was not alone in thinking that Glennie's accounts of Buckle's conversations were inaccurate. *The Athenaeum* criticized *Pilgrim Memories* as follows: "We cannot help thinking that posthumous records of the travel-talk of eminent men are an injustice to their memories."

24. Mrs. A. Huth to her sons, 15th Nov., 1861.

25. Mrs. A. Huth to her sons, 24th Nov., 1861.

26. Mrs. A. Huth to her sons, 11th Dec., 1861.

27. A part of this Catalogue, now in the Author's Collection, is printed in Huth. Huth, II, pp. 150–5.

28. H. T. Buckle to Henry Huth, 28th Feb., 1862.

29. H. T. Buckle to Mrs. Faunch, 15th Jan., 1862. The original of this letter was probably eventually destroyed by its recipient. Before that, Capel somehow got hold of it and copied it exactly, even carefully reproducing the postmark: Cairo 9. Feb. '62. Curiously enough this must be a mistake as Buckle's letter to Mrs. Huth, written at the same time, reached her in London on 6th February. In July 1867 Mrs. Faunch instructed a solicitor, Mr. Charles Butterfield, to demand the return of the letter, her own request for it being unanswered. On receiving Butterfield's peremptory demand, Capel returned the letter and obtained a receipt for it signed by Mrs. Faunch. This correspondence is in the Author's Collection.

30. Marriage Certificate and Death Certificate at Somerset House. Census Returns 1861. Post Office Directory 1865–67 and *Kelly's London Directory* Royal Red Book and Court Register 1874.

31. E. Huth to Mrs. A. Huth, 3rd Feb., 1862.

32. H. T. Buckle to Mrs. A. Huth, 5th Feb., 1862. Huth, II, pp. 113–16, 156–7.

33. H. T. Buckle to Henry Huth, Feb., 1862. Huth, II, pp. 160–2. I have been unable to trace the original of this letter.

34. E. Huth to Mrs. A. Huth, 13th Feb., 1862.

35. Janet Ross. *The Fourth Generation*, 1912, p. 119.

36. Janet Ross. *Early Days Recalled*, 1891, pp. 108, 175.

37. Charles Hale. "Personal Reminiscences of the late Henry Thomas Buckle." *Atlantic Monthly*, April, 1863. Reprinted in Glennie, pp. 492–505.

38. E. Huth to Mrs. A. Huth, 23rd Feb., 1862.

39. E. Huth to Mrs. A. Huth, 28th Feb., 1862. Huth, II, pp. 185–6.

40. Reverend R. Tyrwhitt. *Vacation Tourists and Notes of Travel*. Ed. Galton, 1862–63, p. 356.

41. J. A. Longmore. *The Athenaeum*, 25th Jan., 1873, p. 115.

CHAPTER IV

THE LAST JOURNEY

1. Glennie, pp. 88–9. That this passage makes so little sense is the fault of its author.

2. Glennie, p. 98.

3. Glennie, p. 21.

4. A. H. Huth to Mrs. A. Huth, 16th March, 1862. Author's Collection.

5. H. T. Buckle to Mrs. A. Huth, 17th March, 1862. Huth, II, pp. 197–8.

6. Huth, II, pp. 202–4. For Gray's views on Buckle's conversational powers see above p. 92.

7. E. Huth to Mrs. A. Huth, 15th April, 1862. Author's Collection.

8. H. T. Buckle to Mrs. A. Huth, 16th April, 1862. Huth, II, pp. 212–19.

9. E. Huth to Mrs. A. Huth, 15th April, 1862. Author's Collection.

10. Buckle's Journal, May, 1862. Huth, II, pp. 233–4.

11. H. T. Buckle to Mrs. A. Huth, 14th May, 1862. Huth, II, pp. 239–40.

12. Glennie. *Mr. Buckle in the East, Fraser's Magazine*, 1863. Vol. 68, p. 186. *Pilgrim Memories*, 1880, p. 464.

13. An account of Buckle's death written by T. B. Sandwith in 1868. Huth, II, p. 249. The Hotel de Palmyre, where Buckle died, soon after became the Russian Consulate.

14. T. B. Sandwith to H. Huth, 2nd June, 1862. Author's Collection.

15. T. B. Sandwith to H. Huth, 2nd June, 1862. Author's Collection.

16. An account of Buckle's death written by T. B. Sandwith in 1868. Huth, II, p. 252. The account I have given of Buckle's death and burial is also based on Dr. Barclay's statement and Dr. Nicora's letter to Sandwith, 31st May, 1862. Author's Collection. See also a letter from E. T. Rogers (the Consul at Damascus who was absent at the time of Buckle's death) to Lord John Russell, dated 12th July, 1862, in the Public Records Office, Foreign Office, General Correspondence, Turkey (F.O. 78), Vol. 1686. Consular No. 11.

17. Huth, II, p. 256.

18. *The Athenaeum*, Nos. 2733–36. March–April, 1880. See also the Preface to the third edition of *Pilgrim Memories*, 1880. "The lesser of the two little boys who were under the care of Mr. Buckle, in his and my Eastern Pilgrimage, grown now to Man's estate, has lately published two volumes devoted, at once, to the glorification of Mr. Buckle and to the vilification of myself."

19. John Dickinson to Henry Huth, 11th April, 1866. Author's Collection.

20. Major Evans Bell to Miss Rogers, 8th May, 1866. Author's Collection.

21. Reverend G. Capel to J. S. Mill, 1st June, 1868. M/T, I, p. 111.

22. Reverend G. Capel to J. S. Mill, 12th June, 1868. M/T, I, p. 112. The Common Place Books as finally published were not in fact complete, because Longman considered certain passages unfit for publication, as did Mill and Helen Taylor. M/T, XVII, pp. 17, 23. The omitted passages are about such subjects as venereal disease, homosexuality and monastic vice.

23. K. Hare to H. Taylor, 2nd July, 1868. M/T, XVII, p. 7.

24. H. Taylor to Mrs. A. Huth, 19th Dec., 1868. M/T, uncatalogued.

25. H. Taylor to Mrs. A. Huth, 13th June, 1869. M/T, uncatalogued.

26. H. Taylor to Mrs. A. Huth, 26th June, 1869. M/T, uncatalogued.

27. K. Hare to H. Taylor, 2nd July, 1868. M/T, XVII, p. 7.

28. Reverend G. Capel to J. S. Mill, 1st June, 1868. M/T, I, p. 111.

29. Reverend G. Capel to J. S. Mill, 3rd Nov., 1866. M/T, I, p. 98.

30. H. T. Buckle to Mrs. A. Huth, 16th April, 1862. Huth, II, pp. 216–17.

31. John Buckle to J. S. Mill, 31st Dec., 1868. M/T, I, p. 122. Other extracts from this letter are quoted above, pp. 17, 200. "It is one of the things he (H. T. Buckle) has always been taunted with, that none but women valued him!" E. Shirreff to Helen Taylor, 31st March, 1872. M/T, XVII, p. 63.

32. E. Shirreff to H. Taylor, Jan. 1869. M/T, XVII, p. 48. On most points of detail, for example that Buckle had not read *Don Quixote* in Spanish, John Buckle was wrong and Miss Shirreff was right. Such inaccuracies deprive John Buckle's general criticisms of much claim to credit.

33. E. Shirreff to H. Taylor, 9th Aug., 1869. M/T, XVII, p. 51.

34. E. Shirreff to H. Taylor, 2nd Sept., 1869. M/T, XVII, p. 52.

35. Mrs. A. Huth to H. Taylor, 28th Oct., 1869. M/T, XVII, p. 15. The papers which Mrs. Huth collected were used by her son, Alfred, in writing his biography, and most of them are now in the Author's Collection.

36. E. Shirreff to H. Taylor, 15th Sept., 1869. M/T, XVII, p. 53.

37. E. Shirreff to H. Taylor, 9th Nov., 1869. M/T, XVII, p. 55.

38. H. Taylor to E. Shirreff, 11th Nov., 1869. M/T, XVII, p. 56. Draft Copy.

39. H. T. Buckle to J. Parker, 10th March, 1858. Huth, I, p. 254. See also above p. 35.

40. H. T. Buckle to J. Parker, 22nd March, 1858. Huth, I, p. 256.

41. E. Shirreff to H. Taylor, 3rd Dec., 1869. M/T, XVII, p. 57.

42. H. Taylor to E. Shirreff, 11th Nov., 1869. M/T, XVII, p. 56. See Huth, II, p. 157 for a mention of the Vienna arrangement.

43. E. Shirreff to H. Taylor, 3rd Dec., 1869. M/T XVII, p. 57.

44. H. T. Buckle to Mrs. Grote, 18th Oct., 1861. Huth, II, p. 112.

45. H. Taylor to E. Shirreff, 11th Nov., 1869. M/T, XVII, p. 56.

46. E. Shirreff to H. Taylor, 3rd Dec., 1869. M/T, XVII, p. 57.

47. E. Shirreff to H. Taylor, 3rd Dec., 1869. M/T, XVII, p. 57.

48. E. Shirreff to H. Taylor, 31st March, 1872. M/T, XVII, p. 63.

49. Mrs. A. Huth to H. Taylor, 4th Oct., 1872. M/T, XVII, p. 23. John Buckle also distrusted him. See John Buckle to J. S. Mill, 31st Dec., 1868. M/T, I, p. 122.

50. Glennie, "Mr. Buckle in the East". *Fraser's Magazine*, 1863, Vol. 68, p. 188.

CHAPTER V

THE HISTORY OF CIVILIZATION

Where different passages from the same part of the *History of Civilization* are quoted consecutively, the reference in this work to Buckle's book is given after the last such extract.

1. Buckle, I, pp. 3–5.
2. ,, I, p. 35.
3. ,, I, p. 6.
4. ,, I, p. 327.
5. ,, III, pp. 479–82.
6. ,, II, p. 373.
7. ,, III, p. 186.
8. ,, I, p. 8.
9. ,, I, pp. 8–9.
10. ,, I, p. 18
11. ,, I, pp. 26–9.
12. ,, I, pp. 32–3.
13. ,, I, p. 39.
14. ,, I, pp. 48–9.
15. ,, I, pp. 45–7.
16. ,, I, p. 63.
17. Buckle I, pp. 52–4.
18. ,, I. pp. 65–7.
19. ,, I, pp. 81–2.
20. ,, I, pp. 126–9.
21. ,, I, pp. 137–8.
22. ,, I, pp. 134, 137.
23. ,, I, pp. 140–5.
24. ,, I, pp. 156–7.
25. ,, I, pp. 158–66.
26. ,, I, p. 168.
27. ,, I, pp. 174–5.
28. ,, I, pp. 178–9.
29. ,, I, pp. 180–1.
30. ,, I, p. 189.
31. ,, I, pp. 191, 193.
32. ,, I, p. 209.

33. Buckle I, pp. 219–23.
34. „ I, pp. 225–6.
35. „ I, p. 230.
36. „ I, pp. 243–4.
37. „ I, pp. 254–7.
38. „ I, pp. 272–6.
39. „ I, pp. 280–1.
40. „ I, p. 499.
41. „ I, p. 505.
42. „ II, p. 105.
43. „ I, p. 288.
44. „ I, p. 335.
45. „ I, pp. 350, 358.
46. „ I, pp. 369–73.
47. „ I, p. 387.
48. „ II, pp. 3–4.
49. „ II, pp. 9, 11.
50. „ II, pp. 76–7.
51. „ II, p. 92.
52. „ II, pp. 104–6.
53. „ II, pp. 118–19.
54. „ II, p. 121.
55. „ II, pp. 123–7.
56. „ II, pp. 154, 159.
57. „ II, p. 202.
58. „ II, pp. 184–8.
59. „ II, p. 444.
60. „ II, pp. 463–4.
61. Buckle II, pp. 465–7.
62. „ II, pp. 467–8.
63. „ II, pp. 468–71.
64. „ II, p. 526.
65. „ II, pp. 529–30.
66. „ II, pp. 568–9.
67. „ II, pp. 570–1.
68. „ II, pp. 571–2.
69. „ II, pp. 585–96.
70. „ III, p. 19.
71. „ III, p. 191.
72. „ III, p. 83.
73. „ III, p. 113.
74. „ III, p. 202.
75. „ III, pp. 202–6, 211.
76. „ III, p. 237.
77. „ III, pp. 238–40.
78. „ III, pp. 241–2.
79. „ III, p. 275.
80. „ III, pp. 258, 260.
81. „ III, pp. 231–2.
82. „ III, pp. 272–3.
83. „ III, pp. 275–6.
84. „ III, p. 303.
85. „ III, pp. 461–2.
86. „ III, p. 185.
87. „ III, p. 467.
88. „ III, pp. 469–70.

CHAPTER VI

BUCKLE AND HIS CRITICS

1. Bradley. "The Presuppositions of a Critical History." *Collected Essays*, Vol. I, 1935, p. 20.
2. Bagehot. *Physics and Politics*, 1896, p. 167.
3. Taylor. Vol. I, 1872, p. 50, H. T. Buckle. Mill on Liberty.
4. Buckle, Vol. I, p. 326.

5. Leslie Stephen. *The Fortnightly Review*, Vol. XXVII, 1880, p. 673.

6. Sayce. *Reminiscences*, 1923, p. 33.

7. Benn. *The History of English Rationalism in the Nineteenth Century*, 1906, p. 183.

8. Buckle, Vol. I, p. 51.

9. Buckle, Vol. II, p. 108.

10. Buckle, Vol. I, p. 221.

11. Mark Pattison. *Westminster Review*, October 1857. Reprinted in *Pattison's Collected Essays*, Vol. II, 1857, p. 430.

12. Pareto. *The Mind and Society*, Vol. I, 1916, pp. 223–5.

13. Leslie Stephen. *The Fortnightly Review*, Vol. XXVII, 1880, p. 675.

14. Henry Sidgwick. *A Memoir*, 1906, p. 68.

15. Buckle's considered estimate of the importance of Voltaire and Montesquieu to historical thought is to be found in Chapter VI of the second volume of the *History of Civilization.*

16. Littré. *La Philosophie Positive Revue*, 1867, Vol. I, p. 55. See also: Spencer. *The Classification of the Sciences*, 1864, p. 37.

17. Bernheim. *Lehrbuch der historischen Methode und der Geschichtphilosophie*, Munich, 1914, p. 708.

18. Hutchison Stirling. *The North American Review*, July, 1872, Vol. CXV, p. 72.

19. Hutchison Stirling. *The Journal of Speculative Philosophy*, Vol. IX, October 1875, p. 389.

20. *A Memoir of W. E. H. Lecky* by his wife, 1909, p. 30. Bouillier. *Morale et Progrès*, 1875, p. 204.

21. Mill. *Auguste Comte and Positivism*, 1865, p. 46. Étienne in the *Revue des Deux Mondes*, Vol. LXXIV, 1868, p. 404, affirms that Buckle was not a Comtiste. See Huth, I, pp. 223–32, for a similar argument.

22. Taylor. H. T. Buckle. Mill on Liberty, Vol. I, 1872, p. 24.

23. Étienne. *Revue des Deux Mondes*, Vol. LXXIV, 1868, p. 376.

24. Gratry. *La Morale et la loi de l'Histoire*, Vol. I, 1868, p. 41.

25. Oettingen. *Moralstatistik und die christliche Sittenlehre*, 1868, p. 49.

26. Maine. *The Effect of Observation of India on Modern European Thought*, 1875, p. 13.

27. Robertson, p. 36.

28. Étienne. *Revue des Deux Mondes*, Vol. LXXIV. 1868, p. 371.

29. Trevelyan. *Life and Letters of Lord Macaulay*, Vol. II, 1876, p. 459.

30. Duffy. *Conversations with Carlyle*, 1892, p. 107.

31. Peschel. *The Races of Man and their Geographical Distribution*, 1876, p. 166.

32. Peschel. *The Races of Man and their Geographical Distribution*, 1876, p. 310.

33. Buckle, Vol. I, p. 375.

34. Nordau. (Tr.) M. A. Hamilton. *The Interpretation of History*, 1910, p. 74.

35. The Works of Ruskin. Ed. Notes for Oxford Lectures. Vol. XXII, 1906, p. 500. See Vol. XIII of Nietzche's Complete (translated) Works, 1930, p. 23. For an example of a restrained insult see Mathew Arnold's *Culture and Anarchy*, 1869, p. 171.

36. Gladstone. *Gleanings of Past Years*, Vol. II, 1879, p. 333.

37. Merz. *A History of European Thought in the Nineteenth Century*, Vol. IV, 1914, p. 511. Fränkel. *Buckle und seine Geschichtsphilosophie*, 1908, p. 59. Oettingen. *Moralstatistik und die christliche Sittenlehre*, 1868, p. 171.

38. Annan. *Leslie Stephen*, 1953, p. 156.

39. Dühring. *Kritische Geschichte der Philosophie*, 1878.

40. Flint. *Encyclopaedia Britannica*. See also: Acton. *Historical Essays and Studies*, 1908, p. 320. Leslie Stephen. *The English Utilitarians*, Vol. III, 1900, p. 362.

41. Mark Pattison. *Essays*, Vol. II, 1889. Reprint of article in *Westminster Review*, Oct. 1857, p. 421.

42. Huth, I, p. 152. H. T. Buckle to Reverend G. Capel, 10th Oct., 1857.

43. Buckle, Vol. I, p. 216.

44. Taylor. H. T. Buckle. Mill on Liberty. Vol. I, 1872, pp. 21–2.

45. Laurent. *La Philosophie de l'Histoire*, 1870, p. 234.

46. Bradley. "The Presuppositions of a Critical History." *Collected Essays*, Vol. I, 1935, p. 20.

47. Froude. *Short Studies on Great Subjects*, Vol. I, 1894, pp. 1–21.

48. *The Edinburgh Review*, July, 1861, Vol. CXIV, p. 185. See also: Usinger. *Historische Zeitung*, Vol. XIX, 1868, pp. 33–4, for a similar criticism

49. *A Memoir of W. E. H. Lecky* by his wife, 1909, p. 39.

50. Lecky. *Historical and Political Essays*, 1908, p. 100.

51. Vörlander. *Preussische Jahrbücher*, Vol. IX, 1862, p. 517.

52. Drummond. "Free Will in Relation to Statistics." A Sermon delivered in St. Mark's Chapel, Edinburgh, 15th Jan., 1860.

53. Acton. "Historical Essays and Studies," 1908. Reprint of an article in the *Rambler*, pp. 316–18.

54. *The Edinburgh Review*, April 1858, Vol. CVII, p. 483. Venn in his *Logic of Chance*, 1866, Chapter XVIII, makes the same criticism.

55. Buckle, Vol. II, Footnote, pp. 429–31.

56. Leslie Stephen. *The English Utilitarians*, Vol. III, 1900, p. 355.

57. Froude. *Short Studies on Great Subjects*, Vol. I, 1894, pp. 9–10.

58. Todd. *Theories of Social Progress*, 1926, p. 170.

59. Lange. *History of Materialism*, Vol. III, 1881, p. 246.

60. Fischer. *Ueber das Gesetz der Entwickelung auf psychische*, 1875, p. 114–15.

61. Frauenstädt. *Blätter fur literarische Unterhaltung*, 1st. Oct., 1861, p. 728. For further discussion of Buckle's doctrine of the stationary nature of the moral faculty, see also: Bouillier, *Morale et Progrès*, 1875, Chapter X; and Mill, *Auguste Comte and Positivism*, 1865, p. 114.

62. Pattison. *Memoirs*, 1885, p. 311.

63. Leslie Stephen. *Dictionary of National Biography*.

64. Sayce. *Reminiscences*, 1923, p. 32.

65. Acton. "Historical Essays and Studies", 1908. Reprint of an article in the *Rambler*, 1858, pp. 329–43.

66. Hutchison Stirling. *Darwinianism. Workmen and Work*, 1894, p. 128. It is interesting to compare Stirling's description of the "ordinary volumes" which Buckle quotes with Sayce's description, in which these same books are called "works of the obscurest character".

67. Buckle, Vol. III, pp. 187–9.

68. Lecky. *Historical and Political Essays*, 1908, p. 101.

69. Leslie Stephen. *The Fortnightly Review*, Vol. XXVII, 1880, p. 674. The same criticism is made by Fiske in his *Darwinism*, 1879, p. 197.

70. Lecky. *Historical and Political Essays*, 1908, p. 100.

71. Stein. *Die soziale Frage im Lichte der Philosophie*, 1897, pp. 41–3. Stein regarded Buckle's History favourably, but thought, in Leslie Stephen's phrase, that "he went wrong just from not having the Darwinian Clue".

72. Leslie Stephen. *The Fortnightly Review*, Vol. XXVII, 1880, p. 672. See also his article in the *Dictionary of National Biography*. Ernest Barker: *Political Thought in England*, 1848–1914, pp. 142–5, propounds a similar argument.

73. Frederick W. Maitland, *Life and Letters of Leslie Stephen*. 1899, p. 452.

74. Grant Allen. *Charles Darwin*, 1885, p. 197. See also: Clodd. *Myths and Dreams*, 1885, p. 3.

75. Stein. *Die soziale Frage im Lichte der Philosophie*, 1897, p. 43.

76. Forbes. *The Liberal Anglican Idea of History*, 1952, p. 144. Collingwood. *The Idea of History*, 1946, p. 144. See also Collingwood, Leaflets of the Historical Association, 1932, No. 79, p. 11.

77. *A Memoir of W. E. H. Lecky*, by his wife, 1909, p. 106.

78. *The Edinburgh Review*, Vol. CVII, April 1858, p. 466.

79. Étienne. *Revue des Deux Mondes*, LXXIV, 1868, p. 376.

80. Huth, I, p. 211. Huth gives an outline of what Buckle proposed to write in his subsequent volumes, pp. 204–10.

81. Acton. "Historical Essays and Studies", 1908. Reprint of an article in the *Rambler*, p. 305. See also Morley, *Recollections*, 2 vols., 1917, p. 14.

82. Merz. *A History of European Thought in the Nineteenth Century*, Vol. IV, 1914, p. 511.

83. Martineau. *The Daily News*, 22nd July, 1861. George Eliot, who regarded Buckle as "an irreligious conceited man", recommends his book to Charles Bray on the ground that he would find it suggestive. J. W. Cross. *Life of George Eliot*, 1858, pp. 232, 253.

84. Bernard Shaw. *The Intelligent Woman's Guide to Socialism and Capitalism*, 1928, p. 467.

85. Buckle, Vol. III, p. 395. See Mill. *A System of Logic* (1862 edition or later), pp. 607–8, for an estimate of the importance of the controversy raised by Buckle's History.

86. Leslie Stephen. *Life of Henry Fawcett*, 1886, p. 98.

87. Robertson, p. 21.

88. Gooch. *History and Historians*, 1913, p. 585.

89. Froude. *Short Studies on Great Subjects*, Vol. I, 1894, p. 3.

90. Merz. *A History of European Thought in the Nineteenth Century*, Vol. IV, 1914. "His influence on German thought was probably quite as great as on that of his own country, and perhaps not so soon forgotten." p. 511.

91. Auchmuty. *Lecky*. 1945, p. 12.

92. Winwood Reade. *The Martyrdom of Man*, 1948, p. 25.

93. S. F. Markham. *Climate and the Energy of Nations*, 1942, p. 5.

94. Bernheim. *Lehrbuch der historischen Methode und der Geschichtsphilosophie*, 1914, p. 709.

95. Bowle. *Politics and Opinion in the Nineteenth Century*, 1954, p. 240.

96. Lecky. *Historical and Political Essays*, 1908, p. 102.

97. Mark Pattison. *Essays*, Vol. II, 1889, p. 396.

98. Theodore Parker. *Collected Works*, Vol. XII, 1865, pp. 107–49.

99. *A Memoir of W. E. H. Lecky* by his wife, 1909, p. 25.

100. Benn. *The History of English Rationalism in the Nineteenth Century*, Vol. II, 1906, pp. 175–6, 185.

101. *Fraser's Magazine*, Vol. 66, p. 345.

102. Buckle, Vol. II, p. 422.

BIBLIOGRAPHICAL NOTE

BESIDES the books, articles and manuscripts already mentioned in the Note on Sources, Mr. Packe's biography of John Stuart Mill contains much interesting information about Helen Taylor and many of Buckle's friends and acquaintances. A considerable number of books refer to Buckle in passing and, if this bibliography were to include them all, it would be of inordinate length. The works listed below are confined, with a few exceptions, to the more important of those which are quoted in this book.

ACTON, JOHN. *Historical Essay and Studies*, 1908.

ALLEN, GRANT. *Charles Darwin*, 1885.

Amberley Papers, The. (Ed.) BERTRAND RUSSELL. 2 vols., 1937.

BAGEHOT, WALTER. *Physics and Politics*, 1896.

BARKER, Ernest. *Political Thought in England* 1848–1914, 1942.

BENN, ALFRED WILLIAM. *The History of English Rationalism in the Nineteenth Century*, 2 vols., 1906.

BERNHEIM, ERNST. *Lehrbuch der historischen Methode und der Geschichte*, 1914.

OUILLIER, FRANCISQUE. *Morale et Progrès*, 1875.

BOWLE, JOHN. *Politics and Opinion in the Nineteenth Century*, 1954.

BUCKLE, HENRY THOMAS. *The History of Civilization*, 3 vols., 1899; *Miscellaneous and Posthumous Works of Henry Thomas Buckle* (Ed.) Helen Taylor, 3 vols., 1872.

BURY, J. B. *A History of Freedom of Thought*, 1952; *The Idea of Progress*, 1921.

Chess Player's Magazine, Vol. II, February, 1864.

DARWIN, FRANCIS. (Ed.) *The Life and Letters of Charles Darwin*, 3 vols., 1887.

DUFFY, SIR CHARLES GAVAN. *Conversations with Carlyle*, 1892.

DROYSEN, GUSTAV. *Erhebung der Geschichte zum Rang einer Wissenschaft*, 1863.

DRUMMOND, ROBERT BLACKLEY. *Free Will in Relation to Statistics*, 1860.

Edinburgh Review, The, April, 1858, Vol. CVII; July, 1861, Vol. CXIV.

ELLIS, S. M. (Ed.) *A Mid-Victorian Pepys. The Letters and Memoirs of Sir William Hardman*, 2nd series, 1923.

ELTON, OLIVER. *A Survey of English Literature* 1830–1880, 2 vols., 1932.

ÉTIENNE. *Revue des Deux Mondes*, Vol. LXXIV, 1868.

FISCHER, E. L. *Ueber das Gesetz der Entwickelung auf psychisch ethischem Gebiet*, 1875.

FISKE, JOHN. *Darwinism*, 1879.

FLINT. Article on Buckle, *Encyclopaedia Britannica*, 9th Edition.

FRAUENSTÄDT, JULIUS. *Blatter fur literariche Unterhaltung*, 1st October, 1861.

FRÄNKEL, F. *Buckle und Seine Geschichtsphilosophie*, 1908.

FROUDE, JAMES ANTHONY. *Short Studies on Great Subjects*, 4 vols., 1894.

GLENNIE, J. S. STUART. *Pilgrim Memories, or Travel and Discussion in the Birth-Countries of Christianity with the late Henry Thomas Buckle*, 1880; *Travellers and Correspondents*, 1867; *Fraser's Magazine*, Vol. 66, June, 1859; Vol. 68, August, 1863.

GOOCH, G. P. *History and Historians in the Nineteenth Century*, 1913.

GRATRY, AUGUSTE JOSEPH ALPHONSE. *La Morale et la Loi de l'Histoire*, 2 vols., 1868.

GROTE, MRS. HARRIET. *The Personal Life of George Grote*, 1873.

HALE, CHARLES. *The Atlantic Monthly*, Vol. XI, April, 1863.

HOLYOAKE, GEORGE. *Sixty Years of an Agitator's Life*, 2 vols., 1892; *The Case of Thomas Pooley, the Cornish Well-sinker*, 1857; *Bygones Worth Remembering*, 2 vols., 1905.

HUTH, A. H. *Life and Writings of Henry Thomas Buckle*, 2 vols., 1880.

KENNEDY, CAPTAIN. *The Westminster Chess Club Papers*, June, 1873.

LANGE, FREDERICK ALBERT. (Tr.) Ernest Chester Thomas. *History of Materialism*, 3 vols., 1881.

LAURENT, F. *La Philosophie de l'Histoire*, 1870; *Études sur l'Histoire de l'Humanité*, 1870.

Law Magazine and Law Review, Vol. VII, August, 1859.

LECKY, W. E. H. *Historical and Political Essays*, 1908; *History of European Morals*, 2 vols., 1911.

Lecky, A Memoir of W. E. H. Lecky, By his Wife, 1909.

LITTRÉ. *La Philosophie Positive*, 1868.

LONGMORE, J. A. *The Athenaeum*, No. 2361, 25th January, 1873.

LOWELL, J. R. (Ed.) Charles Norton. *Letters of James Russell Lowell*, 2 vols., 1894.

LYELL, SIR CHARLES. *Life Letters and Journals of Sir Charles Lyell, Bart.*, 2 vols., 1881.

MASARYK, T. G. *Theorie Dějin dle Zásad T. H. Bucklea*, 1884.

MERZ, JOHN THEODORE. *A History of European Thought in the Nineteenth Century*, 3 vols., 1914.

MILL, JOHN STUART. *Auguste Comte and Positivism*, 1865; *A System of Logic Ratiocinative and Inductive*, 1886.

MORLEY, JOHN, VISCOUNT. *Recollections*, 2 vols., 1917.

NORDAU, MAX. (Tr.) M. A. Hamilton. *The Interpretation of History*, 1910.

OETTINGEN. *Moralstatistik und die Christliche Sittenlehre*, 2 vols., 1868.

PACKE, MICHAEL ST. JOHN. *The Life of John Stuart Mill*, 1954.

PARKER, THEODORE. (Ed.) Frances Power Cobbe. *Collected Works*, 12 vols., 1865.

PATTISON, MARK. Essays collected and arranged by Henry Nettleship, 2 vols., 1889; Memoirs, 1885; *Westminster Review*, October, 1857.

PESCHEL, OSCAR. *The Races of Man and their Geographical Distribution*, 1876.

POLLOCK, SIR FREDERICK. *Personal Remembrances of Sir Frederick Pollock*, 2 vols., 1887.

ROBERTSON, J. M. *Buckle and his Critics*, 1897.

ROSS, JANET. *Early Days Recalled*, 1891; *The Fourth Generation*, 1912.

RÜGE. *Geschichte der Civilization in England*, 1868.

SAYCE, REVEREND A. H. *Reminiscences*, 1923.

SPENCER, HERBERT. *An Autobiography*, 2 vols., 1904

STEIN, LUDWIG. *Die soziale Frage im Lichte der Philosophie*, 1897.

STEPHEN, LESLIE. *The English Utilitarians*, 3 vols., 1900; *Dictionary of National Biography*, Vol. III, 1908.

STIRLING, HUTCHISON JAMES. *Darwinianism: Workmen and Work*, 1894; *Journal of Speculative Philosophy*, Vol. IX, October, 1875; *The North American Review*, Vol. CXV, July, 1872.

TIMBS, JOHN. *A Century of Anecdote*, 2 vols., 1860.

USINGER. *Historische Zeitung*, Vol. XIX, 1868.

VENN, JOHN. *Logic of Chance*, 1866.

VÖRLANDER. *Preussische Jahrbücher*, Vol. IX, May, 1862.

WALLACE, D. MACKENZIE. *Russia*, 2 vols., 1877.

WELLS, G. A. *The Critics of Buckle*. Past and Present. April, 1956.

INDEX